Psychoan
Psychoanalytic Therapies

Theories of Psychotherapy Series

Theories of Psychotherapy Series
Jon Carlson and Matt Englar-Carlson, Series Editors

Psychoanalysis and Psychoanalytic Therapies

Jeremy D. Safran

American Psychological Association

Washington, DC

Copyright © 2012 by the American Psychological Association. All rights reserved. Except as permitted under the United States Copyright Act of 1976, no part of this publication may be reproduced or distributed in any form or by any means, including, but not limited to, the process of scanning and digitization, or stored in a database or retrieval system, without the prior written permission of the publisher.

Second Printing March 2013

Published by
American Psychological Association
750 First Street, NE
Washington, DC 20002
www.apa.org

To order
APA Order Department
P.O. Box 92984
Washington, DC 20090-2984
Tel: (800) 374-2721; Direct: (202) 336-5510
Fax: (202) 336-5502; TDD/TTY: (202) 336-6123
Online: www.apa.org/books/
E-mail: order@apa.org

In the U.K., Europe, Africa, and the Middle East, copies may be ordered from
American Psychological Association
3 Henrietta Street
Covent Garden, London
WC2E 8LU England

Typeset in Minion by Circle Graphics, Inc., Columbia, MD

Printer: Maple-Vail Book Manufacturing Group, York, PA
Cover Designer: Minker Design, Sarasota, FL

Cover Art: *Lily Rising,* 2005, oil and mixed media on panel in craquelure frame, by Betsy Bauer

The opinions and statements published are the responsibility of the authors, and such opinions and statements do not necessarily represent the policies of the American Psychological Association.

Library of Congress Cataloging-in-Publication Data

Safran, Jeremy D.
  Psychoanalysis and psychoanalytic therapies / Jeremy D. Safran.
    p. cm. — (Theories of psychotherapy series)
  Includes bibliographical references and index.
  ISBN-13: 978-1-4338-0978-1
  ISBN-10: 1-4338-0978-8
  1. Psychoanalysis. 2. Psychotherapy. I. Title.
  BF173.S257 2011
  150.19'5—dc22
                              2011008323

British Library Cataloguing-in-Publication Data
A CIP record is available from the British Library.

Printed in the United States of America
First Edition

For my daughters, Ayla and Ellie, who like to tease me about having "all those Freud books" lying around the house.

Contents

Series Preface

Some might argue that in the contemporary clinical practice of psychotherapy, evidence-based intervention, and effective outcome have overshadowed theory in importance. Maybe. But, as the editors of this series, we don't propose to take up that controversy here. We do know that psychotherapists adopt and practice according to one theory or another because their experience, and decades of good evidence, suggests that having a sound theory of psychotherapy leads to greater therapeutic success. Still, the role of theory in the helping process can be hard to explain. This narrative about solving problems helps convey theory's importance:

> Aesop tells the fable of the sun and wind having a contest to decide who was the most powerful. From above the earth, they spotted a man walking down the street, and the wind said that he bet he could get this man's coat off. The sun agreed to the contest. The wind blew, and the man held on tightly to his coat. The more the wind blew, the tighter he held. The sun said it was his turn. He put all of his energy into creating warm sunshine, and soon the man took off his coat.

What does a competition between the sun and the wind to remove a man's coat have to do with theories of psychotherapy? We think this deceptively simple story highlights the importance of theory as the precursor to any effective intervention—and hence to a favorable outcome. Without a guiding theory we might treat the symptom without understanding the role of the individual. Or we might create power conflicts with our clients and not understand that, at times, indirect means of help-ing (sunshine) are often as effective—if not more so—than direct ones (wind). In the absence of theory, we might lose track of the treatment rationale and instead get caught up in, for example, social correctness and not wanting to do something that looks too simple.

What exactly *is* theory? The *APA Dictionary of Psychology* defines theory as "a principle or body of interrelated principles that purports to explain or predict a number of interrelated phenomena." In psychother-apy, a theory is a set of principles used to explain human thought and behavior, including what causes people to change. In practice, a theory creates the goals of therapy and specifies how to pursue them. Haley (1997) noted that a theory of psychotherapy ought to be simple enough for the average therapist to understand, but comprehensive enough to account for a wide range of eventualities. Furthermore, a theory guides action toward successful outcomes while generating hope in both the ther-apist and client that recovery is possible.

Theory is the compass that allows psychotherapists to navigate the vast territory of clinical practice. In the same ways that navigational tools have been modified to adapt to advances in thinking and ever-expanding territories to explore, theories of psychotherapy have changed over time. The different schools of theories are commonly referred to as waves, the first wave being psychodynamic theories (i.e., Adlerian, psychoanalytic), the second wave learning theories (i.e., behavioral, cognitive–behavioral), the third wave humanistic theories (person-centered, gestalt, existential), the fourth wave feminist and multicultural theories, and the fifth wave post-modern and constructivist theories. In many ways, these waves represent how psychotherapy has adapted and responded to changes in psychol-ogy, society, and epistemology as well as to changes in the nature of psy-chotherapy itself. Psychotherapy and the theories that guide it are dynamic and responsive. The wide variety of theories is also testament to the dif-ferent ways in which the same human behavior can be conceptualized (Frew & Spiegler, 2008).

It is with these two concepts in mind—the central importance of theory and the natural evolution of theoretical thinking—that we devel-oped the Theories of Psychotherapy Series. Both of us are thoroughly fascinated by theory and the range of complex ideas that drive each model. As university faculty members who teach courses on the theories of psychotherapy, we wanted to create learning materials that not only highlight the essence of the major theories for professionals and professionals in training but also clearly bring the reader up to date on the current status of the models. Often in books on theory, the biography of the original theorist overshadows the evolution of the model. In contrast, our intent is to highlight the contemporary uses of the theories as well as their history and context.

As this project began, we faced two immediate decisions: which theories to address and who best to present them. We looked at graduate-level theories of psychotherapy courses to see which theories are being taught, and we explored popular scholarly books, articles, and conferences to determine which theories draw the most interest. We then developed a dream list of authors from among the best minds in contemporary theoretical practice. Each author is one of the leading proponents of that approach as well as a knowledgeable practitioner. We asked each author to review the core constructs of the theory, bring the theory into the modern sphere of clinical practice by looking at it through a context of evidence-based practice, and clearly illustrate how the theory looks in action.

There are 24 titles planned for the series. Each title can stand alone or can be put together with a few other titles to create materials for a course in psychotherapy theories. This option allows instructors to create a course featuring the approaches they believe are the most salient today. To support this end, APA Books has also developed a DVD for each of the approaches that demonstrates the theory in practice with a real client. Many of the DVDs show therapy over six sessions. Contact APA Books for a complete list of available DVD programs (http://www.apa.org/pubs/videos).

Freudian theory has become synonymous with psychoanalysis. As the original basis for psychotherapy, psychoanalysis has become the starting point in most theories courses and the one theory that others use as a benchmark. Yet many people's knowledge about psychoanalysis does not extend much beyond Freud and the classic approach. A good deal has changed in terms of the practice of psychotherapy, and like other approaches, psychoanalysis has adapted and grown. Jeremy Safran clearly shows how the psychoanalytical or Freudian approach has evolved over the past century in terms of depth of conceptual ideas and responsiveness to the modern practice of psychotherapy. This interesting and insightful book is a worthy vehicle to carry the reader into the new generation of psychoanalytic thought. We are sure the many strategies and clinical examples will help the reader understand why psychoanalysis should still be considered a contemporary psychotherapy.

—Jon Carlson and Matt Englar-Carlson

REFERENCES

Frew, J., & Spiegler, M. (2008). *Contemporary psychotherapies for a diverse world.* Boston, MA: Lahaska Press.

Haley, J. (1997). *Leaving home: The therapy of disturbed young people.* New York, NY: Routledge.

How to Use This Book
With APA Psychotherapy Videos

Each book in the Theories of Psychotherapy Series is specifically paired with a DVD that demonstrates the theory applied in actual therapy with a real client. Many DVDs feature the author of the book as the guest therapist, allowing students to see an eminent scholar and practitioner putting the theory he or she writes about into action.

The DVDs have a number of features that make them excellent tools for learning more about theoretical concepts:

- Many DVDs contain six full sessions of psychotherapy over time, giving viewers a chance to see how clients respond to the application of the theory over the course of several sessions.
- Each DVD has a brief introductory discussion recapping the basic features of the theory behind the approach demonstrated. This allows viewers to review the key aspects of the approach about which they have just read.
- DVDs feature actual clients in unedited psychotherapy sessions. This provides a unique opportunity to get a sense of the look and feel of real psychotherapy, something that written case examples and transcripts cannot always convey.
- There is a therapist commentary track that viewers may choose to play during the psychotherapy sessions. This track gives unique insight into why therapists do what they do in a session. Further, it provides an in vivo opportunity to see how the therapist uses the model to conceptualize the client.

The books and DVDs together make a powerful teaching tool for showing how theoretical principles affect practice. In the case of this book, the DVD *Psychoanalytic Therapy Over Time,* which features the author as the guest expert, provides a vivid example of how this approach looks in practice. In the six sessions on this DVD, Dr. Safran works with a young woman who has suffered from depression and issues surrounding substance use and relationships with abusive men. Safran explores these issues with the client and examines emerging patterns in the therapeutic relationship that may reflect on the client's other past and present relationships.

Psychoanalysis and Psychoanalytic Therapies

1

Introduction

Psychoanalysis is a distinctive form of psychological treatment and a model of psychological functioning, human development, and psychopathology. There is no one unified psychoanalytic theory of treatment but rather a variety of different psychoanalytic theories and treatment models that have developed over more than a century through the writings of a host of different psychoanalytic theorists and practitioners in different countries. Despite this lack of a single unified perspective, it is possible to speak in general terms about certain basic principles that tend to cut across different psychoanalytic perspectives. These include (a) an assumption that all human beings are motivated in part by wishes, fantasies, or tacit knowledge that is outside of awareness (this is referred to as *unconscious motivation*); (b) an interest in facilitating the awareness of unconscious motivations, thereby increasing choice; (c) an emphasis on exploring the ways in which people avoid painful or threatening feelings, fantasies, and thoughts; (d) an assumption that people are ambivalent about changing and an emphasis on the importance of exploring this ambivalence; (e) an emphasis on using the therapeutic relationship as an arena for exploring clients' self-defeating psychological processes and actions (both conscious and unconscious); (f) an emphasis on using the therapeutic relationship as an important vehicle of change; and (g) an emphasis on helping clients to understand the way in which their own construction of their past and present plays a role in perpetuating their self-defeating patterns.

In the early days of psychoanalysis, clients typically saw Freud and his colleagues four to six times per week, and treatment duration was relatively short by today's standards. It was not uncommon for a treatment to last 6 weeks to 2 months. As the goals of psychoanalysis evolved from symptom reduction to more fundamental changes in personality functioning, the length of the average analysis gradually increased over time to the point at which it became common for an analysis to last 6 years or longer.

Many contemporary psychoanalysts still believe that long-term, intensive treatment has important advantages as a treatment modality. As the empirical evidence shows, although circumscribed symptoms can change in short-term, less-intensive therapy, more fundamental changes in personality functioning and underlying psychological structures take time to change (e.g., Howard, Kopta, Krause, & Orlinsky, 1986). Moreover, given that the client–therapist relationship is seen as a central mechanism of change (in a variety of ways that I discuss later), the theory holds that longer term, intensive treatment is necessary to allow this relationship to develop and play a transformative role. Nevertheless, there is a growing recognition that long-term, intensive treatment is not always feasible or even desirable (depending on the nature of clients' problems or their goals). In contemporary psychoanalytic practice, it is thus not uncommon to see clients once or twice a week on a shorter term basis.

Psychoanalysis was the first modern Western system of psychotherapy, and most other forms of therapy evolved out of psychoanalysis, were strongly influence by it, or developed partially in reaction to it. The term *psychoanalysis* was originated by Sigmund Freud (1856–1939), a Viennese neurologist who together with a number of key colleagues (e.g., Wilhelm Stekel, Paul Federn, Max Etington, Alfred Adler, Hans Sachs, Otto Rank, Karl Abraham, Carl Jung, Sandor Ferenczi, Ernest Jones) developed a discipline that combined a form of psychological treatment with a model of psychological functioning, human development, and theory of change. The emergence of this discipline was influenced by a variety of developments taking place at the time in psychiatry, neurology, psychology, philosophy, and social and natural sciences. The development of psychoanalysis was also influenced through interaction with competing models of treatment and psychopathology emerging at the time. In addition, it was influenced by Freud's attempts to address theoretical challenges and critiques posed by those outside the field of psychoanalysis as well as dissenting perspectives and ideas raised by his own students and colleagues (Gay, 1988; Makari, 2008).

Freud's theoretical perspective and ideas about psychoanalytic technique evolved over the course of his lifetime, and although his thinking is often presented as a unified and coherent system of thought, reading his articles and books is more like reading an ongoing work in progress rather than a systematic and unified theory. This style of writing is also true for many other influential psychoanalytic theorists, including Melanie Klein (1955/2002a, 1975/2002b), Ronald Fairbairn (1952, 1994), Donald Winnicott (1958, 1965), and Jacques Lacan (1975/1988a, 1978/1988b).

Although Freud undeniably was the single most influential figure in the initial development of psychoanalysis, many other creative thinkers played a role in its development from the very beginning. Some of their ideas led Freud to sharpen his own thinking in response, some of their ideas were assimilated and modified by Freud in various ways, and some of their ideas were not assimilated by Freud but had a subsequent impact on the thinking of their own students and on future generations of psychoanalysts (Makari, 2008). Although psychoanalysis began with Freud's writing and lectures and the early writing of a small group of colleagues gathered around him in Vienna, by the time of Freud's death in 1939, it was beginning to become an international movement with important centers in Vienna, Zurich, Berlin, Budapest, Italy, France, England, the United States, and Latin America. Each of these centers contributed its own unique influence to the development of psychoanalysis, and a host of different schools and theories of psychoanalysis have evolved in different countries since 1939 (Makari, 2008). Adherents to different schools of psychoanalysis interpret Freud differently, agree and disagree about a variety of major premises, and disagree to vary-ing degrees with different aspects of Freud's theoretical corpus as well as his technical recommendations.

PSYCHOANALYSIS TODAY

Although there is an understandable tendency for many critics to equate psychoanalysis with Freud, it is important to recognize that the value of psychoanalytic treatment and the validity of psychoanalytic theory are not tied to the validity of Freud's thinking. Freud was one person writing in a particular historical era in a specific culture. Some of his ideas were more valid in their original historical and cultural context than they are in contem-porary times, and some were flawed from the beginning. As readers will see later, there are some dramatic differences between the psychoanalysis of Freud's time and that of the present time in North American and the rest of the world. For example, relative to Freud's times, contemporary Ameri-can psychoanalysis has a greater emphasis on the mutuality of the thera-peutic relationship; an emphasis on the fundamentally human nature of the therapeutic relationship; more of an emphasis on flexibility, creativity, and spontaneity in the therapeutic process; and a more optimistic perspective on life and human nature. Contrary to the common misconception, there is actually a substantial and growing evidence base for the effectiveness of psychoanalytically oriented treatments (e.g., Levy, Ablon, & Kaechele, in press; Shedler, 2010) and the validity of various psychoanalytic constructs (see, e.g., Westen, 1998; Westen & Gabbard, 1999). And there has been a growing emphasis on the importance of adapting psychoanalytic theory and practice in a culturally responsive fashion (e.g., Altman, 1995; Gutwill & Hollander, 2006; Perez Foster, Moskowitz, & Javier, 1996; Roland, 1989).

In the United States, psychoanalysis has evolved under the influence of a number of characteristic American attitudes, including a tendency toward optimism and the philosophy of American egalitarianism. Another impor-tant factor is that many of today's leading analysts came of age during the cultural revolution in the 1960s—a time when traditional social norms and sources of authority were being challenged. In addition, a number of promi-

nent feminist psychoanalytic thinkers have challenged many of the patriar-
chal assumptions implicit in traditional psychoanalytic theory, raised
important questions about the dynamics of power in the therapeutic relationship, and reformulated psychoanalytic thinking about gender (e.g.,
Benjamin, 1988; Dimen, 2003; Harris, 2008). Another influence has been a
postmodern sensibility that challenges the assumption that one can ever
come to know reality objectively, maintains a skeptical attitude toward uni-
versalizing truth claims, and emphasizes the importance of theoretical plu-
ralism. A final influence has been the massive influx of clinical psychologists
into postgraduate psychoanalytic training institutes in the past few decades.
This has led to significant and intellectually interesting changes in a discipline that was traditionally dominated by psychiatry.

Unfortunately, many people in the broader mental health field and the
general public are unaware of these changes within psychoanalysis and are
responding to a partial or caricatured understanding of the tradition on
the basis of aspects of psychoanalytic theory, practice, and attitude that are
no longer prominent. Although there are many valid critiques of psychoanalysis in both its past and current forms, I also believe that the current
marginalization of psychoanalysis is partially attributable to certain contemporary cultural biases, especially in the United States, that are not unequivocally healthy ones. These biases include an emphasis on optimism, speed,
pragmatism, instrumentality, and an intolerance of ambiguity. Although all
of these emphases certainly have their value, they can also be associated with
a naïveté that tends to underestimate the complexity of human nature and
the difficulty of the change process. American culture traditionally tends
to gloss over the more tragic dimensions of life, to espouse the belief that we
can all be happy if we try hard enough, and to be biased toward a "quick fix
mentality." Psychoanalysis originated in continental Europe—in a culture
that had experienced centuries of poverty; oppression of the masses by
the ruling classes; ongoing religious conflict and oppression; and generations of warfare culminating in two world wars that were unprecedented in
scale, degree of devastation, and tragedy.

Although American psychoanalysis tends to be more optimistic
and pragmatic than its European counterpart, it still retains many of the

traditional psychoanalytic values, such as the appreciation of human complexity, a recognition that contentment is not necessarily the same as a two-dimensional version of "happiness," and an appreciation that change is not always easy or quick. I believe that a greater understanding of the nature of contemporary psychoanalysis, and a deeper appreciation of the more valuable dimensions of psychoanalytic theory and practice in general, can lead to an enrichment of psychologists' understanding of how best to help people and serve as a corrective to some of our potentially problematic cultural blind spots and biases. And finally, as I discuss later, there has been movement in contemporary psychoanalysis toward recovering some of the culturally subversive, socially progressive, and politically engaged spirit that was once more characteristic of the discipline. My hope is that this book will both introduce a broader readership to some of the more important recent developments in psychoanalytic theory and practice that it may not be familiar with and correct certain misconceptions about traditional psychoanalysis as well.

THE TENSION BETWEEN CONFORMIST AND SUBVERSIVE THREADS IN PSYCHOANALYSIS

For many years, psychoanalysis dominated the mental health care system in the United States and many other countries. From the late 1960s until the present time, however, psychoanalysis in the United States has become increasingly marginalized within both the health-care system and clinical training programs. There are many reasons for the declining fortunes of psychoanalysis. One important factor is that during its heyday, psychoanalysis justifiably earned a reputation as a conservative cultural force with a tendency toward orthodoxy, insularity, arrogance, and elitism. It also earned a reputation as a somewhat esoteric discipline with a limited interest in grappling with the concrete problems that many people deal with in their everyday lives and a limited appreciation of the social and political factors that affect their lives. Instead, it came to be seen by many as a self-indulgent pastime for the financially comfortable.

The fact that psychoanalysis came to earn this reputation is ironic. Although Freud initially began developing psychoanalysis as a treatment for clients presenting with symptoms that other physicians were unable to treat, his ambitions and the ambitions of subsequent psychoanalysts ultimately came to extend beyond the realm of therapy into social theory and cultural critique. Freud and many of the early analysts came from medical backgrounds. Nevertheless, Freud came to feel strongly that psychoanalysis should not become a medical subspecialty and, in fact, prized the cultural and intellectual breadth that could be brought to the field by analysts with diverse education backgrounds and intellectual interests. Many of the early analysts, including Freud, were members of an emerging, educated Jewish middle class whose upward social mobility was made possible by the open, politically progressive policies of the Austro-Hungarian Empire at the turn of the century and who contributed to the development of this culture. As the social theorist Thorstein Veblen (1919) argued, secular Western European Jews at the turn of the century formed a unique group of marginal intellectuals. Alienated from traditional Judaism and not fully accepted into European society even when they assimilated its customs, they developed a characteristically skeptical point of view.

The early analysts thus tended to be members of a liberal, progressive intelligentsia—a traditionally oppressed and marginalized group. They aspired toward social acceptability, but at the same time tended to regard prevailing cultural assumptions from a critical perspective. This critical and in some respects subversive stance went hand in hand with a vision of progressive social transformation. Psychoanalysis began in part as a radical critique of the illness-producing effects of social suppression and consequent psychological repression of sexuality. Freud was deeply interested in broad social and cultural concerns. He was critical of various trappings of the physician's privilege, and until the end of his life he supported free psychoanalytic clinics, stood up for the flexible fee, and defended the practice of psychoanalysis by professionals without medical training. Many of the early analysts were progressive social activists committed to political critique and social justice. Sandor Ferenczi, one of Freud's closest colleagues, critiqued social hypocrisy and conventionalism, founded a free clinic in Budapest, and passionately defended the rights of women and homosexuals. Karl Abraham, Ernst Simmel, and Max Etington set up a public psychoanalytic clinic in Berlin in the 1920s that became a bastion of social and political progressivism (see Danto, 2005).

A number of these analysts were influenced by left wing, socialist thinking. This is not surprising given that they came of age in the politically charged culture of Vienna and Berlin, where the Marxist critique of capitalism was widely discussed in intellectual circles. They viewed themselves as brokers of social change and saw psychoanalysis as a challenge to conventional political codes and as more of a social mission than a medical discipline. Prominent analysts such as Wilhelm Reich (1941), Erich Fromm (1941), and Otto Fenichel (1945), among others, were well-known for their socialist or Marxist commitments and their fusion of psychoanalysis and social concerns.

Another example of this longstanding tradition of the intersection between psychoanalysis and social, political and cultural concerns, is the productive collaboration that took place between psychoanalytic thinkers such as Erich Fromm and Herbert Marcuse, and the tradition of critical theory developed by The Institute for Social Research in Frankfurt. The Institute for Social Research consisted of a group of German social scientists who were interested in critiquing and changing society from an interdisciplinary perspective which synthesized sociology, history, political science, anthropology and psychology. An important premise of critical theory is that all theories are shaped by social and cultural ideologies and that for this reason it is important to critically analyze theory from sociological, historical and political perspectives that can potentially shed light on the role that that theory may play in perpetuating cultural ideologies that can function to further the interests of the privileged class.

Some of the key figures in The Institute for Social Research were Max Horkheimer, Theodor Adorno, Walter Benjamin, and Leo Lowenthal. Their intellectual project was initially inspired by the Marxist analysis of the problems of modernity in terms of the influence of industrial capitalism on the development of contemporary culture. From this perspective, the industrial revolution led to the rise of a middle class that owns the means of production, and which profits from the labor of a much larger working class. Members of the working class as a rule control neither the form nor the pace of their work, nor the fruits of their own labor. They are thus alienated from their intellectual and physical potential. This results in a system in which the wealth and power are concentrated in the hands of the few, at the expense of the exploited working class. As technology becomes more refined, production becomes more automated and the amount of training and skill required by the laborer become increasingly simplified. This contributes to the devaluation of their labor and their experience of alienation and meaninglessness. Laborers become interchangeable units who become dehumanized.

In 1947, Horkheimer and Adorno published their classic book *Dialectic of Enlightenment* (Horkheimer & Adorno, 1947). Written in the shadow of massive atrocities of both Nazi and communist regimes in World War II, Horkheimer and Adorno use a combination of neo-Marxist theory, continental philosophy and psychoanalytic thinking to make sense of how it was possible for the Enlightenment to ironically lead to an unprecedented descent into barbarism rather than a new age of liberation. Central to their thesis is the idea that the advance of science, technology, and instrumental thinking combined with the capitalist emphasis on mass production and systematization, can lead to the development of coldly rational totalitarian systems. In these systems human beings became commodified, objectified, coerced into social conformity, or exterminated if it serves the interests of a coldly rational state apparatus in pursuit of a Utopian ideal.

When many members of the Frankfurt school fled to the United States with the rise of Nazism, they were particularly struck by the role that shared cultural ideology plays in maintaining the status quo under the influence of American consumer culture. They coined the term *culture industry* to refer to the way in which the mass media market ideas and beliefs that create false needs that function to maintain the capitalist system. So for example, we are socialized into believing that if we drink a certain kind of beer or wine, drive a certain kind of car or wear certain clothes we will find love, happiness and contentment. There is also an ideology maintained in the United States that anyone can be successful and rich if they work hard enough. This ideology denies the reality of the different opportunities available to members of different socio-economic classes and blames the individual for his or her failure to transcend the reality of material social conditions. Once again, this serves to maintain the capitalism system and manipulates the "have nots" into acting against their own best interests. This type of critical analysis is particularly timely in light of the growing disparity between the wealthy and the poor in the post-Regan era.

Theodor Adorno also collaborated with a group of psychologists at Berkeley University to conduct a series of empirical studies guided by psychoanalytic thinking, investigating the psychological characteristics that would predispose and individual to support a totalitarian regime (Adorno, Frenkel-Brunswick, & Levinson, 1950). Although they were particularly concerned about the individual and group psychology that had made the rise of facism in Nazi Germany possible, in many ways their analysis is just as relevant to understanding the emergence of right wing conservativism in contemporary American politics. Some of the common characteristics identified included: rigid adherence to conventional middle class values; submissive, uncritical attitudes towards idealized authorities of the ingroup; the tendency to think in rigid "black and white" categories; preoccupation with power and toughness; and the preoccupation with and projection of immoral sexual attitudes and activities among members of the outgroup.

Russell Jacoby (1983) has done a masterful job of demonstrating the way in which many of the European analysts who immigrated to the United States because of the rise of Nazism in Europe downplayed their more politically progressive and socially critical commitments to fit in with American culture and avoid arousing the fears and suspicions of Americans who might have seen them as dangerous foreigners. This was especially true following World War II as the wartime alliance between the United States and the Soviet Union broke down and the rampant fear of communism, socialism, and Marxism reached its heights in the McCarthy era. During this period, émigré psychoanalysts quite reasonably understood that the fight for a politically a progressive psychoanalysis informed in part by a Marxist critique of capitalism was out of step with the times and might easily jeopardize the future of psychoanalysis in North America. They thus kept their political views to themselves and focused on establishing psychoanalysis as a profession.

It is interesting to reflect on the role that the professionalization of psychoanalysis in the United States played in shaping its character. During the second decade of the 20th century, when psychoanalysis was beginning to take root in the United States, the profession of American medicine was struggling to upgrade and standardize the quality of medical training. In 1910, the Flexner Report issued by the Carnegie Foundation criticized medical training in the United States and called for more rigorous admission standards, training, and regulation of the profession. In part as a backlash to this report, the physicians who played a dominant role in developing psychoanalysis in United States were concerned about jeopardizing the future of the profession by training candidates who did not even have a background in medicine. In 1938, a fateful decision was made early by the American Psychoanalytic Association to restrict formal psychoanalytic training to physicians. A concern about protecting the professionalism of psychoanalysis played a role in developing a purist, elitist, and rigid form of psychoanalysis with a veneer of scientific respectability, a discouragement of innovation, and a tendency toward social conservatism.

Over time, as medicine consolidated its privileged status within the health care professions and psychoanalysis became established as a subspecialty of medicine, the social prestige of the psychoanalytic profession grew as well. For residents training as psychiatrists, the rigorous, time-consuming process involved in undergoing psychoanalytic training also contributed to the sense that psychoanalysis was an elite subspecialty within psychiatry. Chairs in most major psychiatry departments were psychoanalysts, and most psychiatry residency training programs provided at least some training in psychoanalytically oriented treatment.

The United States became the center of the psychoanalytic world, and massive amounts of time, effort, and money went into psychoanalytic training and the development of the profession. Psychoanalysis became a lucrative, high-prestige, and socially conservative profession, attracting candidates who often had an interest in becoming respected members of the establishment rather than in challenging it (Jacoby, 1983; McWilliams, 2004). Unlike the original psychoanalysts in Europe coming from backgrounds and educational systems that were typically intellectually rich and scholarly in nature, many of the candidates entering psychoanalytic training in the United States often came from educational systems that were relatively narrow and highly technical in nature. There was thus a tendency for psychoanalysis to be applied as a narrow, technical approach with rather inflexible ideas about correct and incorrect technique, analogous to the way one tends to think of medical procedures. This tendency led to a certain technical rigidity and narrow-mindedness. Over 50 years ago, Robert Knight, then president of the American Psychoanalytic Association, remarked on the more "conventional" character of the psychoanalytic candidates of his era, relative to the more original and individualistic character of the candidates of the 1920s and 1930s. According to Knight (1953), the psychoanalytic candidates of the 1950s were "not so introspective, are inclined to read only the literature that is assigned and wish to get through with the training requirements as soon as possible" (p. 218).

In addition, medical education, with its traditional respect for hierarchy and authority, tended to infuse the training of psychoanalysts with a sensibility that led to an unquestioning acceptance of the words of one's teachers rather than to the development of a critical and reflective spirit. And this same sensibility tended to color the therapist–client relationship in a way that institutionalized and exacerbated the inherent power imbalance in the therapeutic relationship instead of encouraging a more democratic egalitarian relationship (Jacoby, 1983; Moskowitz, 1996).

Many European analysts who fled to Latin American also abandoned or went underground with their radical political sympathies and contributed to the establishment of a more politically conservative psychoanalysis. For example, Marie Langer (whose contributions I discuss later), a Viennese born and trained analyst who immigrated to Buenos Aires in 1942 (see Hollander, 1997), was a committed social and political activist during her college days. She grew up and attended college in the socially progressive culture of Vienna that was further consolidated by the election of the social democratic party. In school she was influenced by the Marxist critique of the exploitive nature of capitalist class relations that inspired the politics of the labor movement and leftist parties, including the ruling social democrats.

By the time she completed medical school and began psychoanalytic training in the 1930s, the rising influence of the Nazi movement forced her to flee Vienna, and eventually she immigrated to Argentina, where she became a founding figure of the Argentine Psychoanalytic Association. For many years, she kept a low political profile and devoted herself to establishing psychoanalysis in Argentina and spreading it across Latin America. She stated, "I think my immersion in professional life and my isolation from left politics was partially a defense against my insecurity as an immigrant and my need to find a niche for myself and my family in a new society" (Hollander, 1997, p. 55). In Argentina and other parts of Latin America, psychoanalysis gradually became the dominant influence in the mental health field just as it did in the United States. By the 1960s, it had succumbed to a type of theoretical rigidity and conservative orthodoxy, similar in some respects to the theoretically orthodox style of American psychoanalysis of that era.

Meanwhile, various forces in play were about to lead to dramatic changes in American psychoanalysis. With the rise of biological psychiatry and the explosion in the development of new psychotropic medications, psychoanalysis began to become less fashionable within American psychiatry. The publication of the *Diagnostic and Statistical Manual of Mental Disorders* (3rd ed.; *DSM–III;* American Psychiatric Association, 1980), which among other things attempted to purge the *DSM* of psychoanalytic thinking, further contributed to the growing marginalization of American psychoanalysis (e.g., Horowitz, 2003). Over time, training curricula within psychiatry residencies shifted away from introducing residents to the basics of psychoanalytic theory and practice. Concurrently, the number of psychiatry residents applying for training in psychoanalytic institutes decreased exponentially over time.

It was around this time that the Division of Psychoanalysis (Division 39) was formed within the American Psychological Association. In 1986, Division 39 filed a class action suit against the American Psychoanalytic Association, arguing that the refusal to admit psychologists as candidates within psychoanalytic training institutes was a violation of the antitrust regulations because, by establishing a monopoly of the field of psychoanalysis by physicians, it was preventing fair competition for clients by psychologists and depriving them of their livelihood. Ironically, by the time the lawsuit was settled, market forces were already opening the doors of psychoanalytic training institutes to psychologists, because as the number of candidates seeking psychoanalytic training continued to dwindle, traditional institutes became eager to recruit psychologists (McWilliams, 2004; Moskowitz, 1996).

In the past 20 years, many of the more significant and innovative contributors to the development of American psychoanalytic theory have been psychologists. Thus, psychologists have in many respects become the torchbearers for psychoanalysis in this country. In making this assertion, I am by no means downplaying the vitally important contributions of a host of contemporary medically trained psychoanalysts, such as Glen Gabbard, James Grotstein, Theodore Jacobs, Otto Kernberg, Thomas Ogden, Owen Renik, and Robert Wallerstein. Nevertheless, the explosion in sheer quantity of creative contributions by psychologists to psychoanalysis over the past 30 years and the paradigm-shifting impact of these contributions are undeniable. This new breed of psychoanalytic theorists and researchers have played a vital role in transforming psychoanalysis into a less insular and more intellectually vital discipline, grounded in an appreciation of contemporary developments in a broad range of social sciences, including psychology, sociology, philosophy, political science, and philosophy. The revitalizing influence of psychology on psychoanalysis is attributable to a number of factors. First, there is more of an emphasis in clinical psychology training programs on the development of critical-thinking skills, in contrast to residency training in psychiatry, which places a greater emphasis on memorization of facts and technical mastery. Moreover, training in psychology does place more emphasis on the study of basic psychological, developmental, and social processes that in theory should be relevant to understanding both psychopathology and the process of change. In addition, psychologists receive more training in empirical research methodology than do psychiatrists. Although this does not necessarily lead psychologists to maintain empirical research programs after going into psychoanalytic training, it does help to hone their critical thinking skills and to deepen their appreciation of the limits of various theoretical constructs.

There is another important variable influencing the changing character of American psychoanalysis. Given that pursuing formal psychoanalytic training in today's culture is less likely to be a pathway to professional prestige or financial success, the typical candidate is more likely to be drawn to the field for intrinsic reasons. Especially given the increasingly marginal status of psychoanalysis within the general culture and within mainstream clinical psychology, those attracted to the field are less likely to buy into prevailing cultural and professional values and assumptions and are more likely to approach things from a critical perspective. Thus, ironically, the marginalization of psychoanalysis provides a potential catalyst for innovative thinking. In this respect, important aspects of the emerging sensibility in contemporary American psychoanalysis may be closer in nature to the sensibility of the early psychoanalysts (who, as I previously indicated, were members of a marginalized group) than that of American psychoanalysis in its heyday during the 1940s, 1950s, and early 1960s.

PSYCHOANALYSIS VERSUS PSYCHODYNAMIC THERAPY

Traditionally psychoanalysts have made a clear distinction between *psychoanalysis* versus what is referred to as *psychoanalytic* or *psychodynamic therapy* (I will use the two terms interchangeably). The term *psychoanalysis* has been reserved for a form of treatment with certain defining characteristics or parameters. The term *psychodynamic therapy* has been used to refer to forms of treatment that are based on psychoanalytic theory but that lack some of the defining characteristics of psychoanalysis. Over the years there has been some controversy over which parameters of psychoanalysis are defining criteria and which are not.

A common stance has been that psychoanalysis (as opposed to psychodynamic therapy) is longer term (e.g., 4 years or more), intensive (e.g., a minimum of four sessions per week), and open ended (i.e., no fixed termination date or number of sessions). In addition, traditional psychoanalysis came to be characterized by a specific therapist stance that involves (a) an emphasis on helping clients to become aware of their unconscious motivation; (b) refraining from giving the client advice or being overly directive; (c) attempting to avoid influencing the client by introducing one's own belief and values; (d) maintaining a certain degree of anonymity by reducing the amount of information one provides about one's personal life or one's feeling and reactions in the session; (e) attempting to maintain the stance of the neutral, objective observer rather than a fully engaged participant in the process; and (f) a seating arrangement in which the client reclines on a couch and the therapist sits upright, out of view of the client. This traditional conceptualization of some of the key characteristics of psychoanalysis came to be known as *classical psychoanalysis*.

HOW DID THE DISTINCTION BETWEEN PSYCHOANALYSIS AND PSYCHODYNAMIC THERAPY EMERGE?

As psychoanalysis became the dominant form of treatment in various countries including the United States, analysts experimented with treating a broader range of clients than had initially been the case. As a result, it became necessary to modify various treatment parameters to adapt the approach to clients with different characteristics and needs. Some clients find it too threatening, anxiety provoking, or destabilizing to explore their unconscious motivation and benefit more from structure, advice, and help with problem solving. Some require active reassurance and find the therapist's reluctance to provide direction or exert direct influence too frustrating or anxiety provoking. Some feel uncomfortable lying on a couch and experience it as a form of submission to the therapist. Some do not have the time or the financial resources to attend frequent sessions per week or long-term treatment. To adapt to the needs of these clients, therapists experimented with modifying all of these parameters. And these modified versions of psychoanalysis came to be termed *psychodynamic therapies*.

As psychoanalysis evolved as a discipline, it became important for analysts to distinguish what they came to think of as "real" or "pure" psychoanalysis from the various modified versions of psychodynamic treatment that were emerging. Undergoing formal psychoanalytic training is a rigorous, demanding, and time-consuming activity. It involves taking many years of coursework, receiving extensive clinical supervision, and undergoing a lengthy personal psychotherapy (referred to as a *training analysis*). Many of the therapists practicing psychodynamic treatment were psychiatry residents with a more limited exposure to formal psychoanalytic training who were working in a public hospital setting with clients who were uneducated or more psychologically impaired. A type of professional hierarchy evolved in which the more affluent, educated clients who were able to function in a private practice setting and were more suitable for a traditional analysis were referred to the experienced and more highly trained analysts. This combined with a type of professional guildism reinforced the tendency to maintain a clear-cut distinction between "pure psychoanalysis" and psychodynamic therapy, which tended to be viewed as a diluted or degraded form of psychoanalysis that was not completely distinguishable from the type of help that any untrained or minimally trained helper could provide.

Although the political reasons for maintaining a clear distinction between psychoanalysis and psychoanalytic or psychodynamic therapy are understandable, inevitably psychoanalytic training developed somewhat of a cultish and elitist quality to it, and the various parameters traditionally distinctive of "real" psychoanalysis (e.g., the use of the couch, a minimum number of sessions per week, refraining from giving advice or self-disclosing) developed somewhat of a ritualistic quality to them. As indicated earlier, over time a considerable amount of energy has gone into debating what the essential defining characteristics of a real psychoanalysis are.

Although it is premature to say that debates of this kind have ceased to exist, I think it is fair to say that many psychoanalysts no longer make such rigid distinctions. My own perspective is that although the distinction between psychoanalysis and psychodynamic or psychoanalytic treatment has more to do with the politics of the discipline and professional elitism than any theoretically justifiable criteria, it is a mistake to assume that all of the parameters associated with a traditional psychoanalysis are of no value. For example, the traditional analytic stance of attempting to maintain anonymity can alienate clients, especially in contemporary American culture, which tends to be less formal and hierarchical. At the same time, undisciplined self-disclosure on the therapist's part can be problematic as well. Many clients really do need and value advice and active direction, but too much advice can interfere with clients' ability to develop their own resources and perpetuate a stance of helplessness. Some clients benefit from short-term treatment, but many really do need longer term treatment. I believe that the tendency to pathologize the practice of long-term psychoanalytic treatment or view it as a problematic form of dependency in part reflects an overemphasis in our culture on the value of individualism and a devaluation of the type of interdependency more characteristic of traditional cultures.

For many clients, one therapy session per week is adequate. But there is something about the type of intensity of the therapeutic relationship that can develop when treatment takes place more frequently that really does facilitate certain aspects of the change process. I treat most of my clients sitting across from them (without the use of the couch). But I have found that using the couch can facilitate certain therapeutic processes that can be valuable, such as helping clients to direct their attention inwards toward more important experiences that are subtle in nature and less easily accessible. Notwithstanding the potential benefits of the couch, there are treatments or times in a treatment when an ongoing process of face-to-face encounter between the therapist and client can play a central role in the change process. For example, if the client comes to treatment with problems in intimacy, the ability to explore the quality of emotional contact between the therapist and client on a moment-by moment-basis can be important. It can also be critical for the therapist to be able to see the client's face to develop a nuanced sense of what he or she is feeling and to be able to attune empathically. Or it can be important for the client to have face-to-face contact with the therapist to be able to gauge his ongoing emotional reactions. As I discuss later, psychoanalysts are increasingly coming to see the process of ongoing mutual affective regulation between client and therapist as an important change process, and this process is facilitated when there is visual contact between them. Without this visual contact, it is more difficult for both therapist and client to monitor one another's nonverbal behavior and engage in an ongoing process of mutual responsiveness to and influence of one another's affective experience.

2

History

Sigmund Freud was born in 1856 in a relatively poor but upwardly mobile Jewish family in a small town in what was then the Austro-Hungarian Empire, approximately 150 miles from Vienna. Despite his broad interests growing up, he eventually chose to study medicine, in part because of the allure of science as a possible road to fame and prestige combined with optimism about science as the ultimate path to knowledge. Freud's development of psychoanalytic theory and practice was influenced by a number of cultural and intellectual trends and scientific models that dominated European circles in the late 19th and early 20th centuries (Gay, 1988; Makari, 2008). One important foundation for Freud's more abstract theoretical ideas can be found in the dominant tradition in German neurology during Freud's medical training, which was based on the belief that all psychological phenomena could be understood in neurophysiologic and mechanistic terms. This emphasis on the importance of ultimately grounding psychology in neurophysiology remained a key influence in Freud's thinking throughout his life. Although prescient in his anticipation of today's booming interest and remarkable developments in neuropsychology and

23

the brain sciences, many of the dominant neurophysiological models of Freud's era are considered outdated by contemporary scientific standards. Freud's effort to synthesize psychology with developments that were current in the fields of biology and neurophysiology played a central role in the formulation of what is referred as his *drive theory* of motivation. In drive theory, Freud assumed that human beings are fundamentally asocial in nature and that the primary motivation is to maintain psychic energy at a constant level. Psychic energy is, for Freud, a force that lies on the boundary between the physical and biological and that drives or propels intrapsychic processes and action. According to Freud, once psychic energy is activated (through either an internal or external event), there is a need to discharge it in order to maintain a constant level of psychic energy in the system. This discharge can take place in various ways (e.g., becoming preoccupied with a person, an idea, or a fantasy, or the eruption of symptoms).

Because of various historical circumstances, the field of psychoanalysis was isolated from the natural sciences until recent years, during which there has been a massive resurgence of interest in the synthesis of psychoanalysis and neuroscience research. As a result, many of neurobiological aspects of Freud's thinking (what he referred to as *metapsychology*) were not modified by mainstream analysts in light of newer developments in the natural sciences. This contributed to the perpetuation of various aspects of psychoanalytic theory that have been justly criticized over the past 30 years.

Another formative influence on Freud's early thinking, acquired in his time studying in Paris with renowned French neurologist Jean-Martin Charcot, was his exposure to what were then recent developments in French neurology and psychiatry that were beginning to explore the role that the splitting of consciousness can play in psychopathology (Gay, 1988). Charcot had established an international reputation through his use of hypnosis (or what was referred to as *mesmerism*) with hysterics. *Hysterics* were clients who presented with a variety of dramatic physical problems that could not be accounted for on an organic basis. These clients tended to complain of problems such as paralysis of the limbs, blindness, deafness, and physical convulsions (Gay, 1988). Today this particular pattern of symptom presentation and the associate diagnosis is much less common.

Freud returned to Vienna as a proponent of Charcot's, and he began to synthesize French and German influences on his thinking. Subsequently, Freud was to build on and then critique Charcot's position. In 1886, Freud began collaborating with an older colleague, Josef Breuer, a mentor and patron of Freud's when he was in medical school. Breuer was a highly respected physician in Vienna known for his dramatic successes treating clients with hysteria. His approach involved encouraging them to talk about themselves and helping them to remember traumatic experiences in their lives that they had forgotten. Breuer found that when these clients were able to recall these experiences in an affectively charged fashion, their symptoms would diminish.

Freud and Breuer came to believe that hysterical symptoms were the result of suppressed affect or emotional experience that had been cut off at the time of the trauma and thus had to express itself in the form of physical symptoms. Freud came to believe that by using hypnotic techniques to help clients to recover memories of the trauma and to experience associated affect that had been suppressed at the time, the client could be cured. In 1893–1895, Breuer and Freud published *Studies in Hysteria* together—a book consisting of a number of case histories and a theoretical section outlining their current thinking about the psychological origins of hysteria (Breuer & Freud, 1893–1895/1955).

By the time *Studies of Hysteria* was published, however, Freud was already distancing himself from Breuer, whom he felt he had outgrown, and he had begun to refine both his thinking and treatment of hysteria (Makari, 2008). At first Freud believed that many neurotic symptoms were ultimately attributable to a history of childhood sexual abuse, a perspective that Breuer did not share. Over time, Freud shifted his view to believe that although sexual abuse could play a role in the development of psychological problems, recovered memories of sexual abuse were often at least partially constructed and reflected unconscious or repressed childhood sexual fantasies propelled by sexual instincts (Gay, 1988; Makari, 2008).

At the turn of the century, Freud began to pursue a long-standing interest in the role of dreams as a potential window into unconscious aspects of the human psyche. Freud's (1900/1953) publication of *The Interpretation of*

Dreams eventually caught the attention of the highly respected Eugene Bleuler, the director of the Burgholzi Institute in Zurich. The Burgholzi Hospital (which specialized in the treatment of patients with schizophrenia) was widely known and respected throughout Western Europe as a prominent medical and scientific establishment. Bleuler had a number of talented young psychiatrists on his staff, including Carl Jung. Under Bleuler's guidance, Jung was already establishing an important reputation in the scientific community for adapting research methodology from experimental psychology to study unconscious processes through word association tests. Bleuler encouraged Jung to read Freud, and an alliance began to develop between Freud, Jung, Bleuler, and the group of psychiatrists in Zurich working with Bleuler. Because of the prominence of Bleuler and his colleagues within mainstream psychiatry, this alliance ultimately played a critical role in contributing to the acceptance of psychoanalysis in scientific circles throughout Western Europe (Makari, 2008).

In 1909, Freud and Jung were invited by the American psychologist G. Stanley Hall to give a series of lectures at Clark University in Worcester, Massachusetts. The lectures were well attended and warmly received by a number of prominent American intellectuals, psychiatrists, neurologists, and psychologists. This warm reception laid the ground for the subsequent assimilation of psychoanalysis by American culture and ultimately for the transformation of the United States into one of the most important centers of psychoanalysis in the world (Gay, 1988; Hale, 1971, 1995; Makari, 2008).

World War I had an important impact on the personal lives of the psychoanalysts living in continental Europe as well as on the development of psychoanalysis. During the war, the practices of many analysts, including Freud, dried up, and they lived in poverty and under severe government rationing of food. All publishing and professional activity came to a halt, and many analysts who were physicians were conscripted by the military as emergency physicians. The years leading up to World War II and the ultimate declaration of war in 1939 were to have an even more profound effect on the lives of most psychoanalysts living in continental Europe and on the development of psychoanalysis. In Germany, the growing influence of Nazism from 1930 until Hitler's installation as dictator of Germany in 1933 led to the persecution of vast numbers of continental analysts who were Jewish. Those who had the good fortune to escape immigrated to countries throughout the world. The United States was the most common destination, but both England and Latin America became important destinations as well. All three regions became important centers for psychoanalysis that ultimately led to a growing number of theoretical and technical innovations in psychoanalytic thought influenced in different ways by different cultures over time (Gay, 1988; Makari, 2008). In the United States, the military began relying heavily on psychoanalytically oriented psychiatrists and psychologists to conduct psychological assessments and treat psychologically traumatized soldiers, and this had a massive impact on the growth of American psychoanalysis (Hale, 1995).

THE EVOLUTION OF EARLY PSYCHOANALYTIC THINKING

In this section, I briefly summarize the evolution of early psychoanalytic theory from the late 1890s to the mid-1920s. I begin with Freud's early use of hypnosis to help patients recover traumatic memories and continue on to discuss the innovation of fundamental psychoanalytic principles such as free association, resistance, and transference. By 1923, Freud had developed his structural model of the mind, which distinguishes between three different psychic agencies: the id, the ego, and the superego.

Free Association

Although Freud's early forays into psychoanalysis used mesmerism or hypnosis to help clients recover lost memories and associated emotions, over time he found this technique to be unreliable. Although some clients were good candidates for hypnosis, many were simply not sufficiently suggestible. Instead of hypnotizing his clients, Freud began to encourage them to "say everything that comes to mind without censoring." This was the origin of the psychoanalytic principle of free association, in which clients are encouraged to attempt to suspend their self-critical function and verbalize fantasies, images, associations, and feelings that are on the edge of awareness.

Over time Freud and the early analysts came to believe that it was vital to make a clear distinction between psychoanalysis and the tradition of hypnosis out of which it had emerged. In addition to the unreliability of hypnotic techniques, Freud came to distrust the accuracy of many recovered memories. In addition, as analysts gained more clinical experience, they began to find that it was not uncommon for a symptom that remitted as a result of hypnosis to return after a short period of time.

Another factor influencing the theoretical emphasis on clearly distinguishing psychoanalysis from hypnosis and suggestibility was the evolving conception of both the nature and goals of psychoanalysis. Despite a growing interest in the use of psychoanalysis by a number of medical practitioners, hypnosis had not completely shed its public image as a form of quackery, and Freud and his colleagues were eager to establish psychoanalysis as a treatment that was based on scientific principles. In addition, there was a growing sense that one of the important goals or values of psychoanalysis involved the pursuit of truth. Hypnosis helps people through suggestion or through fostering a certain type of belief. In contrast, the goal of psychoanalysis was supposed to be helping people to become more skeptical and to face uncomfortable truths about themselves. Psychoanalysis came to be seen as a kind of counterindoctrination (to a type of social and cultural brainwashing) rather than a form of indoctrination (Reiff, 1966).

Freud acknowledged that psychoanalysis retained an element of suggestion insofar as the client's initial positive feelings about the analyst and hopes about the analyst's potency play important roles in motivating him or her to persist in the face of difficult and sometimes painful analytic work. These positive hopes and expectations were seen as deriving from the client's fantasies about the healing powers of the therapist, on the basis of the client's view of his or her parents as powerful. But ultimately the goal was for the therapist to analyze all aspects of the client's projected fantasies about the therapist, so that the client could develop a more realistic perspective on the analyst—one that would not perpetuate a situation in which the client continued to see himself or herself as a powerless figure dependent on the greater power of a larger-than-life authority figure.

This emphasis on distinguishing psychoanalysis from suggestion came to exert an important influence on subsequent developments in thinking about both the mechanisms of change and the preferred interventions. With respect to the mechanisms of change, the emphasis was placed on the importance of insight and understanding as the curative factors, and the impact of more human qualities of the therapist and the relational factors became downplayed. With respect to interventions, the key intervention came to be the analyst's interpretation, which involved introducing the client to aspects of his or her unconscious that the client was unable to access on his or her own. Advice, suggestion, reassurance, and encouragement were downplayed because they blurred the boundaries between the truth-seeking aspects of psychoanalysis versus the element of suggestion and would potentially compromise the client's autonomy by encouraging dependence on the analyst.

Resistance

Inevitably, Freud discovered that his clients were not always able to follow his instructions to free associate. This led to the development of the notion of *resistance*, which was initially conceptualized as the client's reluctance or inability to collaborate with the therapist in the prescribed fashion. Freud initially dealt with resistance by using his authority as the doctor to encourage clients to overcome their resistance and say whatever came to mind regardless of their tendency toward self-censorship. Subsequently, he and other analysts came to believe that the therapeutic exploration of the resistance was a vitally important therapeutic task in and of itself.

Transference

A third noteworthy stage in the ongoing evolution of Freud's thinking was the development of the concept of *transference*. Freud began to observe that it was not uncommon for his clients to view him and relate to him in ways that were reminiscent of the way they viewed and related to significant figures in their childhoods—especially their parents. He thus began to speculate that they were "transferring" a template from the past onto the present situation. For example, a client with a tyrannical father might begin to see the therapist as tyrannical.

At first, Freud saw this transference as an impediment to treatment. He speculated that transference was a form of resistance to remembering traumatic experiences. The idea was that the client would act out the previous relationship in the therapeutic setting rather than remember it. Over time, however, Freud came to see the development of the transference as an indispensable part of the psychoanalytic process. By in a sense reliving the past in the analytic relationship, the client provided the therapist with an opportunity to help him or her develop an understanding of how past relationships were influencing the experience of the present in an emotionally immediate way. This conceptualization of the potential value of transference provides additional justification for the notion of the therapist retaining a neutral and uninvolved stance. The idea emerged that the analyst, by maintaining a certain degree of anonymity (through withholding information about his or her own life or personal reactions), could function as a type of ambiguous stimulus or blank screen that would encourage the development of the transference and decrease the possibility that it would be contaminated by the therapist's real characteristics.

The Abandonment of Seduction Theory

Another critical stage in the evolution of Freud's thinking was a shift in his belief that sexual trauma always lies at the root of psychological problems toward an emphasis on the role of fantasy and instinctual drive. Eventually he came to abandon his theory that all of his clients had been sexually abused as children and instead developed the theory of childhood sexuality and instinctual drive. Consistent with the work of sexuality researchers of his time, such as Havelock Ellis and Albert Moll, Freud began to believe, in contrast to the commonsense view that childhood is a time of sexual innocence, that children actually experience sexual or at least presexual feelings from the beginning and that these stem from instinctual sources (Makari, 2008). Freud came to believe that these presexual feelings lead children to have fantasies about having sexual encounters with adults. As children mature, these fantasies become pushed out of memory or repressed because they are experienced as too threatening.

Freud speculated that often memories of sexual trauma are actually the product of reconstructed memories that are based on childhood sexual fantasies rather than real sexual trauma. Although Freud did not come to believe that real sexual abuse or trauma are never the source of the neurotic problems, he did come to place less emphasis on them and no longer saw them as the ubiquitous core of all neurotic problems.

This shift away from seduction theory to an emphasis on unconscious fantasy is a controversial one from a contemporary perspective that mirrors the ongoing controversy taking place in psychology these days about the reality of recovered memories of sexual abuse. Given the current recognition that child sexual abuse is much more common than it was once thought to be, Freud's shift in emphasis from seduction theory to drive theory is seen by many critics as particularly problematic. In addition, Freud's growing emphasis on the role that endogenous drives play in the development of emotional problems led to a neglect of the role that environmental factors, such as the quality of caretaking, play in the developmental process. Although this neglect has subsequently been remedied in many psychoanalytic theories, it still remains a feature of some schools of psychoanalytic thought.

The Development of Structural Theory

In 1923, Freud published *The Ego and the Id*, which lays out the foundations for what subsequently became known as his *structural theory* (S. Freud, 1923/1961). In this paper, he distinguished between three different psychic agencies: the id, the ego, and the superego. The id is the aspect of the psyche that is instinctually based and present from birth. The id presses for immediate instinctual gratification without any regard for realistic concerns about the realities of the immediate situation. The ego gradually emerges out of the id and functions to represent the concerns of reality. In this model, the ego plays the role of enabling the individual to adapt to the concerns of reality. It is thus more rational in nature. Although the id presses for immediate sexual gratification, the ego takes into concern the suitability of the situation for satisfying one's instinctual desires, and it also allows the individual to delay instinctual gratification or to find ways of channeling instinctual needs in a socially acceptable fashion (e.g., skillfully seducing the object of one's sexual desire or redirecting one's sexual desire in a more appropriate direction).

The *superego* is the psychic agency that emerges through the internalization of social values and norms. Although some aspects of the superego can be conscious, other aspects are not. One important function of the ego is to mediate between the demands of the id and the superego. For reasons that I will not go into here, the superego often becomes overly harsh and demanding and can lead to self-destructive feelings of guilt and a punitive and rejecting stance toward one's own instinctual needs and wishes. One of the goals of analysis traditionally has been to help the individual become more aware of the overly harsh nature of his superego so that he becomes less self-punitive.

When instinctually derived wishes begin to emerge that are unconsciously experienced as dangerous because they are incompatible with the demands of the superego, the ego signals their imminent emergence with anxiety. This anxiety triggers the use of various psychic processes to keep the wishes, fantasies, and associate feelings out of awareness. I discuss these psychic processes, which are referred to as *defenses*, in greater detail later. A fundamental premise emerging out of this structural perspective is that there is an ongoing dynamic tension between one's instinctually derived wishes and one's defenses against them. When this tension or conflict is managed in a relatively healthy way, the individual is able to be sufficiently aware of both his needs and wishes and the anxieties they evoke and to find a constructive and adaptive way of negotiating this tension. However, when this conflict is managed in a maladaptive way, various forms of psychopathology can emerge.

PSYCHOANALYSIS BEYOND FREUD

By the time of Freud's death in 1939, several different psychoanalytic traditions were beginning to emerge, influenced by a number of seminal theorists writing in a range of different countries and cultural traditions.

In this section, I briefly review some of these traditions, including ego psychology, Kleinian and post-Kleinian theory, object relations theory, interpersonal psychoanalysis, relational psychoanalysis, and Lacanian psychoanalysis.

The Development of Ego Psychology in Britain and the United States

Freud's structural theory and some of the theoretical developments in his thinking that led up to it ultimately gave rise to an important tradition of psychoanalysis that came to be known as ego psychology. The unofficial leader of the ego psychology tradition was Freud's daughter, Anna Freud, who moved to London in 1938 with her father a year before he died. Under the influence of analysts such as Anna Freud (1936), Wilhelm Reich (1941), and Otto Fenichel (1945), an important thread of ego psychological thinking emerged that placed considerable emphasis on the need for understanding and exploring the defensive functioning of the ego prior to any attempt at exploring unconscious drives, fantasies, or wishes. The rationale for this practice is the assumption that as long as the client's current maladaptive modes of defensive functioning remain unchanged, any attempts to explore and release unconscious instinctual material will be futile. The reason for this is that the same factors that have led the wishes to be buried in the unconscious in the first place will still be intact.

In the United States, the European émigré Heinz Hartmann (1964) became one of the key figures in another strand of ego psychology that was particularly interested in broadening psychoanalysis beyond a psychotherapeutic tradition into a more general theory of psychological development and psychic functioning. Hartmann and his colleagues were particularly interested in the adaptive aspects of the ego and in the investigation of the various ways in which the ego helps the individual adapt to reality. Ego psychology became the dominant tradition of psychoanalysis in North America. During its heyday in the 1940s, 1950s, and early 1960s, any theoretical or technical developments that diverged too far from mainstream ego psychology were in danger of being branded as heretical, and their proponents were in danger of becoming marginalized by mainstream psychoanalysis.

Some of the most significant, clinically relevant American psychoanalytic writing of the time came out of the New York Psychoanalytic Institute and the perspective that was synthesized and articulated particularly clearly by Jacob Arlow and Charles Brenner (e.g., Arlow & Brenner, 1964). In contrast to Heinz Hartmann, who was interested in developing psychoanalysis into a general psychology, or Erik Erikson (1950), who was particularly interested in themes such as the process of identity development, Arlow and Brenner (1964) emphasized the ubiquity of intrapsychic conflict in all aspects of the individual's functioning. For example, whereas Hartman argued that there are aspects of the ego that are sufficiently independent of the id to be completely rational and conflict free, Arlow and Brenner (1964) argued that all aspects of the individual's functioning must be understood as compromises between underlying unconscious, instinctually based wishes and defenses against them.

The Development of Kleinian and Object Relations Theory in Britain

A second major psychoanalytic tradition emerging out of some of Freud's more mature thinking came to be known as *object relations theory*. When Anna Freud and her father arrived in London in 1938, there was already an influential British school of psychoanalysis emerging under the leadership of the Austrian émigré Melanie Klein (1882–1960). Klein, who had been analyzed by Freud's close colleagues Sandor Ferenczi (1873–1933) and Karl Abraham (1949), had immigrated to London in 1926. Originally a child analyst, Klein was particularly interested in understanding the early relationship between the mother and the infant, and she developed a line of theory that laid the groundwork for understanding the way in which psychological maturation involves a process of developing internal representations of our relationships with significant others. Klein's thinking also laid the groundwork for subsequent theoretical developments in psychoanalysis that viewed human beings as fundamentally interpersonal creatures who have a phylogenetically based relationship to the mother and to other human beings.

Object relations theory places a central emphasis on the way in which our internal representations of our relationships with significant others influence the way in which we perceive relationships, choose romantic partners and friends, and shape our relationships with others. These internal representations are referred to as *internal objects* or *internal object relations*. Much of the writing about the process through which internal objects or internal object relations are developed (a process referred to as *internalization*), although clinically rich, is conceptually complicated and can be ambiguous and difficult to grasp (Eagle, 1984; Schafer, 1968). Because of the conceptual problems associated with this literature, there is a growing interest in the conceptualization of internalization that has emerged out of attachment theory. John Bowlby (1907–1990), the originator of attachment theory, was a British psychoanalyst and psychiatrist who was particularly interested in studying child development. I describe Bowlby's model of internalization later in the book. One major difference between the conceptualization of internalization emerging out of attachment theory and the thinking of objects theorists is that models deriving from attachment theory and developmental research tend to assume that internal working models are based on the representation of actual interactions that have taken place between the infant and significant others. In contrast, object relations theory assumes that internal models are shaped by a combination of these real experiences with unconscious wishes and fantasies and other intra-psychic process that are not reality based.

Once Anna Freud arrived in London and began the process of establishing her own power base, the theoretical controversies between Kleinians and Freudians became intense and vitriolic, threatening the survival of the relatively new British Psychoanalytic Society. During a series of what were characterized as "controversial discussions," Freudians critiqued many of the central Kleinian ideas. These discussions revolved around critiques of fundamental Kleinian assumptions such as the degree to which elaborate unconscious fantasies can be attributed to infants and the Kleinian tendency to emphasize interpretations of deep unconscious fantasies in both children and adult clients, without an adequate exploration of defenses that are closer to the client's conscious awareness. These discussions (or more accurately, heated debates) ultimately led to further clarifications in both Kleinian and Freudian thinking.

A so-called gentleman's agreement was forged between Freudians and Kleinians in which it was agreed that the two traditions would coexist within the British Psychoanalytic Society. Throughout the 1940s and 1950s, some of the more innovative theoretical and technical work emerged out of the work of Klein and her followers, who became particularly interested in working with difficult, treatment-resistant cases. Some of the more prominent Kleinian analysts who emerged during this period included theorists such as Hannah Segal, Herbert Rosenfeld, Joan Riviere, Susan Isaacs, Esther Bick, and Wilfred Bion (for a review, see, e.g., Sayers, 2001).

A third group of psychoanalytic theorists emerging out of the British Psychoanalytic Society consisted of analysts who were influenced by both Freudian and Kleinian ideas but were unwilling to formally align themselves politically with either tradition. These analysts, who became known as the British Independents or the Middle Group, consisted of theorists such as Ronald Fairbairn, Michael Balint, Donald Winnicott, Marion Milner, Masud Khan, and John Bowlby (for an excellent survey of the British Independent tradition, see Rayner, 1991). Some of the key qualities associated with the work of these Middle Group analysts were an emphasis on the importance of spontaneity, creativity, and therapist flexibility and the value of providing clients with a supportive and nurturing environment. Many developments coming out of the Kleinian and Middle Group traditions have subsequently been assimilated into more recent developments in American psychoanalysis. Winnicott (1958, 1965) in particular has become an important inspiration to many contemporary North American psychoanalysts who place an important emphasis on creativity, spontaneity, and authenticity. And John Bowlby's work has given rise to the extremely fertile area of attachment theory and research. It is also worth noting in passing that Sandor Ferenczi, who indirectly influenced and anticipated some of the more recent developments in American psychoanalysis, had an important influence on the thinking of the British Independents through his protégé, Michael Balint.

Different object relations theorists (e.g., Fairbairn, 1952, 1994; Klein, 1955/2002a, 1975/2002b) have different models of internalization. For example, Klein theorized that internal objects emerge out of the interaction of real experiences and unconscious fantasies that are instinctively derived. According to her, people are born with instinctually based passions related to both love and aggression that are linked to unconscious fantasies and images about relationships with others. The unconscious fantasies linked to these instincts exist prior to any actual encounter with other human beings and serve as the scaffolding for the perception of others.

In Klein's thinking, instinctually based aggression plays a particularly important role. She believed that infants experience their own aggression as intolerable. For this reason, they need to fantasize that this aggression originates in the other (typically the mother in Klein's thinking) rather than in themselves. Klein uses the term *projective identification* to designate the intrapsychic process through which feelings originating internally are experienced as originating from the other. These unconscious fantasies of aggressive, persecuting others (referred to as *internal objects* by Klein) become part of the infant's psychic world. These aggressive "bad" internal objects then color their perception of significant others who they see as dangerous and persecuting.

To retain some perception of the other as potentially good and not persecutory, infants unconsciously split the image of the other or the internal object into good and bad aspects. The good aspect is thus able to remain uncontaminated by the bad aspect. Over time, as a result of both cognitive and emotional maturation and ongoing encounters with real significant others, the child is able to begin integrating the good and bad objects into one whole and to reown aggression as emerging from the self. Klein is not a systematic theorist. Much of her writing has a feeling of trying to put into words intuitions gleaned from years of clinical experiences that do not lend themselves easily to explicit conceptual articulation.

Fairbairn theorized that internal objects are established when the individual withdraws from external reality because the caregiver is unavailable, frustrating, or traumatizing, and instead creates a type of internal reality as a substitute. According to Fairbairn, to the extent that one has unsatisfying relationships with actual significant others, one becomes preoccupied with fantasized relationships, which become represented unconsciously. These fantasized relationships become important building blocks for one's experience of the self because the self is always experienced in relationship to others, whether in fantasy or reality. From Fairbairn's perspective, the problem is that these defensive attempts to control significant others by developing fantasized relationships with them, rather than real ones, are ultimately only partially successful. The reason for this is that the depriving or traumatizing aspects of the significant other that provide the raw material for the unconscious fantasy or internal object inevitably end up becoming part of the internal structure or enduring psychic organization that is developed.

The Movement Toward Psychoanalytic Pluralism in North America

As indicated previously, unlike the British system that formally institutionalized the existence of three different psychoanalytic traditions, coexisting to some extent on equal if not necessarily harmonious terms, the system in the United States formally recognized the existence of only one psychoanalytic tradition: ego psychology. American ego psychologists were by and large unfamiliar with British object relations theory, and American theorists diverging too far from mainstream ego psychology either resigned from or were forced out of the American Psychoanalytic Association and started their own schools of thought. These schools of thought had little, if any, influence on mainstream American psychoanalysis.

One of the most notable mavericks was Harry Stack Sullivan (1892–1949), an iconoclastic American-born psychiatrist who had never received any formal psychoanalytic training. Sullivan (e.g., 1953) developed his own model of psychoanalytically oriented psychiatry, which was strongly influenced by a type of social field theory emerging out of the Chicago School of Sociology and symbolic interactionist thinking. Unlike Freud, Sullivan theorized that the need for human relatedness is the most fundamental human motivation, and he deprivileged the role of sexuality in his thinking. He also believed that it is impossible to understand the individual out of context of relationships with others, and that this principle extends to the therapeutic relationship as well. In contrast to mainstream psychoanalysts, Sullivan argued that everything transpiring in the therapeutic relationship needs to be understood in terms of both the client's and the therapist's ongoing contributions, rather than exclusively in terms of the client's psychology or the transference. Although Sullivan published very little (most of his books consist of posthumously published lectures), he had a formative influence on the training of American psychiatrists, primarily through his lectures and supervising.

Sullivan befriended and became somewhat of a mentor to another American-born psychiatrist, Clara Thompson (1957). With Sullivan's encouragement, Thompson went to Europe to seek training with Sandor Ferenczi, who in his own way was transitioning toward a more interpersonal perspective in his more mature work. Sullivan and Thompson ultimately formed an alliance with Erich Fromm. Fromm, a European-born and trained psychoanalyst with a background as a sociologist, had an interest in the synthesis of psychoanalysis and sociological and political thinking. In addition, over time he increasingly came to incorporate humanistic and existential ideas into his thinking (e.g., Fromm, 1941). Fromm's perspective placed considerable emphasis on the importance of the authentic human encounter in the therapeutic relationship.

In 1946, Sullivan, Thompson, and Fromm founded the William Alanson White Institute in New York. The White Institute subsequently became the foremost center of American interpersonal psychoanalysis. The development of interpersonal analysis was thus influenced by a combination of the distinctive interests and sensibilities of its three cofounders. Although this tradition was ignored by mainstream American psychoanalysis, it nevertheless nurtured and kept alive an important tradition of thinking, which was ultimately to have an important impact on mainstream American psychoanalysis in the 1980s and 1990s.

Another important figure who came to play an important role in the movement toward a more pluralistic perspective in North American psychoanalysis was Heinz Kohut (1984). Kohut was a European émigré who completed his medical training in Vienna in 1939 and then immigrated to Chicago, where he completed both his residency in psychiatry and his formal psychoanalytic training. For a number of years, Kohut was a well-respected mainstream ego psychologist. As his thinking and clinical work evolved, however, he became particularly interested in the treatment of narcissism, and over time his theoretical formulations diverged increasingly from mainstream psychoanalytic ideas. Kohut became particularly interested in understanding the processes through which the individual develops a cohesive sense of the self, an experience of inner vitality, and a capacity for self-esteem. He placed an increasing emphasis on the role that the therapist's empathic stance plays as a mechanism of change in and of itself, and in the centrality of this process in repairing ruptures in the therapeutic relationship when they occur as a result of the therapist's inevitable lapses in empathy.

Rather than focusing on developing adaptive compromise formations, Kohut became increasingly interested in helping clients to develop a cohesive sense of self and a sense of inner vitality and engagement in meaningful life projects. This emphasis on transforming an inner sense of emptiness into one of vitality and authenticity mirrored important developments taking place in the work of important British Middle Group theorists such as Michael Balint and Donald Winnicott. Ultimately Kohut broke away from the mainstream and founded the tradition of self psychology.

The development of relational psychoanalysis was another important stage in the ultimate fragmentation of the monolithic psychoanalytic perspective that dominated American psychoanalysis in the 1950s and early 1960s. A key publication that helped to crystallize developments that were already taking place and to catalyze the emergence of a new paradigm was Jay Greenberg and Stephen Mitchell's (1983) book, *Object Relations in Psychoanalytic Theory*. This book provides a scholarly examination and critique of the work of a broad range of different psychoanalytic theorists from both the United States and Britain. It provides an ingenious framework for schematizing the relationship between various key psychoanalytic theorists and for understanding both the intellectual and sociopolitical factors leading to the evolution of their approaches. Greenberg and Mitchell (1983) argued that the entire history of psychoanalysis can be understood as the attempt by various theorists to develop an interpersonal model of motivation and functioning without discarding Freud's model of motivation, which is based on his drive theory.

Greenberg and Mitchell's book accomplished a number of objectives. First, it established a legitimate role for the tradition of American interpersonal psychoanalysis within the mainstream psychoanalytic tradition by drawing parallels between what Sullivan was trying to accomplish theoretically and what other more "legitimate" mainstream psychoanalysts were attempting to achieve (e.g., Heinz Hartmann, Edith Jacobson, Margaret Mahler, Otto Kernberg). By illustrating the way in which a range of different theorists, including Sullivan, were attempting to elaborate on the interpersonal aspects of psychoanalysis that were implicit in Freud's thinking but not conceptualized in a theoretically systematic and coherent fashion, the authors paved the way for incorporating some of the insights emerging from interpersonal theory into mainstream psychoanalysis. Related to this, they introduced Sullivan's interpersonal perspective to an audience of ego psychologists who were by and large unfamiliar with it. Just as important, they began introducing both interpersonal analysts and American ego psychologists to the seminal work of British object relations theorists such as Klein, Fairbairn, and Winnicott.

Klein and Post-Kleinian Traditions in Europe and Latin America

Because this book is aimed primarily at an American audience, I have focused for the most part on developments in psychoanalytic thinking that have to date had the greatest influence on the American psychoanalytic tradition. I would be remiss, however, if I did not at least make reference to two additional developments that have been remarkably influential in other parts of the world and that are increasingly coming to have an impact on American psychoanalysis. The first development can be designated as Kleinian and post-Kleinian thinking. A host of innovative thinkers in various parts of Europe and Latin American have built on Kleinian thinking in creative and clinically useful ways. Of particular note is the Kleinian or neo-Kleinian emphasis on careful moment-by-moment monitoring of the extent to which the client is making constructive use of the therapist's interventions, as well as the potential role that the client's feelings of badness and inadequacy and envy of the therapist's apparent goodness and bountifulness can play in his or her inability to make constructive use of therapeutic interventions (e.g., Joseph, 1989). Examples of extremely influential Kleinian and post-Kleinian theorists in Latin America and continental Europe include Heinrich Racker, Willi and Madeline Baranger, Leon Grinberg, Horacio Etchegoyen, Ignacio Matte-Blanco, and Antonino Ferro (cf. Etchegoyen, 1991; Ferro, 2002). Many of these theorists have also been profoundly influenced by the prominent neo-Kleinian analyst Wilfred Bion (1970).

Lacanian Theory

A final major psychoanalytic tradition is Lacanian and post-Lacanian theory. This tradition, which originated in the work of the French psychoanalyst Jacques Lacan (1901–1981), played a central role in the development of French psychoanalysis. It has also become highly influential in Latin America (especially Argentina) and has had an important influence on psychoanalysis in continental Europe and increasingly in England. In the United States, the influence of Lacanian analysis has traditionally been limited to the areas of literary criticism, the humanities, and feminist thinking. But Lacanian concepts are beginning to make their way into American clinical psychoanalysis as well. Lacan is notoriously difficult to understand, in part because his thinking is embedded in the context of the French intellectual tradition that is stylistically very different from the Anglo-American intellectual tradition.

Lacan (1975/1988a, 1978/1988b) was extremely critical of the American tradition of ego psychology, which he viewed as betraying Freud's most radical and important insights about the centrality of unconscious processes and of emphasizing conventionality and adaptation to society. In contrast to American ego psychologists who emphasized the adaptive aspects of the ego, Lacan argued that the ego (i.e., one's sense of "I") is an illusion. According to Lacan, our identity or sense of "I-ness" is forged out of a misidentification of ourselves with the desire of the other. This begins in our childhood when we attempt to satisfy the desire of others, initially as incarnated in the desires of the mother; in other terms, one could say that we develop a sense of who we are through the construction of an identity that is designed to satisfy the needs and fantasies of our parents. Unlike Winnicott (or for that matter, humanistic psychotherapists), however, Lacan, does not believe that there is a true self waiting to be discovered, underlying the illusory sense of "I" that we experience. Instead, there is emptiness or what Lacan refers to as a *lack*—a fundamental sense of alienation from the self. This fundamental experience of alienation or lack stems from a variety of sources. One of the most important ones is that our experience cannot be symbolized or communicated without the medium of language. The very process of symbolizing our experience through language, however, results in a distortion of this experience and contributes to the experience of alienation.

If there is no true self waiting to be discovered or uncovered, what is the essence of cure from a Lacanian perspective? I believe that Lacanian theory is ambiguous on this point. On one hand, Lacan emphasized the importance of developing a true ownership of one's own desire and a separation from the desire of the other. On the other hand, he argued that desire by its very nature can never be satisfied. There is thus a level at which Lacan appears to be saying that an important goal of analysis is to accept this intrinsic lack and to come to terms with it (for a similar interpretation of Lacan, see Moncayo, 2008).

Finally, I think it is valuable to consider the cultural context and historical period during which Lacan became influential in France. Unlike North America, France did not take a serious interest in psychoanalysis until the 1960s. The French experienced a cultural revolution in the 1960s similar in some respects to the cultural revolution in the United States, but different in other respects. In May–June 1968, an uprising took place in which students seized control of their high schools and universities and workers took over their factories. Inspired by socialist thinking (which has always had a greater influence in Europe than North America), these students and workers had a vision of challenging the entrenched hierarchy and bureaucratic structure of the French middle-class establishment and of paving the way for a new, liberal, and more progressive society that allowed for a greater role for participatory democracy, as well as personal liberation from the rigidly defined roles and rules of society. This was a heady and exciting time in French cultural life filled with a sense of new possibilities. In Sherry Turkle's (1992) words:

> The streets of France were flooded with people talking to each other as they claimed they had never talked with each other before. They spoke of their sexuality, of their dissatisfactions with family life and formalities, of their desire for more open communication. The hierarchies and bureaucratic structures which are so much a part of French life were, for the moment, forgotten. Questions about authenticity and alienation were experienced as real, immediate and tangible. (p. 64)

Lacan developed an iconic status in French culture. He was notorious for his radical challenge to conventional rules and for his attacks on traditional hierarchies within the psychoanalytic establishment. Furthermore, Lacan strongly promoted accepting candidates from a wide range of educational backgrounds into psychoanalytic training and challenged existing psychoanalytic orthodoxies and forms of authoritarianism. His intellectual engagement with well-known French left-wing intellectuals (many of whom attended his immensely popular lectures) also contributed to his popularity. In a sense, psychoanalysis in France blossomed and emerged as a progressive and revolutionary force at precisely the same time as psychoanalysis in the United States was playing the role of a conservative cultural institution on the decline.

In Latin America, Lacanian psychoanalysis began to emerge as an important cultural force in the climate of political ferment leading up to the emergence of the dictatorships of the 1970s and 1980s. Unlike the situation in France, countries such as Argentina and Brazil already had well-established psychoanalytic establishments by this time. The dominant psychoanalytic associations were beginning to splinter into conservative apolitical factions, and a younger generation of analysts felt that an apolitical or accommodationist stance in the face of oppressive totalitarian regimes was indefensible. The antiauthoritarian, politically subversive elements of the Lacanian tradition, as well as its connection to left-wing intellectual circles, played important roles in enhancing its appeal. With the downfall of the various dictatorships in Latin America in the early to mid-1980s, Lacan's influence blossomed more fully (Plotkin, 2001).

Lacanian psychoanalysis played an important role in breaking up the hegemony of the traditional psychoanalytic institutes in Latin America in the same way that traditions such as self psychology and relational psychoanalysis did in the United States. And last but not least, the Lacanian deemphasis of the importance of either medical training or standardized training curricula and uniform institutional credentialing procedures opened the profession up to a much broader range of potential training candidates. This was particularly important for the large number of psychologists trained in university programs who became licensed and practiced as psychologists without undergoing the long-term and intensive training typical of American clinical psychology students (Plotkin, 2001).

3

Theory

What are the values and goals of psychoanalysis and psychoanalyti-cally oriented therapy? As I have already indicated, there is no sim-ple answer to this question given the host of different psychoanalytic traditions and the evolving nature of psychoanalysis. Nevertheless, I will attempt to articulate some of the key values represented within a range of diverse psychoanalytic traditions, some of them complementary and some existing in tension with one another.

PSYCHOANALYSIS AS A BOUNDARY DISCIPLINE

Psychoanalysis has been classified alternatively as a medical discipline, a science, an interpretive or hermeneutic system, a philosophical system, and a form of cultural criticism. Whereas Freud was intent on establishing psy-choanalysis as a science, many contemporary critics have argued that it is a "failed science" (e.g., Grunbaum, 1984). At the same time, there is a ten-dency among many contemporary proponents of psychoanalysis to argue that the attempt to think of psychoanalysis as science was misguided in the first place and that psychoanalysis is more accurately conceptualized as a hermeneutic or an interpretive discipline. Although there is no doubt that many psychoanalytic concepts have not been tested empirically, and many are unverifiable to begin with, there are nevertheless a host of empirical studies supporting a range of different psychoanalytic concepts (for a review of some of this empirical literature, see, e.g., Westen, 1998; and Westen & Gabbard, 1999). As I discuss later, there is also a substantial and growing body of research supporting the effectiveness of psychoanalytic treatment (for excellent reviews of this research, see, e.g., Shedler, 2010; and Levy, Ablon, & Kaechele, in press).

Notwithstanding this growing evidence base, debates such as whether it is best to conceptualize psychoanalysis as a science or a hermeneutic discipline will inevitably continue. I believe that the reason for this is that psychoanalysis lies on the boundary between a variety of different intellectual and scientific disciples. This liminal status has led to considerable confusion about how to think about psychoanalysis, but it has also been an important source of vitality.

PSYCHOANALYSIS AND THE NATURE OF THE GOOD LIFE

To begin thinking about the goals of psychotherapy, it is essential to make some assumptions about what psychological health looks like. And these assumptions are inevitably influenced by values and beliefs about the nature of what constitutes the "good life." Different forms of psychotherapy and different psychoanalytic traditions hold different assumptions about the nature of the good life and by implication the goals of psychoanalysis. Freud's oft-quoted remark that "psychoanalysis transforms neurotic misery into ordinary unhappiness" is seen by some as reflecting a pessimistic perspective on life. But it can also be seen as embodying a certain form of wisdom. Freud believed that life by its very nature involves various forms of suffering: illness, loss of loved ones and friends, disappointments, and ultimately death. It is essential, however, to distinguish what might be termed *existential suffering* from self-imposed neurotic suffering.

From Freud's perspective, one of the goals of psychoanalysis is to help people learn to grapple with life's inevitabilities with a certain degree of equanimity and dignity.

As I discuss in greater detail later in this chapter, many contemporary psychoanalysts have emphasized the goal of living life with vitality. Dimen (2010), paraphrasing the author Andrew Solomon, said that "good treatment restores vitality, not happiness" (p. 264). In addition, for many contemporary psychoanalysts there is also an emphasis on challenging potentially oppressive normative emphases on singular and conventional definitions of "mental health" and on replacing them with a respect for and appreciation of the infinite number of different ways of being in this world and a celebration of this diversity (e.g., Corbett, 2009; Dimen, 2010; Harris, 2008). In the words of the influential British psychoanalyst, Donald Winnicott (1958): "We are poor indeed if we are only sane" (p. 150).

As Cushman and Gilford (2000) argued, in many respects psychoanalysis goes against the grain of many values that are characteristic of our culture and that are reflected in such developments as the managed care system and the evidence-based treatment movement. According to them, the advent of the managed care system, the evidence-based treatment system, and the dominance of the health-care system by the cognitive–behavioral tradition reflect such values as clarity, activity, speed, concreteness, practicality, realism, efficiency, systematization, consistency, independence, and self-responsibility.

Psychoanalysis, in contrast, tends to value such dimensions as complexity, depth, nuance, and patience. This emphasis on patience, acceptance, and allowing things to unfold in their own way can be traced back to some aspects of Freud's early thinking and is an important thread that is expressed in different ways in different psychoanalytic traditions. Freud cautioned analysts that the "furor sanandi" (an excessive zeal to cure) could interfere with the therapist's ability to assume the kind of attitude of patience and acceptance that is necessary to be truly helpful. Wilfred Bion (1970) is famous for speaking about the importance of approaching every session "without memory or desire" in order to allow the "emotional truth" of what is taking place to emerge (p. 57).

The downside of this type of perspective is that it can lend itself to the type of never-ending analysis that is caricatured in Woody Allen movies and that clients have valid reasons to be concerned about. In fact, some very prominent analysts have argued that this attitude can too often degenerate into a failure to grapple with the question of what is genuinely helpful to clients and is one of the factors that has led to the declining popularity of psychoanalysis (Renik, 2006). On the other hand, there is a certain wisdom embodied in this emphasis that can serve as a valuable corrective to the contemporary Western tendency to overestimate our capacity for individual efficacy and mastery and that fails to recognize the limitation of our ability "have it all."

Complexity, Ambiguity, and Curiosity

Psychoanalysis tends toward the view that at a fundamental level, human beings are complex creatures whose experience and actions are shaped by multiple and often conflicting conscious and unconscious determinants, as well as by social and cultural forces. Related to this is an emphasis on the importance of tolerance of ambiguity. Psychoanalytic thinking assumes that given the complexity of human experience, there is a fundamental ambiguity to the therapeutic process. This sense of ambiguity forecloses the possibility of pat understandings of what is going on with one's client or in the therapeutic process. This can lead to a fair amount of anxiety for novice therapists who want to feel that they can understand what is going on in a definitive fashion and have clear guidelines for practice. The positive side of this fundamental ambiguity is a genuine curiosity in watching the process emerge and allowing one's understanding to unfold and evolve over time (McWilliams, 2004). This can be associated with a genuine respect for the complexity of human nature and a feeling of humility in the face of the ultimate unknowability of things.

The Ethic of Honesty

Freud believed in the importance of shedding one's illusions and coming to accept the inevitabilities of life. He believed that self-deception is ubiquitous, and he valued the process of self-reflection and truth seeking (in the sense of searching for one's real motives). In a sense, one could say that psychoanalysis is associated with an ethic of honesty (e.g., McWilliams, 2004; M. G. Thompson, 2004). Clients are encouraged to strive to be truthful with themselves about their own motives, and this type of honesty is expected of therapists as well.

Once we accept the idea of unconscious motivation, we begin to recognize that we are all at some level strangers to ourselves. We begin to see that we therapists are just as susceptible to self-deception as our clients are. It is not unusual for trainees in supervision to find out that they were intervening in a certain way because of feelings that they were completely unaware of (e.g., competitiveness, insecurity, irritation, a desire for control) and that our rational or theoretical understanding of why we are acting as we are as therapists is often only part of the story or an after-the-fact justification.

Conducting psychotherapy from a psychoanalytic perspective thus inevitably involves an ongoing process of self-discovery and personal growth for therapists. It is difficult to work with clients, especially challenging ones, without being willing to explore one's own contribution to what is going on in the therapeutic relationship in an ongoing fashion and a willingness to reflect on why we are doing what we are doing in a given session. Many contemporary psychoanalysts believe that in many successful treatments, both the client and the therapist change. Practicing psychoanalysis is thus not for the faint of heart.

A Search for Meaning, Vitality, and Authenticity

Freud's emphasis was on becoming aware of our irrational, instinctually based wishes and then renouncing or taming them through our rational faculties. One important shift in the goals of psychoanalytic thinking, especially in North America, involves an emphasis on the importance of creating meaning and revitalizing the self. This shift may in part be a result of changing cultural and historical conditions. This shift in cultural sensibility corresponds to an important shift in the cultural landscape from Freud's time to ours. Psychoanalysis was born during an era when individualism was in the process of becoming more pronounced. In the Victorian culture of Freud's time, the self was viewed as dangerous and an emphasis was placed on self-mastery and self-control (Cushman, 1995). Over the last century, the culture of individualism has continued to evolve, and the individual has become increasingly isolated from the community. This is a double-edged sword. On the one hand, the more individuated person of contemporary culture is freer of the potentially suffocating influence of community. On the other hand, he or she is cut off from the sense of meaning and well-being that potentially flows from being integrated with a wider community.

The disintegration of the unifying web of beliefs and values that traditionally held people together and that give life its meaning has resulted in the emergence of what Philip Cushman (1995) referred to as the *empty self.* This empty self experiences the lack of tradition, community, and shared meaning as an internal hollowness; a lack of personal conviction and worth; and a chronic, undifferentiated emotional hunger. In contemporary Western culture, psychological conflicts are thus more likely to involve a search for meaning and a hunger for intimate and meaningful relationships than a conflict between sexual instincts and cultural norms (S. A. Mitchell, 1993; Safran, 2003).

This search for meaning is linked to a process of individuation—a process of both discovering and deciding what one really believes in, rather than simply accepting consensual social values. Philosophers and historians tell us that the concept of authenticity is a relatively novel invention that emerged in 18th-century Europe (Guignon, 2004; Taylor, 1992). Its emergence was associated with the rise of the culture of Romanticism. The Romantic movement can be understood as a backlash against the Enlightenment. It was an attempt to recover a sense of oneness and wholeness lost with the rise of modernity. The Romantic movement holds that truth is discovered not through scientific investigation or by logic but through immersion in one's deepest feelings. There is a distrust of society in the Romantic movement and an implicit belief in the existence of an inner "true self" that is in harmony with nature. Conventional social rituals are seen as artificial and empty, and as potentially stifling authenticity. Consistent with this sensibility, there is an important thread in contemporary psychoanalytic thinking that views the therapist's authentic responsiveness to the client as an important element in the change process. The therapist's ability to act spontaneously or to improvise in response to the demands of the moment is viewed as a potential antidote to the devitalizing effects of social ritual and conformity in people's lives (e.g., Ringstrom, 2007; Stern et al., 1998). Irwin Hoffman has persuasively argued that it is important not to emphasize the value of spontaneity at the expense of ritual, and vice versa. He argues instead for the value of thinking in terms of the dialectical interplay between ritual and spontaneity in the therapeutic process. A detailed discussion of Hoffman's perspective is beyond the scope of this book but the interested reader is referred to Hoffman (1998).

Reflection-In-Action Versus Technical Rationality

At a time when there is a growing emphasis in the psychotherapy field on the importance of developing evidence-based practices that can be delivered in a standardized fashion, there is an important trend in contemporary psychoanalytic thinking that emphasizes the unique nature of every therapeutic encounter and the impossibility of developing "standardized" interventions or principles of intervention. The idea that professional knowledge consists of "instrumental problem solving made rigorous by the application of scientific theory and technique" is referred to as *technical rationality* by Schon (1983, p. 21). Interestingly, Schon (1983) and others conducting research on differences in the problem-solving styles of experts versus novices (e.g., Dreyfus & Dreyfus, 1986) have found that skilled practitioners across a wide range of disciplines (musicians, architects, engineers, managers, psychotherapists) do not problem solve in a manner consistent with this model of technical rationality. Instead, they engage in a process of what Schon termed *reflection-in-action*. This involves an ongoing appraisal of the evolving situation in a rapid, holistic, and (at least partially) tacit fashion. It involves a reflective conversation with the relevant situation that allows for modification of one's understanding and actions in response to ongoing feedback.

It has become increasingly common for contemporary psychoanalytic thinkers to argue that this notion of reflection-in-action provides a better framework for conceptualizing the therapeutic activities of a skilled therapist than does the model of technical rationality (Aron, 1999; Hoffman, 2009; Safran & Muran, 2000). The therapist can no longer look toward a unitary and universal set of principles to guide his actions. Instead, he is confronted with a multiplicity of theoretical perspectives that he can use to help him reflect on how best to act in this particular moment with this particular client. Any guidelines derived from theory must ultimately be integrated with the therapist's own irreducible sub-jectivity (Renik, 1993) and with the unique subjectivity of the client to find a way of being that is facilitative in a given moment.

KEY CONCEPTS

In this section, I outline some of the central concepts of psychoanalytic thinking. Most, if not all, of these concepts have evolved over time. In addition, whereas some of these concepts originated in the early days of psychoanalytic thinking, others emerged at later stages in the evolution of psychoanalytic theory.

The Unconscious

The concept of the unconscious is central to psychoanalytic theory. Over time psychoanalytic conceptualizations have evolved, and these days differ-ent models of the unconscious are emphasized by different psychoanalytic schools. Freud's original model of the unconscious was that certain memo-ries and associated affects are split off from consciousness because they are too threatening to the individual.

As Freud's thinking about the unconscious evolved, he began to distin-guish between two different principles of psychic functioning that are always taking place at the same time: secondary process and primary process. Sec-ondary process is associated with consciousness and is the foundation for rational, reflective thinking. It is logical, sequential and orderly. Primary process, which operates at an unconscious level, is more primitive in nature than secondary process. In primary process, there is no distinction between past, present, and future. Different feelings and experiences can be condensed together into one image or symbol, feelings can be expressed metaphorically, and the identities of different people can be merged. The "language" of primary process does not operate in accordance with the rational, sequential rules of secondary process or consciousness. Primary process can be seen operating in dreams and fantasy.

Over time Freud came to think of the unconscious not only in terms of traumatic memories that had been split off but also in terms of instinctual impulses and associated wishes that are not allowed into awareness because we have learned that they are unacceptable through cultural conditioning. These instincts and associated wishes are often related to the areas of sexuality and aggression. For example, a woman has sexual feelings toward her sister's husband but disavows them or pushes them out of awareness because she experiences them as too threatening. A man has angry feelings toward his boss but pushes them out of awareness because they are too threatening. Freud referred to the process through which unacceptable wishes are kept out of awareness as *repression*.

This perspective ultimately became formalized and elaborated further by Freud with his distinction between the id, the ego, and the superego. It is important to point out, however, that although this conceptualization had an important influence on the development of subsequent psychoanalytic theory, many contemporary psychoanalysts no longer find it to be particularly useful. Charles Brenner, one of the major architects of mainstream American ego psychology in the 1950s, explicitly rejected the usefulness of this model of the mind as early as the mid-1990s (Brenner, 1994) in favor of a model that simply sees intrapsychic conflict as ubiquitous.

Many contemporary interpersonal and relational psychoanalysts find it more useful to think of the mind as consisting of multiple self-states that may to varying degrees be in conflict with one another and that emerge in different relational contexts (e.g., Bromberg, 1998, 2006; Davies, 1996; Harris, 2008; S. A. Mitchell, 1993; Pizer, 1998). In this perspective, there is no central executive control in the form of the ego. Consciousness is a function of a coalition of different self-states. It is thus an emergent product of a self-organizing system that is influenced in an ongoing fashion by current interpersonal context. From a developmental perspective, experience taking place in the context of interpersonal transactions that are intensely anxiety provoking or traumatic can be kept out of awareness. But there is no hypothetical psychic agency keeping it out of awareness. Instead, there is a failure to attend to the experience and construct a narrative about it (Stern, 1997, 2010). It is thus this failure of attention and construction that leads to the splitting off or dissociation of aspects of experience. And just as the interpersonal context leads to the dissociation of experience in the first place, we need others to help us attend to and construct a narrative about it. As Donnel Stern (2010) put it in his most recent book, the therapist thus serves as an essential "partner in thought" for the client.

Whether the unconscious is conceptualized in traditional Freudian terms, or in terms of aspects of experience that are not symbolized (or self-states that are dissociated), the concept of the unconscious is central to psychoanalytic thinking. For most psychoanalysts, one of Freud's most important insights is that "we are not masters of our own house." We are all motivated by forces outside of our awareness.

Fantasy

Psychoanalytic theory holds that people's fantasies play an important role in their psychic functioning and the way in which they relate to external experience, especially their relationships with other people. These fantasies vary in the extent to which they are part of conscious awareness—ranging from daydreams and fleeting fantasies on the edge of awareness to deeply unconscious fantasies that are defended against. In Freud's early thinking, these fantasies were linked to instinctually derived wishes and served the function of a type of imaginary wish fulfillment. In this view of fantasies, they are typically linked to sexuality or aggression. Over time Freud and other analysts developed a more elaborate view of the nature of fantasy that sees fantasies as serving a number of psychic functions, including the need for the regulation of self-esteem, the need for a feeling of safety, the need for regulating affect, and the need to master trauma. Because fantasies are viewed as motivating our behavior and shaping our experience, yet for the most part operate outside of focal awareness, exploring and interpreting clients' fantasies is viewed as an important part of the psychoanalytic process.

One- Versus Two-Person Psychologies

An important development that has taken place across a range of different psychoanalytic schools has been a shift from what has come to be termed a *one-person psychology* to a *two-person psychology*. Freud's original view of the therapist as an objective and neutral observer who could serve as a blank screen onto whom the client projects his transference has been replaced with a view of the therapist and client as coparticipants who engage in an ongoing process of mutual influence at both conscious and unconscious levels. The conceptual shift has important implications for the evolution of many of the concepts we discuss later (e.g., resistance, transference, countertransference), as well as for psychoanalytic technique, because it implies that the therapist cannot develop an accurate understanding of the client without developing some awareness of his ongoing contribution to the interaction. Although the therapist's goal still remains one of ultimately understanding and helping the client, this cannot be accomplished without an ongoing process of self-exploration on the therapist's part. This is especially the case with difficult or more disturbed clients, who tend to evoke complex feelings and reactions in others that may remain unconscious. But the process of exploring one's own contributions to the therapeutic relationship can help to illuminate subtle aspects of psychic functioning and interpersonal style in less disturbed clients as well.

Knowledge and Authority

Traditionally psychoanalysis has emphasized the therapist's ability to know things about clients that they cannot know about themselves, both because we are all inevitably blinded by our own limits to conscious awareness and because therapists are in a privileged position with respect to understanding things as a result of their training, expertise, and own personal growth. This emphasis on the therapist's superior understanding of things is tied to a conception of the role relationship between client and therapist that tends to exacerbate the already existing power imbalance of the therapeutic relationship. This unfortunately can lead to abuses of the therapist's authority as well as to an experience of being denigrated or patronized for the client, who is already feeling vulnerable in this respect because of the inherent power imbalance. Because the client is in the position of the one seeking help from the therapist, he or she is inevitably in a one-down situation.

Other issues to be considered are the nature of the therapist's expertise, the kind of specialized knowledge he or she has (if any), and how this intersects with the dimension of power and authority in the therapeutic relationship. In Freud's time, it was assumed that therapists had a type of objectivity that clients did not have and that because of clients' unconscious conflicts and inability to break through their own defenses and become aware of unconscious experience, therapists both by virtue of their specialized training and personal analysis and their ability to see clients from the outside had the ability to interpret clients' unconscious conflicts.

As discussed earlier, in contemporary psychoanalytic thinking there has been a shift toward a two-person psychology and a greater emphasis on the mutuality of the therapeutic relationship. The therapist to some extent has been deprived of his or her status as the expert on the client's unconscious. Moreover, with the increasing emphasis on the therapist's inevitable embeddedness in the interpersonal field and lack of self-transparency, there is more of a sense that reality is "up for grabs" in the therapeutic relationship.

Defenses

A defense is viewed as an intrapsychic process that functions to avoid emotional pain by, in one way or another, pushing thoughts, wishes, feelings, or fantasies out of awareness. For example, the client who speaks about an interpersonal loss, such as the death of a parent, and has no conscious awareness of any associated feelings is engaging in a defensive process. A variety of intrapsychic processes can be used to keep threatening wishes, feelings, and self-experiences out of awareness. These processes or mechanisms are termed *defenses*. In the heydays of ego psychology, a systematic attempt was made to conceptualize and categorize the various defenses that people use. Common examples of defenses that have become part of the language of popular culture include *intellectualization* (in which the individual talks about something threatening while keeping a distance from the feelings associated with it), *projection* (in which a person attributes a threatening feeling or motive he or she is experiencing to the other person), and *reaction formation* (in which the individual denies a threatening feeling and proclaims he or she feels the opposite, e.g., somebody who is feeling irritated with a friend says, "I could never be angry with you!").

An important defense that has not entered the popular lexicon is referred to as *splitting*. Splitting takes place when an individual attempts to avoid his perception of the other as being good from being contaminated by negative feelings by splitting his representation of the other into two different images (an all-good image and an all-bad image). Melanie Klein believed that this defense is commonly used at certain stage of development by infants to allow them to feel safe with their mothers. Rather than developing a complex representation of the mother that entails both her desirable and undesirable qualities, two separate representations of the mother are established: one that is all good and the other that is all bad. The infant thus alternates between seeing the mother as all good or all bad, depending on which representation is dominant in any given moment. According to Klein, the ability to integrate the good and bad representations of the mother is a developmental achievement. This involves developing the ability to tolerate ambivalent feelings about the other.

Clients who have more severe psychological disturbances (e.g., borderline clients) never achieve this ability as adults and as a result are more likely to use splitting as a defense than are psychologically healthy individuals. Splitting tends to have a more serious impact on individuals' everyday functioning than other defenses have, because individuals who commonly use it experience dramatic fluctuations in their perception of and feelings about others. These individuals thus fluctuate between idealizing others as perfect and then demonizing them and seeing them as evil. These intense fluctuations make it very difficult to maintain stable relationships with others and difficult to hold onto a stable image of the therapist's trustworthiness.

Resistance

Resistance is conceptualized as the tendency for the individual to resist change or act in a way that undermines the therapeutic process. What is the difference between defense and resistance? Resistance is the way in which defensive processes manifest in the therapy session so as to interfere with the therapist's goals or agenda. For example, the client's inability to think of anything to say while in the session may be understood as a form of resistance. The tendency to consistently come late for sessions or to forget about sessions can be thought of as a form of resistance. In both of these examples, a primary motivating factor may be the unconscious wish to avoid emotional pain (e.g., the pain associated with exploring threatening feelings or the fear of changing). This tendency to avoid pain or fear manifests in a behavior that thwarts or impedes the therapist's agenda and the process of treatment.

There are many different potential sources of resistance, including the avoidance of threatening feelings being evoked by the therapeutic process, the equation of change with the experience of self-annihilation, a fear that trusting the therapist will lead to abandonment and more pain, envy of the therapist, or negative feelings toward the therapist that are in part a function of the individual's dynamics.

The concept of resistance, although potentially valuable, can also be problematic. One problem is that the term *resistance* tends to have a connotation of the client doing something wrong, insofar as he or she is not cooperating with the therapist in the therapeutic process. The concept can thus have a blaming or pathologizing quality to it. Over time, an important shift in analytic theory and technique has taken place in which resistance has come to be seen not as an obstacle but as an intrinsic mode of the client's psychic functioning or aspect of his or her character that needs to be illuminated and understood rather than bypassed. Moreover, greater emphasis has been placed on the self-protective aspects of resistance. There has thus been an important shift toward conceptualizing the notion of resistance in empathic and affirmative terms. One way of thinking about resistance is to recognize that we are all complex beings with complex and contradictory needs and motivations and that there is a natural tendency to be ambivalent about changing. We begin therapy both wanting to change and to stay the same (Bromberg, 1995). This desire to stay the same (which is typically unconscious) can be grounded in many factors, including a fear of losing our identities and a fear that if we give up our habitual ways of defining ourselves and relating to others, we will experience both complete abandonment and a loss of a sense of self.

Even if resistance is formally conceptualized in empathic or affirmative terms, however, there is a natural tendency for therapists to experience resistance as problematic because it obstructs their therapeutic goals and agendas. It is thus not uncommon for therapists to become frustrated or irritated with clients when resistance emerges and to respond in an attempt to break through or interpret away the resistance in order to move on with the work of therapy. It can thus be helpful to remember that the process of exploring the resistance is the essence of the therapeutic process rather than the work that needs to be done to get to the point at which one can begin therapy.

Another important evolution in the conceptualization of resistance reflects the previously mentioned shift from a one-person psychology to a two-person psychology. Whereas a one-person psychology locates the source of the resistance in the client, a two-person psychology emphasizes that the therapist often plays an important role in the emergence of resistance. Resistance often emerges in part as a perfectly understandable reaction to the therapist's mistakes or lack of accurate empathic understanding. Resistance can also be a function of more subtle contributions of the therapist to the interaction. For example, a therapist who unconsciously fears dealing with feelings of grief may collude with a client in not fully exploring feelings about the loss of a loved one. A therapist may collude with the client in the process of keeping the conversation at an intellectual level because the theme resonates with painful experiences in the therapist's own life. The exploration or interpretation of resistance thus often involves an exploration of the therapist's contribution to the resistance (Safran & Muran, 2000).

Transference

Like most psychoanalytic concepts, the notion of transference has evolved considerably since Freud first developed it in 1905. Transference refers to clients' tendency to view the therapist in terms that are shaped by their experiences with important caregivers and other significant figures in their developmental backgrounds. Thus, early developmental experiences establish templates or schemas that shape the perception of people in the present. Although this tendency to view others through schemas that were established through experiences with one's parents is true for all new relationships, the role of the therapist tends to be imbued with a particular set of expectations by virtue of the fact that the therapist is in the role of the helper. The client is thus particularly likely to be in a dependent role viz-a-viz the therapist, and the therapist has a greater likelihood of functioning as a stand-in for a parental or authority figure than another person selected at random.

The therapeutic relationship thus provides an opportunity for the client to, in a sense, bring the memory of the relationship with the parent or other significant figure from the past (aspects of which are often unconscious) to life through the relationship with the therapist. This provides the therapist with an opportunity to help clients gain insight into how their experiences with significant figures in the past have resulted in unresolved conflicts that influence their current relationships. Because transference involves a type of reliving of clients' early relationships in the present, the therapist's observations and feedback can help them to see their own contributions to the situation in an emotionally alive way. The resulting insight will have an experiential quality to it that will lead to change rather than a purely intellectual understanding that has no ultimate impact on the client.

Early conceptualizations of transference assumed that it involves a distortion of objective reality. It was common to make a distinction between transferential aspects of the therapeutic relationship that are distorted versus nontransferential perceptions that are more accurate or reality based. With the growing influence of a two-person psychology, transference has come to be viewed as the joint product of the client's perceptions and the therapist's characteristics and actions. This is a critical shift in conceptualization, and its importance cannot be overestimated. In the more traditional conceptualization of transference, the assumption is that the client's psychological problems make it difficult for him or her to perceive objective reality accurately, and therapists have the ability to provide more objectively based feedback that can correct the client's distorted perceptions.

There are two problems with this perspective. First, the assumption that the therapist is the ultimate authority on reality exacerbates the inherent power imbalance in the therapeutic relationship and contributes to the client's feelings of being disempowered and the therapist's potential abuse of this power imbalance. Second, although it is inevitably the case that the client's perceptions of the therapist will be influenced by past experiences, it is problematic to assume that his or her perceptions of the therapist are distorted. What if the client's perception that the therapist is critical or withholding (or shy, sadistic, or flirtatious) has some basis in the therapist's actual characteristics? Or what if certain aspects of the client's behavior elicit reactions on the therapist's part that are consistent with the client's expectations? For example, a client who anticipates that therapist will be abusive in the same way as his or her father or mother had been may act in a hostile way toward the therapist, thereby eliciting hostile or abusive behavior from the therapist. The client's perception of the therapist as abusive is thus not a distortion. It is the client's construction of the current situation influenced by a combination of factors.

Countertransference

The therapist's countertransference is his or her counterpart to the client's transference. Freud conceptualized the therapist's *countertransference* as the therapist's feelings and reactions to the client's transference that are a function of his or her own unresolved unconscious conflicts. Thus, for example, a male therapist whose mother tended to play the role of the martyr may have extremely strong negative reactions to a client who plays a similar role. A therapist whose father was extremely competitive with him may have intensely competitive feelings toward a competitive client. From Freud's perspective, countertransference reactions were an obstacle to therapy, and the therapist's task was to analyze or work through his or her own countertransference in personal supervision, in therapy, or through self-analysis.

These days, countertransference tends to be defined more broadly as the totality of the therapist's reactions to the client (including feelings, associations, fantasies, and fleeting images). In the same way that a two-person psychology makes it impossible to view transference exclusively as the client's distortion, it is also incompatible with conceptualizing counter-transference as stemming exclusively from the therapist's unresolved conflicts. Client characteristics and subtle communications to the therapist in the room can also contribute to the countertransference. Although this view of countertransference as providing the therapist with potentially valuable information about the client can be extremely useful therapeutically, it is not without its own potential dangers. There is a tendency in some psychoanalytic writing to assume that countertransference experience provides an infallible source of information about the client's unconscious experience and to underemphasize the therapist's own unique contribution to the countertransference.

Different theorists emphasize different ways of making use of counter-transference. On one end of the spectrum, some analysts recommend selectively disclosing certain aspects of their subjective experience with the client as a way of deepening the exploratory process. Some go as far as to share personal dreams that might be relevant. Others are more cautious about the disclosure of the countertransference experience to clients and instead emphasize the value of a type of internal work in which one reflects on one's experience privately and makes use of it to help formulate one's thinking about what might be going on between the client and therapist and what implications this might have for understanding the client (e.g., Bollas, 1992; Jacobs, 1991; Ogden, 1994).

It is not unusual for trainees to raise questions about the potential value of countertransference as a source of information about the client. For example, imagine a situation in which I have just found out that one of my children has developed a chronic illness. It is highly likely that this knowledge is going to have an important impact on the type of experience I will have with any client I see. And yet the particular form and shading of my experience will also be influenced by the client I am working with. With one client, I may be more aware of feelings of helplessness and sadness. With another, my feeling may tend toward rage at the cosmic injustice of my situation.

Enactment

Enactments are conceptualized as repetitive scenarios played out in the relationship between client and therapist that reflect the unconscious contributions of both persons' personal histories, conflicts, and characteristic ways of relating to others. Because client and therapist are always influencing one another at both conscious and unconscious levels, they inevitably end up playing complementary roles in these scenarios. The process of collaborating in the exploration of how each of them is contributing to these scenarios provides clients with an opportunity to see how their own relational schemas contribute to the enactment and to play out new scenarios with other important human beings in their lives, thereby contributing to a modification of their current relational schemas.

The traditional psychoanalytic wisdom was that the therapist should avoid participating in these enactments and instead try to maintain a neutral position from which he or she can interpret the client's transference toward the therapist, thereby helping the client to see how the present is being shaped in maladaptive ways by his or her own unconscious assumptions, projections, and previous developmental experiences. A common position in contemporary psychoanalytic thinking, however, is that the therapist cannot avoid participating in these enactments no matter how psychologically healthy or mature he or she is because (a) people are inevitably influenced by complex nonverbal communications from others that are difficult to decode and (b) therapists, like other human beings, are never fully transparent to themselves.

 One problem with aspiring to therapeutic neutrality as an ideal is that it sets up unrealistic standards that lead us to place impossible demands on ourselves that make it more difficult to accept and become aware of aspects of our own contribution to the enactment that we experience as shameful or unacceptable. This lack of self-acceptance makes it more likely that we will need to dissociate aspects of our own self-experience, thus making it more difficult to ultimately recognize the nature of our participation in the enactment and to disembed from it.

Furthermore, even if it were possible to avoid participating in enactments with our clients, the ability to do so would deprive us of the experience of participating in our clients' relational worlds and developing a lived experience of what their relational world feels like. The process of participating in these enactments thus allows us, in Philip Bromberg's (1998) words, to know our clients "from outside in." Those things that our clients cannot express to us linguistically or verbally are communicated through nonverbal behavior and action, and the only way we can come to know important dissociated aspects of the client's internal experience is to play a complementary role in their relational scenarios and experience the feeling of playing this role.

The Therapeutic Alliance

The concept of the *therapeutic alliance* originated in early psychoanalytic theory. Although Freud did not use the term explicitly, he did emphasize the importance of establishing a good collaborative relationship with the client. In a seminal paper, Richard Sterba (1934) established the groundwork for subsequent thinking about the alliance by arguing that therapy involves a process of developing the capacity for self-observation by identifying with the therapist's observing function.

Perhaps the best-known psychoanalytic formulation of the alliance was articulated by Ralph Greenson in the United States. Greenson (1965) spoke about the importance of distinguishing between the transferential aspects of the therapeutic relationship, which are distorted, and the alliance, which is based on the client's rational, undistorted perception of the therapist and on a feeling of genuine linking, trust, and respect. Greenson emphasized that the caring, human aspects of the therapeutic relationship play a critical role in allowing the client to benefit from the interventions of psychoanalysis.

Many contemporary psychotherapy researchers have found Edward Bordin's (1979) transtheoretical conceptualization of the alliance to be particularly useful. Bordin conceptualized the alliance as consisting of three interdependent components: tasks, goals, and bond. According to him, the strength of the alliance is dependent on the degree of agreement between client and therapist about the tasks and goals of therapy and on the quality of the relational bond between them. The *tasks* of therapy consist of the specific activities (either overt or covert) that the client must engage in to benefit from treatment (e.g., exploring dreams, exploring the transference). The *goals* of therapy are general objectives toward which the treatment is directed (e.g., symptom reduction, personality change). The *bond* element of the alliance refers to the degree of trust the client has in the therapist and the extent to which he feels understood by the therapist. The bond, task, and goal components of the alliance are always influencing one another. So, for example, to the extent that there is an agreement between client and therapist about tasks and goals, the bond will be strengthened. To the extent that the therapeutic tasks or goals do not initially make sense to the client, a strong bond will make it easier to develop some agreement or working consensus.

Building on Bordin's (1979) thinking as well as developments in relational psychoanalysis, I and my colleagues have argued that it is more useful to think of the alliance as an ongoing process of negotiation between client and therapist about therapeutic tasks and goals because this emphasizes the importance of mutual attempts by both client and therapist to find ways of working together, rather than placing the burden of responsibility on the client to accommodate to the therapist's way of working (see, e.g., Safran & Muran, 2000). This ongoing process of negotiation, which is only partially conscious, is an important element of the change process in and of itself. It can provide clients with the opportunity to learn that it is possible to negotiate one's needs with the needs of the other, rather than dealing with conflicts by either denying one's own needs or adopting a rigid stance toward relationships. The ongoing negotiation of the alliance in therapy thus helps the client to learn that healthy relationships do not have to involve a denial of the other's subjectivity on the one hand and/or an experience of self-effacement or compromise of one's sense of integrity on the other.

The Therapist's Stance

Classical psychoanalytic thinking prescribed very clear guidelines for the therapist's stance in therapy consisting of abstinence, anonymity, and neutrality. *Abstinence* refers to the therapist's refraining from gratifying clients' wishes and requests when their fulfillment is seen as interfering with the therapeutic process. It is important to remember here that early psychoanalytic thinking was influenced by Freud's experience of working with hysterical clients who had a tendency to develop erotic transferences toward him (and other analysts), and he cautioned therapists against gratifying clients' erotic wishes rather than helping them to understand what was underlying them.

Anonymity refers to a therapeutic stance that is designed to minimize the disclosure of personal information by the therapist to minimize the therapist's influence on the type of transference that develops. The meaning of therapist *neutrality* has shifted over time, but it essentially refers to a therapist stance that is guided by the ideal of objectivity, a respect for the client's autonomy, and a reluctance to influence the client in any way. The principle of neutrality is influenced in part by the previously discussed traditional emphasis on distinguishing analysis from suggestion and an emphasis on the truth-finding aspects of analysis.

Although these guidelines still exert some influence on today's psychoanalytic thinking, their implementation has been modified if not completely abandoned by a number of theorists. For example, with respect to the principle of abstinence, although it may be countertherapeutic to agree to a borderline client's request to meet for coffee between sessions, it can be therapeutic to agree to speak to a client in crisis by phone between sessions or to provide a particular client with advice. It all depends on the client's unique needs and the specific context.

With respect to the principle of anonymity, the shift toward a two-person psychology and the recognition that the therapist is always conveying information about himself or herself even if attempting to remain anonymous (e.g., through nonverbal behavior, through the type of interventions he or she makes, through decisions about when to remain silent and when to speak) has decreased the emphasis on neutrality as an essential element of the therapist's stance. Nevertheless, contemporary psychoanalytic therapists attempt to retain an ongoing disciplined reflectiveness about the potential impact of disclosing various types of information to the client.

For example, will answering my client's request for information about my personal background, my personal life, or my current feelings about him or her facilitate or hinder the therapeutic process? Why is my client asking this particular question now? And what emotional impact does my client's question have on me? Two different clients may ask the identical question (e.g., a question about where I live or how many children I have), and yet with the first client I feel perfectly comfortable answering, and with the second client I feel intruded on. With one client, the process of spontaneously disclosing my current feelings about him or her as a way of deepening the process of exploration may be facilitative. Another client may experience this disclosure as intrusive. I elaborate in greater detail on the topic of therapist self-disclosure in the next section.

Self-Disclosure

As psychoanalytic thinking about the topic of therapist neutrality has evolved, so too has thinking about the topic of self-disclosure. In the heyday of mainstream classical psychoanalysis, it was believed that the therapist should be extremely cautious about any form of self-disclosure because it might potentially "contaminate" the transference by influencing it through personal information about the therapist. This led at times to extreme positions such as a reluctance to answer any questions about details of the therapist's life outside of the therapy session (e.g., questions about whether the therapist has ever struggled with issues similar to the client's, questions about the therapist's marital status, children, hobbies, where the therapist is going for a vacation) or the therapist's thoughts or feelings during the session (e.g., what are you thinking or feeling right now?).

Although this perspective on self-disclosure has the advantage of offering unambiguous guidelines and can be facilitative in certain contexts, it has the downside of limiting the therapist's flexibility and in some cases being unnecessarily off-putting and alienating to the client. As the mainstream in North America moved toward more of a two-person psychological perspective, questions of when to self-disclose and when not to self-disclose became both topical and controversial. These days, the controversy has subsided to some extent, with definitive answers to the question being replaced with the ubiquitous "it depends." It depends on the type of self-disclosure, it depends on the unique qualities and needs of the client, it depends on what a particular form of self-disclosure means to both client and therapist, and so forth.

Under some circumstances, it can be extremely facilitative for the therapist to self-disclose. For example, it may be helpful for the client to know that the therapist has struggled or is struggling with similar issues, or it may be reassuring for a single client to know that the therapist is single or is married. The therapist's willingness to answer an innocuous question may reduce a sense of artificial distance or formality and facilitate the development of the alliance.

In other cases, therapist self-disclosure can interfere with the therapeutic process or have unintended and potentially harmful consequences. As clients, we have ambivalent and conflicting needs about knowing our therapists (Aron, 1996). On the one hand, there is the desire for intimacy, the desire to feel close to the therapist, or the desire to reduce the power imbalance by knowing that the therapist is a human being just as we are. On the other hand, we can have the conflicting desire to maintain some aspects of the anonymity of the therapist so that we do not have to worry about the therapist's needs or so that we can maintain the therapist in the role of the helper who has special qualities that will allow him or her to be of assistance to us.

Another form of self-disclosure involves revealing aspects of one's personal thinking or feelings within the session. This form of self-disclosure (often referred to as *countertransference disclosure*) can provide a useful way both of providing the client with his or her impact on another human being and may also play a vital role in initiating an exploratory process (Ehrenberg, 1992; Safran & Muran, 2000). For example, a therapist who becomes aware of feeling particularly cautious or tentative with a client may, in a curious and inquiring manner, say, "I'm not sure what exactly is going on, but I find myself being very cautious, and tentative with you . . . it feels almost as if I'm walking on eggshells."

Countertransference disclosures of this type can be a useful way of putting into words something that is taking place implicitly in the therapeutic relationship, thereby holding it up to the light of day where it can be examined. It is not uncommon in everyday exchanges for people to unconsciously act in ways that subtly impact on others or elicit complex and contradictory reactions that are difficult to understand or put into words. For example, someone may act in a subtly demeaning way toward others that engenders feelings of inadequacy or competitiveness in them. Or someone may habitually have a lively, humorous bantering style that keeps others off balance and at a distance. The implicit rules of everyday social discourse do not sanction trying to talk about these subtle interactions. As a result, there is a type of ongoing mystification that is perpetuated in relationships, especially for people who are likely to be particularly self-defeating. One of the tools that the therapist has at his disposal is the role-conferred sanction to break the normal rules of social discourse and to step back and attempt to talk about that which normally goes unexplored.

This provides therapists with a tremendously valuable tool for facilitating self-awareness in their clients. Like other forms of self-disclosure, however, countertransference disclosure can be either facilitative or hindering, depending on the particular context. For example, a client whose parents were narcissistically self-absorbed may experience the therapist's countertransference disclosure as a form of narcissistic self-absorption on the therapist's part and as a neglect of the client's needs. A narcissistic client's sense of self may be so fragile that he or she cannot tolerate attending to the subjectivity of the other and may experience the therapist's countertransference disclosure as overwhelming or threatening. It is thus always important for the therapist to be responsive to the needs of the specific client and the unique context when using countertransference disclosure.

Emotion and Motivation

As previously discussed, the concept of *drive* is central to Freud's view of motivation. For Freud, drive is an instinctually derived force that exists on the boundary between the psychological and the biological. It is a psychic representation of stimuli originating from within the organism that makes a demand on the mind for work. It is thus a form of psychic energy. In

Freud's mature thinking, there are two primary drives: a life instinct and a death instinct. Motivation is conceptualized as a complex interaction between these two drives and also as a product of attempts to reestablish situations that have resulted in satisfaction by facilitating the discharge of psychic energy in the past. There is no systematic model of emotion in Freud's thinking. As previously discussed, Freud's drive model was anchored in neurophysiological theory and evolutionary models that were commonly accepted in his time but have since been superseded by other theoretical and empirical developments. Although there have been a number of attempts to develop revised or alternative motivational models by psychoanalysts over the years, the most common trend in contemporary psychoanalytic thinking is to replace drive theory with a motivational perspective that is grounded in contemporary developments in emotion theory and research (Safran & Muran, 2000). In this perspective, emotions play a central role in human motivation. Emotions are conceptualized as a form of internally generated information that provides us with feedback about ourselves as biological organisms in interaction with our environment. Certain basic emotions are biologically wired into the human organism through an evolutionary process, and these emotions and elaborations of them that result from learning play an adaptive role in the survival of the species. Emotions function to safeguard the concerns of the organism. Some of these concerns are biologically programmed, and these correspond to core motivational systems (e.g., Ekman & Davidson, 1994; Frijda, 1986; Greenberg & Safran, 1987; Safran & Greenberg, 1991).

For example, Lichtenberg (1989) theorized that there are five core motivational systems: (a) the need for psychic regulation of physiological requirements, (b) the need for attachment and affiliation, (c) the need for assertion and exploration, (d) the need to react aversively through antagonism or withdrawal, and (e) the need for sensual and sexual pleasure (e.g., attachment, curiosity). Other concerns are a result of learning. Many of these learned concerns are the result of values that result from learning about subgoals that will satisfy the needs of the attachment system. For example, one can learn that one needs to be dependent to maintain a connection with the attachment figure, or others might learn that a type of precocious maturity is important or that sexual desirability plays a role.

Attachment Theory

John Bowlby believed that Freud's motivational model was inadequate, and he set on the course of systematically developing a motivational model that has become increasingly prominent in mainstream developmental psychology. Bowlby's motivational model combines certain basic psychoanalytic ideas with infant observation research, ethology, and control systems theory (an interdisciplinary branch of engineering and mathematics that deals with the behavior of dynamic systems). Attachment theory has generated a tremendous amount of empirical research in the last few decades and in fact has become one of the most fertile research areas emerging out of psychoanalytic theory. Because articles and books on attachment theory are voluminous (see, e.g., Cassidy & Shaver, 2008, for an excellent review), I will risk oversimplifying things by restricting myself here to detailing a few fundamental propositions of attachment theory and exploring the way it fills an important niche in the psychoanalytic perspective on unconscious motivation.

According to Bowlby, humans have an instinctively based need (what attachment theorists refer to as a *motivational system*) to maintain proximity to their primary caregivers (referred to as *attachment figures;* Bowlby, 1969, 1973, 1980). This motivational system, designated the *attachment system,* serves an adaptive function in that it increases the possibility that the infant will be able to obtain the caretaking and protection that are essential for its survival. To maintain proximity to the attachment figure, infants develop representations of their interactions with their attachment figures that permit them to predict what type of actions will increase the possibility of maintaining proximity to attachment figures and what type of actions will threaten the relationship. Bowlby referred to these representations as *internal working models.* For many years, Bowlby's work was ignored by mainstream psychoanalytic theorists, who regarded his thinking as simplistic and mechanistic. Nevertheless, through the work of a number of empirically minded collaborators studying mother–infant interactions, Bowlby's work became increasingly influential within mainstream developmental psychology. Of particular note in this respect is the research of Mary Ainsworth (Ainsworth, Blehar, Waters, & Wall, 1978), who developed the Strange Situation laboratory procedure for observing mother–infant interactions and reliably classifying the attachment status of 1- to 2-year-old infants. This procedure was subsequently to become the paradigmatic method in attachment research. The subsequent development of the Adult Attachment Interview by Mary Main and her collaborators (e.g., Main, Kaplan, & Cassidy, 1985) has allowed researchers to assess adults' internal working models of attachment through a structured interview and reliable coding system. The development of the Adult Attachment Interview thus became another critical turning point in the evolution of attachment research, and it has subsequently given rise to a vast body of empirical research with immensely rich clinical implications (e.g., Steele & Steele 2008). The integration of attachment theory and research with psychoanalysis has now become commonplace (see, e.g., Fonagy, 2001; Holmes, 2010), and Bowlby's work is coming to assume its rightful place within the psychoanalytic world. Now that we have gone over the theory and concepts behind psychoanalytic therapy, I explain in some detail the process of therapy.

4

The Therapy Process

Psychoanalytic therapy is a rich and complex process. In this chapter, I articulate some of the elements of this process and provide case examples illustrating the key aspects of the approach, beginning with the principles of intervention.

PRINCIPLES OF INTERVENTION

In this section, I discuss the therapy process at the level of principles of intervention. In other words, what are the general principles that guide the psychoanalytic therapist's approach to therapeutic intervention, and what are the specific interventions that he or she uses?

Formulation

One broad schema that is useful especially for clinicians in training is the notion of level of personality organization. In this perspective, clients are viewed as functioning along a continuum with respect to how psychologically mature or healthy their level of ego organization is—beginning at the psychotic level of organization at the lower end, moving up to a borderline level in the middle, and a neurotic level of organization at the higher end of the spectrum. In arriving at a formulation of this type, the clinician takes into account such factors as the client's characteristic style of defense mechanisms, ego strengths and weaknesses, capacity for insight, and the nature of his or her internal object relations. For example, some defenses (e.g., intellectualization) are viewed as more mature than others (e.g., splitting). Examples of ego strengths include impulse control, judgment, capacity for sustained work, and reality testing.

The topic of case formulation in psychoanalysis is a complex one, and a vast literature has been devoted to outlining different considerations relevant to it. To begin with, given that there are multiple psychoanalytic theories rather than a uniform psychoanalytic approach, each psychoanalytic theory will lead the therapist to focus on certain phenomena rather than others and to formulate the same case in different ways. Thus, one can formulate a case from the perspective of ego psychology, various models of object relations theory (e.g., Klein, Fairbairn, Winnicott), interpersonal theory, self psychology, Lacanian theory, intersubjectivity theory, or relational psychoanalysis.

Ego psychology or modern conflict theory (the contemporary American version of ego psychology) tends to formulate clinical problems in terms of the conflict between unconscious wishes and defenses against them. For example, an individual wishes to assert himself and defends against his wish by being overly accommodating; an individual wishes for intimate connection, but she defends against this wish by dissociating it and acting in a counterdependent fashion.

Object relations and interpersonal/relational theories tend to formulate cases in terms of internal object relations that lead the individual to play out repetitive self-destructive patterns. For example, a client who had a tyrannical father develops an internalized representation of male authority figures as dangerous to stand up to and impossible to please. A woman whose father divorced her mother when she was 3 years old and abandoned the family develops an internalized representation of men as emotionally unavailable and a pattern of being attracted to emotionally unavailable romantic partners, in part as a way of recapturing the love of the father who abandoned her. A man with an emotionally intrusive mother develops an internalized representation of women as emotionally intrusive and develops a pattern of avoiding intimacy with romantic partners.

There is no reason that a clinical formulation cannot synthesize both conflict and relational models. For example, Matthew has an internalized representation of others as intolerant of aggression, and has developed a pattern of defending against his aggressive impulses and acting in an overly accommodating way. This relational pattern leads others to take advantage of him, which incurs resentment, which in turn has to be disowned. Although Matthew is not aware of angry feelings, he nevertheless expresses them in a passive–aggressive fashion. This evokes aggressive responses from others, which he feels are unwarranted. This further intensifies Matthew's feelings of being an impotent victim.

The process of formulation involves combining information from a number of different sources. The therapist looks for recurrent themes that occur in the stories that clients tell about their current relationships and their past relationships (including their relationships with their parents). The therapist also pays attention to patterns or themes that are beginning to emerge in the therapeutic relationship. This requires therapists to attend to subtle fluctuations in their own ongoing feelings and experiences and to engage in an ongoing reflection of the nature of their own participation in the relationship.

Although there are multiple theoretical perspectives to guide case formulation from a psychoanalytic perspective and many different dimensions that are considered relevant to arriving at an adequate formulation, there is also a long-standing tradition within psychoanalysis of the importance of not letting one's formulations bias or interfere with one's ability to be open to emergent information. Freud himself in early technical papers wrote about the importance of the therapist learning to cultivate an attitude of evenly hovering attention so that the therapist is able to hear and see things that are not necessarily consistent with his or her expectations (S. Freud, 1912/1958). But there is a tension even within Freud's writing between his emphasis on the importance of the therapist cultivating a tolerance of uncertainty and ambiguity and his own tendency to write up his cases in a fashion that from the perspective of a contemporary sensibility has a quality of certainty, reminiscent of the way in which all the pieces are pulled together when a mystery is solved in a Sherlock Holmes story.

Nevertheless, this emphasis on the importance of the discipline of maintaining an open and receptive attitude can be found in the writing of various analysts subsequent to Freud, including Theodor Reik (1948), Wilfred Bion (1970), to some extent Donald Winnicott (1958, 1965), and recently such analysts as Thomas Ogden (1994) and Christopher Bollas (1992). The emphasis is on maintaining an open, receptive mind that takes in information not just from the client but also from one's own unconscious experience.

There has been a shift in recent years toward the importance of being cautious regarding the dangers of approaching the client with an overly tight or coherent formulation that does not easily lend itself to revision in the face of new information. This is particularly evident in the work of some British Independent theorists (e.g., Bollas, 1992; Coltart, 2000; Parsons, 2000) and in the writing of American relational thinkers who emphasized the importance of learning from one's client and being receptive to acknowledging one's own ongoing contributions to enactments (Aron, 1996; Bromberg, 1998; S. A. Mitchell, 1988, 1993, 1997).

Donnel Stern (1997, 2010), for example, argued that a good psychoanalytic process involves (what the philosopher Gadamer referred to as) a fusion of horizons in which both client and therapist come to a shared perspective on reality by allowing themselves to be influenced by one another. An important thread in contemporary theory emphasizes that one can never have an objective understanding of how the other is, because any understanding that develops will inevitably be influenced by the enactment in which one is engaged. Philip Bromberg emphasized that there are limits to what one can learn about one's clients on the basis of their verbal reports because they themselves are not able to verbalize aspects of their experience that are split off or dissociated (Bromberg 1998, 2006). From this perspective, the only way to truly understand our clients is to enter into their relational worlds and play out various scenarios with them in an unconscious way. Clients who have dissociated their experience are often only able to communicate it through their actions. This is because the experience is only represented at a nonverbal, motoric level as a type of implicit relational knowing. It is thus only by allowing ourselves to be used by our clients in this way and experiencing and reflecting on our own countertransference that we are able to make contact with dissociated aspects of their experience.

The notion that we could have an adequate and comprehensive formulation of our clients prior to actually establishing a relationship with them and allowing our understanding to emerge out of these relationships is anathema. In a more traditional perspective, the therapist's adequate formulation of clients' core themes and psychodynamics allows them to make interpretations that will help them to achieve insight into their unconscious conflicts. In contrast, the general perspective I have outlined suggests that understanding, relating, reflecting, and communicating about what is taking place in the therapeutic relationship are all part of one seamless process, rather than a serious of stages in which formulation leads to accurate interpretations, which in turn leads to change through insight.

Empathy

From a contemporary psychoanalytic perspective, the most fundamental intervention is empathy. The ability to identify with our clients and immerse ourselves in their experience is critical in the process of establishing an alliance. In addition, this capacity to identify ourselves with our clients and communicate our empathic experience to them is a central mechanism of change in and of itself. The topic of empathy was traditionally neglected in psychoanalytic writing, in which the emphasis was placed on the importance of making "accurate interpretations." With Heinz Kohut and the development of self psychology, however, the topic of empathy was placed in the foreground. Kohut argued that it is not enough for an interpretation to be "accurate"; it also has to be experienced as empathic by the client.

Kohut highlighted the importance of what he termed *vicarious introspection,* that is, the process of placing oneself in the client's shoes and attempting to develop a sense of the client's phenomenological experience.

In addition, he emphasized the role that the therapeutic process of empathic mirroring can play in helping clients to develop a cohesive sense of self. The growing influence of mother–infant developmental research on psychoanalytic thinking has added another dimension to the psychoanalytic perspective on empathy. For example, Daniel Stern's (1985) research on affect attunement in mother–infant relationships has provided a model for understanding the way in which the therapist's ability to attune and resonate to the client's affective experience can help the client to articulate and make sense of his or her own emotional experience.

Interpretation

Historically, one of the most important interventions at the psychoanalytic therapist's disposal has been what is called an interpretation. An interpretation has traditionally been conceptualized as the therapist's attempt to help clients become aware of aspects of their unconscious intrapsychic experiences and relational patterns. From a more traditional perspective, the distinction between interpretation and empathic reflection can be conceptualized in the following fashion. Whereas empathic reflection is the therapist's attempt to articulate meaning that is implicit in what the client is saying, interpretation is the therapist's attempt to convey information that is outside of the client's awareness.

Traditionally a distinction has been made between the accuracy of an interpretation in the sense of the extent to which an interpretation corresponds to a "real" aspect of the client's unconscious functioning versus the quality or usefulness of an interpretation (useful in the sense that the client can make use of the interpretation as part of the changes process). In theory, an interpretation can be accurate without being useful. The dimension of quality is spoken about in a variety of ways—for example, timing (Is the context right? Is the client ready to hear it?), depth (To what extent is the interpretation focused on deeply unconscious material versus material that is closer to awareness?), and empathic quality (To what extent is the interpretation delivered in a way that is sensitive to the impact it has on the client's self-esteem? To what extent does it contribute to the client's experience of being genuinely understood?).

Traditionally interpretations have been conceptualized as falling at different levels along the continuum of depth to surface. A deep interpretation is one targeted at material that is deeply unconscious for the client. An interpretation that is closer to the surface end of the continuum is targeted at experience that is almost accessible to consciousness, but not quite. From this perspective, an empathic reflection can be conceptualized as an interpretation targeted toward the surface end of the continuum.

Whereas to some extent it is true that the usefulness of an interpretation is mediated by the degree to which the experience being interpreted is close enough to conscious awareness for the client to be on the verge of articulating it, it is important not to rule out the potential value of deeper interpretations. For example, one of the hallmarks of a Kleinian interpretation has traditionally been that it is often geared toward interpreting deeply unconscious material that is remote from the client's experience.

It is not uncommon for clients to complain about experiences with therapists who have made deep interpretations that made no sense to them and were experienced as frightening, overwhelming, or disturbing. Nevertheless, it has been my experience that deep interpretations of this sort can be experienced as helpful by clients, especially when the therapist is able to address unconscious anxieties and primitive unconscious fears (e.g., fears related to destructive rage and aggression or annihilation of the self) that feel too unbearable for the client to tolerate. In situations of this type, a therapist's ability to approach unbearable experience in a confident way without feeling overwhelmed can feel reassuring and containing to the client. Here the quality of the therapist's presence and state of mind while making the interpretation is a critical factor. In other words, the therapist's willingness to touch on nameless dreads without being overwhelmed by whatever feelings they stir up in him or her can provide the client with a sense of safety and security that typically eludes the client.

Elyn Saks (2008), in a wonderful memoir of her own personal struggle with schizophrenia, speaks about her experience with a skilled Kleinian analyst (whom she calls Mrs. Jones) who helped Saks with her interpretations of the role that factors such as Saks's deep unconscious envy and her projection of angry and hostile feeling onto others play in producing her psychotic symptoms. To quote Saks:

> I met with Mrs. Jones three times a week. . . . I reported my delusions and the forces beyond my control that were unbearably evil. I was malicious, I was bad, I was a destroyer of worlds. She was not afraid; she did not look at me with alarm in her eyes. She did not judge, she only listened, and reflected back to me what she heard telling me what *she thought it meant.* (p. 185; italics added)

Following is a dialogue between Saks and Mrs. Jones.

Mrs. Jones: Tell me about your difficulties at university.

Saks[1]: I'm not smart enough. I can't do the work.

Mrs. Jones: You were first in your class in Vanderbilt. Now you're upset about Oxford because you want to be the best and are afraid you can't be. You feel like a piece of shit from your mother's bottom.

Saks: I'm closing the curtains from now on because people across the street are looking at me. They can hear what I'm saying. They are angry. They want to hurt me.

Mrs. Jones: You are evacuating your angry and hostile feelings onto those people. It is you who are angry and critical. And you want to control what goes on in here.

Saks: I *am* in control. I control the world. The world is at my whim. I control the world and everything in it.

Mrs. Jones: You want to feel in control because in fact you feel so helpless.

According to Saks:

> While the content of what Mrs. Jones said to me was not always a comfort (more often than not it, it was startling, and had the effect of catching me up short), her presence in the room was. So calm, so reasonable,

---

[1]Although this dialogue is quoted from Saks (2008), I have changed Saks's use of the first person "I" to "Saks" to avoid any confusion in the present context.

no matter what I said to her, no matter how disgusting or horrible, she never recoiled from what I said. To her, my thoughts and feelings were not right or wrong, good or bad; they just were. (Saks, 2008, pp. 92–93)

A number of factors influence the extent to which an interpretation is experienced as empathic. First, to the extent that the interpretation is in the neighborhood of feelings or thoughts that are on the edge of consciousness for the client, the client is more likely to feel understood because it seems to "fit" or make sense to the client and captures an important aspect of the client's experience that he or she can't articulate. An interpretation that captures or crystallizes a feeling that the client is unable to articulate can be experienced as empathic in the sense that the client feels "known," perhaps in a way that he or she usually doesn't. This is particularly important when the therapist is giving voice to feelings or experiences that are semi-inchoate for the client and contributing to his or her feelings of confusion and isolation.

Interpretations are most likely to be helpful when the therapist is able to interpret a disavowed aspect of experience in a way that the client experiences as validating, supportive, and affirming. For example, a therapist who is able to interpret underlying experiences of sadness and pain and who is at the same time able to empathically resonate with these feelings (not just imagine the client's perspective at a conceptual level, but also temporarily identify with the experience at a personal and emotionally compelling level) will contribute to the client's sense of feeling connected and affirmed. In situations of this type, the therapist's state of mind (i.e., the extent to which the therapist feels empathically connected to the client or not) is just as important, if not more important, than the specific content of his or her interpretation. Similarly, the therapist who is able to interpret disowned feelings of anger and to temporarily identify with the client in this experience will help the client to feel understood and affirmed in his or her experience of anger.

To the extent that there is a strong therapeutic alliance and the client trusts the therapist, an interpretation that is potentially threatening can be experienced in a more benign way because it is being delivered by somebody whose good will and intention the client trusts. It also is important to bear in mind that the immediate relational context colors the meaning of anything that the therapist says (S. A. Mitchell, 1993). Interpretations with exactly the same words can be experienced as critical or caring, depending on whether the client feels respected by and cared for by the therapist.

Any intervention must be understood in terms of its relational meaning. In other words, when the therapist makes a specific content interpretation to the client (e.g., "It is hard for you to trust people because of your history of abandonment and it is hard for you to trust me right now"), the meaning of this particular interpretation will be mediated by the history of the client's own relationships with others, by the therapist's own unique history, and by the meaning of this type of interpretation to the therapist given his or her own particular dynamics (e.g., Is the therapist somebody who tends to identify with people who experience this particular client's dilemma because of his or her own particular issues?), and the way both client and therapist are feeling about themselves and one another in this moment. A deep interpretation about the client's unconscious motives may be experienced as disrespectful or disempowering. Alternatively, it may be experienced as tremendously reassuring. It can cast the therapist in the position of the one who knows and be experienced as reassuring for a client who is desperately seeking a powerful authority who has the answers.

Clarification, Support, and Advice

Despite the traditional psychoanalytic emphasis on refraining from providing excessive reassurance or advice, many contemporary psychoanalytic therapists find that such support can play a vitally important role in the change process. Although ideally we do wish to promote our clients' ability to trust in themselves, there is also a recognition that in many circumstances a genuine word of reassurance can be vitally important for a client who is struggling with a difficult situation or feeling shaky. Similarly, a word of well-timed advice to a client who is feeling genuinely overwhelmed or confused or is in a state of crisis can be an extremely important intervention. A traditional psychoanalytic concern has been that when therapists give advice or share their opinions with clients, this imposes undue influence on them and risks compromising their autonomy. Critics such as Owen Renik (2006), however, have argued that the practice of withholding one's opinions as a therapist is disingenuous, because our beliefs implicitly influence the message we convey to our clients without giving them a chance to fully reflect on our position and disagree with us if they wish. A willingness on the therapist's part to give advice, especially when asked for it, is consistent with reducing the power imbalance, because we are "playing our cards straight up" with our clients rather than engaging in a process of mystification.

Interpretation of Transference and Countertransference

One of the most important forms of interpretation is referred to as a *transference interpretation*. This is an interpretation that focuses on the here and now of the therapeutic relationship between the client and the therapist. The reason that transference interpretations are considered to be particularly important is that they have the advantage of drawing the client's attention to something that is happening in the moment. A transference interpretation thus has an immediate and experiential quality to it. By drawing the client's attention to the way in which their perceptions and actions are shaping their experience of things in the here and now, therapists provides them with an opportunity to actually observe themselves in the process of shaping their experience of the situation. They thus begin to experience themselves as agents in the construction of reality. Transference interpretations can focus exclusively on the therapeutic relationship or explore similarities between what is taking place in the therapeutic relationship and other relationships in the client's life (both present and past). For example, Doris, a divorced woman in her mid-30s, consistently complains about romantic partners being emotionally unavailable and has just been speaking about her supervisor as not being sufficiently supportive. For the last few sessions (including this one), I have had the sense that Doris is feeling frustrated with me, so I say, "I wonder if there is any similarity between your experience with your supervisor and the way in which you are experiencing our relationship in this moment?" Interpretations that do not involve a focus on the here and now of the therapeutic relationship can run the risk of leading to an intellectualized understanding. It is one thing to conceptually or intellectually understand one's own role in a self-defeating pattern and another to have an experientially grounded, emotionally immediate understanding.

For many contemporary psychoanalytic therapists, transference interpretations have become inseparable from the process of the exploration of the transference/countertransference matrix. Consistent with an emphasis on a two-person psychology, transference is not conceptualized as a distorted perception arising in a vacuum but as one element in an ongoing transference/countertransference enactment. In practice, then, transference interpretations often involve an ongoing collaborative exploration of who is contributing what to the relationship. In my own writing, I have used the term *metacommunication* to designate this process of collaborative exploration (e.g., Safran & Muran, 2000). Metacommunication consists of an attempt to step outside of the relational cycle that is currently being enacted by treating it as the focus of collaborative exploration, a process of communicating or commenting on the relational transaction or implicit communication that is taking place. It is an attempt to bring ongoing awareness to bear on the interaction as it unfolds. There are many different forms of metacommunication. A therapist can offer a tentative observation about what is taking place between him or her and the client (e.g., "It seems to me that we're both being cautious with each other right now . . . does that fit with your experience?"). A therapist can convey a subjective impression of something the client is doing (e.g., "My impression is that you're pulling away from me right now"). Or the therapist can disclose some aspect of his or her own experience as a point of departure for exploring something that might be taking place in the therapeutic relationship (e.g., "I'm aware of feeling powerless to say anything that you might feel is useful right now"). Any disclosure of this type must be considered the very first step in an ongoing process of exploring the transference/countertransference cycle. The therapist does not begin by assuming that his or her feelings are in any way caused or evoked by the client, but rather that they may offer clues as to something that is unconsciously being enacted in the relationship.

It is also important to bear in mind that clients can experience straightforward traditional interpretations of the transference as a criticism or as a form of one-upmanship, especially in situations in which the therapeutic alliance is strained. In other words, they can be experienced by clients as the therapist's attempt to take himself or herself out of the equation by insinuating something to the effect of, "The tension we're having in our relationship right now is your fault and I've got nothing to do with it." This is particularly likely to occur in situations in which the therapist is caught in an enactment and is unconsciously using the interpretation to deny any responsibility for what is going on or is defensively blaming the client for a mutually constructed pattern in the therapeutic relationship.

Nontransference Interpretations

Although I have been emphasizing the value of transference interpretations because of their emotional immediacy, it is important not to minimize the potential value of interpretations that don't make reference to the therapeutic relationship. In some situations, making a well-timed, well-worded interpretation about an event taking place in the person's relationships outside of the therapy situation can be particularly useful. This is especially true if the client is confused about what is taking place in the situation and is receptive to considering the possibility that a specific unconscious conflict is playing a role. For the interpretation to be helpful, however, the context has to be such that the client really does experience the interpretation as a new and emotionally meaningful way of looking at the situation, rather than just as an intellectualized and arid attempt to understand what is going on. It is difficult to specify exactly what type of context facilitates this sense of newness other than to say that the client needs to be experiencing a genuine sense of confusion and a search for understanding, and the interpretation must be phrased in such a way that it facilitates further exploration rather than shutting down. For example, Peter, a successful professional in his 40s, began treatment after his wife discovered that he was having an affair with a female coworker and threatened to leave him. He immediately ended the affair and sought therapy in the hope of understanding what had led him to have an affair in the first place. This was the only time he had ever had an affair, and he experienced it as completely out of character for himself and a form of compulsion or addiction that he had no control over. After spending several sessions getting to know him, I began to get a sense of a man with considerable disowned anger who was feeling devalued by and emotionally isolated from his wife. I began to interpret his affair as an attempt on his part to reaffirm his sense of potency and lovability and as an expression of disowned anger at his wife. He experienced this interpretation, combined with the process of beginning to develop greater ownership of his needs for validation and for emotional intimacy and of his anger, as extremely helpful.

Another reason that extratransference interpretations can be valuable is that clients are coming to treatment to deal with problems in their everyday lives, not with problems in their relationships with their therapists. To the extent that the therapist focuses exclusively on transference interpretations, the client may have difficulty finding relevance to his or her everyday life. Of course in practice, this potential problem is often reduced by making transference interpretations that involve establishing a link between what is taking place in the therapeutic relationship and what is taking place in the client's everyday relationships. Although this type of interpretation can be extremely helpful, as previously indicated the potential danger is that the client will experience this linking of the two relationships as an attempt to blame him or her for what is going on in the therapeutic relationship by saying, in essence, "You're doing the same thing with me that you do with everyone else in your life." The therapist thereby refuses to accept responsibility for his or her own contribution to what is taking place in the therapeutic relationship. This can be especially likely to happen if the alliance is tenuous or there is a therapeutic impasse. In such situations, it can be useful to carefully explore what is taking place in the therapeutic relationship on its own terms, with a genuine openness to understanding how each partner is contributing to what is taking place, rather than to rush to establish links with relationships in the client's everyday life.

Genetic Transference Interpretations
and Historical Reconstruction

A third major type of interpretation is referred to as a *genetic transference interpretation*. A genetic transference interpretation involves conveying a hypothesis about the role that one's developmental experiences have played in shaping one's current conflicts. For example, the therapist may interpret the client's tendency to be overprotective of other people, thereby denying his or her own needs, as stemming from the client's history of protecting a depressed and fragile mother.

Because psychoanalysis originated with the exploration of the client's past, there has been a tendency at different points in psychoanalytic thinking to overestimate the importance of making genetic transference interpretations. The problem with an excessive emphasis on interpretations of this type is that it can lead to an intellectualized understanding of the potential influence of the past on the present without resulting in a real change. Notwithstanding this potential problem, a good genetic transference interpretation can play a valuable role in helping the client to begin to replace a sense of confusion and perplexity with some sense of meaning and understanding. It can also help to reduce the client's tendency to excessive self-blame by helping him or her to see that current problems are a meaningful and understandable result of an attempt to cope with a difficult or traumatic childhood situation. For example, Howard, a male client in his mid-20s, experienced a lack of direction in his life, a chronic low-level depression, and a sense of inadequacy. His father was an extremely successful business executive whom my client described as charismatic and always the center of attention. When Howard was 8 years old, his father and mother divorced. Although Howard maintained a relationship with his father, he felt he was never able to obtain his approval. Over time, it emerged that whenever Howard would tell his father about something he had accomplished or was excited about, he had the impression that his father belittled him. In one session, I suggested to Howard that perhaps his father felt the need to "put him down" because of his own need to be the center of attention and an associated feeling of being threatened by any success his son might have. Howard found this interpretation extremely helpful, and it opened the door for exploring important associated feelings.

Of course, too much emphasis on tracing the historical roots of one's current self-defeating patterns can lead to a type of preoccupation with the past and a tendency to blame others rather than to develop a sense of agency that can promote change. This is, however, by no means inevitable, and to the extent that it does take place it can and should be explored in the same way that any defense is explored.

The Use of Dreams

Dream interpretation was once considered central to psychoanalytic practice. Freud referred to dreams as the "royal road to the unconscious," and some of his most important early breakthroughs in psychoanalytic theory and practice emerged out of the interpretation of his own dreams and the dreams of clients. Freud considered dreams to be a form of wish fulfillment and had a well worked out methodology for working with dreams. Since Freud's time, a variety of different psychoanalytic models have been developed for conceptualizing the meaning of dreams and for working with them. One particularly useful approach to dream interpretation was developed by Fairbairn, who conceptualized all figures in a dream to represent different aspects of the self. For example, I once had a female client who was terrified to sleep at home alone when her husband was away. At such times it was common for her to have dreams in which she was being chased by an axe murderer. When I suggested that she experiment or play around with the possibility of seeing herself in the role of the axe murderer, she was able to contact some of the aggressive feelings associated with being in the role and ultimately to contact disowned feelings of anger toward her husband for abandoning her during his frequent business trips.

Although a variety of different psychoanalytic approaches to the interpretation of dreams have developed over time, I think it is fair to say that dream interpretation no longer plays the central role in North American psychoanalytic theory and practice that it once did. To some extent the exploration of transference/countertransference enactments has become more central. Nevertheless, most psychoanalysts and psychoanalytic therapists including myself do find it particularly useful to work with dreams under certain circumstances. One situation in which dreams can be particularly useful is when clients have difficulty contacting and expressing their inner life during treatment. In this type of situation, suggesting to clients that they begin to pay attention to and write down their dreams is a way of providing material for the treatment that emerges spontaneously while the client is asleep and is not subject to the same type of defensive processes that otherwise can drastically constrain the range of experiences. Of course, the client's recording of the dream and subsequent recounting of it in the session involves a process of reconstruction, but the fashion in which it is reconstructed can be of interest in and of itself. Another situation in which working with dreams can be particularly interesting is one in which the client reports a particular vivid dream or one with striking or startling imagery and associated affect.

When listening to dreams, I find it useful to avoid any preconceptions about what different aspects of dreams may symbolize or preconceived ideas as to how to work with them. I attempt to listen to the dream with a type of receptive openness and allow the dream to work on my own feelings, fantasies, and unconscious experience. I pay attention to the client's way of talking about the dream and to fluctuations in the client's emotional experiences during the recollection. I often stop the client at specific points and ask what he or she is experiencing. I may start by asking what the client thinks of the dream. Sometimes his or her interpretation makes perfect sense to me, and sometimes I find that the ideas that pop into my mind are radically different from the client's formulation. At such times I am curious about the large discrepancy between our interpretations, and I may relay some of my own thoughts and ideas and explore how the client responds. I may ask the client to recount the dream a second time, slowly, and stop the client at various points along the way by asking what comes up for him or her.

Perhaps most important, I emphasize to clients that there are an infinite number of ways of interpreting any dream and that dream material allows us an opportunity to engage in a kind of interactive play during which we can experiment with different ways of looking at things and explore how these different alternatives influence both of our understandings. I emphasize that the things that come up for me when my clients recount a dream may well reflect more about my psychology than theirs, and I invite them to nevertheless join me in the process of using my reactions, fantasies, associations, and thoughts as a stimuli to help them reflect on their experience in ways that may deepen it. I view dream work as a kind of coconstructive process that allows clients and therapists to engage in a playful way of working with the material. This type of play makes use of intuition and the ongoing process of mutual influence that is taking place as a vehicle for creating meaning together in a way that is not constrained by the type of logical, linear thinking that conversations about clients' everyday experience often are. And as is always the case, I pay particular attention to aspects of the dream that could be construed as implicit allusions to our relationship or to me (referred to as *allusions to the transference* by psychoanalysts). I provide a clinical illustration of this process later, when I discuss the case of Simone, a young woman whom I saw in long-term psychoanalytic treatment.

Working With Resistance and Defense

Relatively early on in psychoanalytic thinking, the interpretation of resistance and defense came to be viewed as a vitally important technical issue. Although early in his career Freud attempted to overcome or bypass resistance by motivating the clients to explore repressed memories and experiences despite their internal resistances, analysts soon came to believe that the analysis or interpretation of resistance was central to the work of treatment rather than a prelude to the uncovering of unconscious memories, fantasies, and wishes. This shift was facilitated by Freud's articulation of the structural model in 1923 and various theoretical and technical developments emerging out of structural theory. One such development was the tradition of ego psychology that became particularly interested in exploring the various ways in which the ego plays an active role in defending against unconscious impulses.

A central axiom in the ego psychology tradition is that analysis proceeds from surface to depth. In other words, we always begin by analyzing the client's resistances and defenses and only gradually more toward interpreting underlying impulses, fantasies, and wishes as they become more accessible through the process of resistance analysis. As previously discussed, from a psychoanalytic perspective the exploration of resistance is intrinsic to the change process. Clients inevitably have conflicting feelings about changing, and these conflicts manifest in a variety of different ways at different points in the treatment. Moreover, resistance stems from an infinite number of different sources (e.g., fear of changing, fear of loss of self, avoidance of painful feelings, negative feelings about the therapist or the therapeutic process, the need to individuate from the therapist, secondary gain [i.e., benefits resulting from maintaining the current symptoms], attachment to old patterns of relating, fear of losing the unconscious, symbolic connection to one's attachment figures).

Common ways in which resistance is expressed in treatment include coming late for sessions, missing sessions, extensive periods of silence or uncommunicativeness, filling the session with superficial chatter or social conversation, failure to pay fees, compliance, and what is referred to as a "flight into health" (i.e., experiencing a rapid and transient reduction in one's symptoms as a way of avoiding exploring deeper issues). Some actions or ways of being in treatment may signal or facilitate progress in some contexts but may function as resistance in others. For example, the client's reporting of dreams may function as an important way of deepening the therapeutic process by communicating feelings and themes that are not consciously accessible to the client. But a client who ritualistically begins every session by reporting dreams may be avoiding the exploration of important feelings or themes in the here and now.

Defense Interpretation

Innumerable articles and books have been written about the technique of defense interpretation. Following are brief descriptions of some of the principles involved.

1. The therapist conveys the rationale for interpreting defenses as part of the process of establishing an alliance around the task of defense analysis. For example, I might say to my client,

> People often automatically or unconsciously find ways of avoiding feelings, thoughts, wishes, or fantasies that are threatening to them as a way of avoiding distressing feelings such as pain or shame. For example, sometimes people have difficulty staying in contact with feelings of sadness because of a fear that they will be overwhelmed by them or that they will never pass. One of my jobs as a therapist will be to help you become aware of times that you are doing this, as well as how you are doing it, so that you have more of an ability to choose whether you are willing to stay with a particular feeling, fantasy, or wish instead of unconsciously avoiding it. A fuller awareness of these aspects of your experience will help you to develop a better understanding of what's motivating your actions and will also potentially provide you with important information that helps us understand more fully what things really mean to you and what you're really wanting in any given situation.

2. Once a rationale has been conveyed to the client, the therapist begins the task of monitoring the various types and ways in which the client cuts off or avoids his experience and begins the process of drawing his attention to avoidances or defensive maneuvers. For example,

> I notice that as you talk about your wife leaving you, your voice becomes very even, and you begin to talk in somewhat of a monotone. Do you have any awareness of this?" "I notice that as you talk about your feelings about our sessions right now, that you're looking down. Do you have any awareness of this?

Sometimes the client is able to become aware of the defensive maneuvers the therapist is attempting to immediately draw attention to, and the therapist can then follow up with questions such as the following: "Any sense of what was going on in inside of you at that moment?" or even more directly, "Any awareness of avoiding anything in this moment?" If the client is able to become aware and begin to explore an internal experience, the therapist can then follow up with probes such as, "Any sense of what might be difficult about focusing on these feelings?"

3. In situations in which clients are not able to initially become aware of their defensive maneuvers, it can be helpful to reiterate the rationale for exploring defenses and then remind them that you will try to direct their attention to them when they occur again. By continuing to draw clients' awareness to their defenses as they occur in the present moment, the likelihood of their observing them in real time is increased. This provides clients with an opportunity to attend to the moment and actually engage in an experientially based discovery process rather than merely speculating. Therapists can help clients to explore what the processes are through which they defend against their experience (e.g., changing topics, contracting muscles to minimize feelings, intellectualizing) and what the unconscious fears, beliefs, and expectations are that prohibit the experience of certain feelings, wishes, and fantasies.

4. Over time the process of defense interpretation has become more exploratory, dialogical, and collaborative in nature and less "interpretive" (in the sense of therapists simply pointing out clients' defenses to them). The term *exploration of defenses* rather than *defense interpretation* thus might be more accurate. It is also worth noting that there is no static, finite list of defenses that exist outside of the context and function that a given act may be serving in a specific moment. Thus, for example, a preoccupation with talking about the past can sometimes serve as a defense against exploring the present. Other times a focus on the present can serve as a defense against exploring the past. Sometimes anger can be a defense against sadness; other times sadness is a defense against anger. The therapist's judgment of the contextual function of anything the clients says or does is always critical for assessing whether it is serving in a defensive fashion.

5. In addition, it is worth noting that although it is important for therapists to always attend to the style and manner of the client's presentation and to engage in an ongoing assessment of the extent to which he or she is contacting or avoiding an emergent experience in the moment, it is not always advisable to interpret or explore defenses whenever they

take place. Sometimes the process of exploring defenses is experienced as too confrontative or critical by clients and can interfere with their ability to gradually move into contacting their emergent experience at a pace that feels safe to them. In other words, sometimes clients need the therapist to support their defenses or to ally with them in order for them to feel safe enough to begin disclosing their inner experience. Defense interpretation should thus be used tactfully, sparingly, and judiciously.

Working Through Therapeutic Impasses

There is a growing emphasis in the psychoanalytic literature on the theoretical and technical importance of working through therapeutic impasses when they emerge (cf. Safran & Muran, 2000). Over time the emphasis has shifted from a perspective in which impasses in the therapeutic process are viewed as a function of the client's resistance to one in which impasses are viewed as a two-person interactive process in which client and therapist become locked into a complementary "doer or done to" position from which it feels impossible for either to escape. Benjamin (2004), Davies (2004), and Aron (2006), among others, have written eloquently about how there are times in the treatment process during which both client and therapist are trapped because neither is able to acknowledge the possible validity of the other's perspective without feeling that they themselves are wrong or bad in some fundamental and unacceptable way. For example, the client accuses the therapist of being sadistic, and the therapist feels that he is being abused by the client. Although it might be possible for the therapist to mouth the words "yes, you're right, I'm being abusive," the problem is that he doesn't really experience himself as sadistic and therefore it would be impossible for him to acknowledge his sadism in a genuine fashion.

In situations of this type, neither client nor therapist is able to genuinely acknowledge the validity of the other's perspective because it feels that doing so would involve a type of self-violation or compromise of his or her own integrity. How can the interaction begin to shift out of a frozen position in which there is no alternative to either (a) the client's perspective being valid and the therapist's perspective being unimportant or lacking validity, or (b) the therapist's perspective being valid and the client's perspective being invalid or unreasonable? The therapist's task is to facilitate a movement to a third position (i.e., an alternative to the binary choice of "you're right and I'm wrong" or "I'm right and you're wrong"). This process requires an internal shift within the therapist that has a quality of "surrendering" or "letting go" of a position he or she needs to hold onto tenaciously because of underlying and sometimes unconscious fears or threats of acknowledging dissociated aspects of self-experience (Safran & Muran, 2000). For example, perhaps the therapist in the first illustration finds it too threatening or intolerable to experience aspects of himself that are indeed sadistic. Perhaps the therapist in the second illustration is threatened by fully acknowledging to herself complex feelings of anger and shame around the experience of "being taken advantage of."

To the extent that therapists are able to acknowledge and accept dissociated aspects of their own experience, they begin to experience the psychological freedom to fully appreciate and empathize with the validity of the client's subjective experience without experiencing an internal compromise or a sacrifice or submersion of their own subjectivity. This shift thus involves a movement toward a type of intersubjectivity, in which one is able to experience the other as a subject rather than an object, while at the same time holding onto one's own subjectivity (Benjamin, 1988, 1990, 2004).

Termination

Termination is considered to be one of the most important phases of treatment. A well-handled termination can play a vital role in helping clients to consolidate any gains that have been made in treatment. Conversely, poorly handled terminations can have a negative impact on the treatment process. In a treatment that is not time limited, the topic of termination can be initiated by either client or therapist. Often termination is initiated by the client who feels that he has achieved his goals or who is frustrated with a lack of progress. Ideally, though, by the time termination actually takes place, the client and therapist will have spent some time talking openly and constructively about the process, and the decision to terminate will be mutual. Often clients who are contemplating termination will have difficultly bringing it up directly, and it is important for the therapist to be attuned to cues that the client may be considering ending treatment. For example, the client begins to consistently arrive late for sessions or cancels sessions, seems less engaged in treatment, or asks general questions about how long people typically stay in treatment.

Ideally, the decision to terminate is made collaboratively by client and therapist and marks the end of a treatment that has been helpful and satisfying. In real life, termination in open-ended treatment is often somewhat messier than the idealized way it is presented in many textbooks. Often termination is the result of extraneous factors (e.g., the client moves to another city). In other situations, termination takes place when the client becomes frustrated with what he or she perceives as a lack of progress and decides to take a break or seek another therapist.

When the factors leading up to termination are not extraneous, it is more common for clients to initiate termination than therapists. This may be because therapists can have more ambitious goals for change that are guided by theoretical concerns, or it may be because the client becomes dissatisfied with the treatment. There are also occasions when both client and therapist feel that the client has achieved the initial therapeutic goals, and the client is the first one to recognize this and to bring it up. When the client brings up the topic of termination in a fashion that feels premature or precipitous for the therapist, it is important for the therapist to carefully explore the client's reasons for wishing to terminate. Sometimes, for example, the client initiates the topic of termination because of feelings of dissatisfaction with the treatment or anger or disappointment with the therapist but has difficulty bring this up directly with the therapist. In such situations it is the therapist's task to provide a climate that maximizes the client's sense that the therapist is genuinely interested in and receptive to hearing any concerns about the treatment that the client has and that it is safe to talk about negative feelings or concerns. At the same time it is critical for the therapist not to push too hard for answers, thoughts, or feelings that the client is reluctant to talk about. The therapist needs to convey respect for the client's right to privacy and respect for the validity of his or her ultimate decision.

Sometimes the client will initiate termination by failing to show up for a scheduled session and is subsequently reluctant to schedule a make-up session. In this situation it is preferable for the therapist to encourage the client to return for at least one final session, during which the client can talk more freely about his or her concerns and the therapist can learn more fully about what has been going on for the client. This session may or may not lead to the client staying in therapy. Even if it does not, however, it increases the possibility that the client will leave therapy with a more meaningful sense of closure than he or she might otherwise.

An important thread to analytic work involves looking beneath the surface explanation to find deeper meaning or unconscious motivation. If the therapist explores the client's reasons for initiating termination in a sensitive and respectful manner, with a genuine receptivity to hearing negative or ambivalent feelings about the therapy or therapist, in some circumstances it can lead to the exploration of feelings such as resentment, mistrust, or disappointment, which if listened to empathically can strengthen the therapeutic relationship and lead to the client's recommitment to therapy. Alternatively, the client may wish to leave treatment because he or she is feeling too intimate with, vulnerable to, or dependent on the therapist.

When, however, the therapist fails to accept at face value the client's stated reasons for wanting to leave and repeatedly attempts to badger the client into admitting feelings or motivations that he or she either doesn't experience or is unaware of, the client can feel undermined, coerced, or pathologized. The therapist thus needs to strike a balance between, on the one hand, trying too hard to hold on to a client who wants to terminate and, on the other hand, failing to adequately explore the client's underlying motivations for terminating.

When the process of exploring the client's desire to leave treatment does lead to a final decision to terminate, it is useful to establish a contract to meet for a certain number of final sessions to provide an opportunity to terminate in a constructive fashion. This process of termination involves a number of different principles, such as reviewing the changes that have taken place in treatment, constructing a shared understanding of the factors that have led to change, helping the client to recognize his or her own role in the change process, creating a space that allows the client to express a range of feelings about the termination and the treatment (both positive and negative), using various interventions to facilitate the exploration of these feelings, exploring or interpreting defenses against experiencing these feelings, exploring potentially painful feelings around loss or fear of separation, and exploring any feelings of disappointment with the treatment and accepting them in a nonjudgmental and nondefensive fashion.

Exploring Ambivalent Feelings

It is normal for clients who are terminating therapy to have ambivalent feelings about the treatment and the therapist, just as it is normal for human beings to have ambivalent feelings about all relationships. Clients may experience a range of feelings, including gratitude for the changes that they have made in their lives, fear of ending treatment, relief at no longer having to be therapy, sadness about the loss of the therapist, abandonment, disappointment about the changes that have not taken place, and resentment toward the therapist because of the failure to realize some of their initial treatment goals or other disappointments with the therapy and the therapist. None of these feelings are mutually exclusive. It is important for the therapist to provide a safe place for clients to explore and express the full range of feelings they may have about termination to allow them to obtain a greater degree of closure about the experience of therapy. Some clients may have difficulty acknowledging any negative feelings because of fears (both conscious and unconscious) that they will spoil the positive feelings or hurt or anger the therapist. Other clients may have difficulty contacting and expressing feelings of gratitude. To the extent that therapists are genuinely open to hearing negative feelings, clients may find it easier to contact positive feelings when they otherwise may have difficulty doing so. It also helps clients to learn that ambivalent feelings are tolerable. By the same token, it is important for therapists not to shrug off positive feelings expressed by the client. The process of experiencing and expressing gratitude and having it graciously acknowledged by the other is an important part of the growth process.

Working Constructively With Countertransference Feelings During Termination

Termination is bound to be fraught with a range of feelings for therapists in the same way as it is for clients. It is inevitable that, as therapists, we want to be helpful to our clients and successful with their treatment. It can thus be extremely difficult to deal with any discomfort that may emerge when clients are not as pleased with the treatment outcome as we would like them to be. Negative feelings are particularly likely to emerge for the therapist when he has experienced a client who is unilaterally terminating as difficult to work with, especially when the therapist has struggled unsuccessfully in an attempt to meet the client's needs or has been an ongoing object of criticism or passive–aggressive behavior by the client. In such situations it can be difficult for the therapist to tolerate negative sentiments from the client without wanting to blame the client for any lack of progress. This in turn may take work on the therapist's part, either in personal therapy or supervision, to become more accepting of his her own personal failures and limitations. And yet it is critical to remember that for the client, the opportunity to feel that the therapist failed and to express negative feelings about this without retaliation and without feelings of having excessively hurt or destroyed the therapist may be a valuable part of the change process. It may, for example, help the client to know that the feelings of the other do not need to be protected or that negative feelings are not toxic and do not have to be hidden. This in turn can help to free the client internally to ultimately be able to experience feelings of closeness and gratitude toward the therapist and others.

Cultivating a Climate That Tolerates Ambiguity and Lack of Closure

An important aspect of the termination process involves making sense of the entire experience of therapy and establishing a sense of closure. But it is also important for the therapist to recognize and convey an appreciation for the fact that there are limits to the extent of closure that can be obtained on the journey that the therapist and the client have taken together and on their relationship. Life is a work in progress, and the meaning of the time the client has spent in therapy and the meaning of the relationship that he has developed with the therapist will evolve over time as the client has other life experiences. The therapist often has a sense that over the course of treatment, certain threads running through the client's life story and way of being in the world have emerged, been more clearly fleshed out, and been made sense of, whereas other threads have remained more vague or elusive.

Some themes that play out in the therapeutic relationship and unfold over time, or patterns of relating to one another that are frustrating or troubling, can be worked through constructively and understood in ways that help clients gain a sense of movement and mastery in their life. Other themes are less clearly understood by the end of therapy and remain mysteries that may make more sense to the client in the light of subsequent experiences and changes that occur later in the client's life. Learning to live with ambiguity and a lack of complete closure is an important developmental achievement. In fact, the empirical research on the topic of wisdom has suggested that this type of tolerance of ambiguity is a more advanced cognitive–affective developmental stage (Sternberg & Jordan, 2005). The cultivation of this ability to tolerate such ambiguity can be an important byproduct of therapy, especially if the therapist is able to see the cultivation of this type of tolerance as one of the byproducts of a "good enough" termination.

CHANGE MECHANISMS

Now that I have discussed principles of intervention, I discuss some of the underlying mechanisms that are hypothesized to be active in the change process. For example, how do interpretations contribute to change? Why is empathy important? What are the various ways in which the therapeutic relationship contributes to change? What is the role of emotion in the change process? What about nonverbal communication? To what extent does change take place at a conscious level?

Making the Unconscious Conscious

Psychoanalytic theory postulates a host of different change mechanisms, and a multitude of new ways of conceptualizing the change process continue to emerge as psychoanalytic theories evolve and proliferate. At the most basic level, there is an understanding that change often has something to do with making the unconscious conscious or, in Freud's oft-cited axiom, "Where id has been there shall ego be." Although Freud's understanding of the nature of the change process evolved over the course of his lifetime, central to his mature thinking was the idea that change involves becoming aware of our instinctual impulses and related unconscious wishes and then learning to deal with them in a mature, rational, or reflective fashion. Thus, for Freud, a central premise is that we are driven by unconscious wishes that we are unaware of, and this lack of awareness compromises psychological freedom and perpetuates self-defeating behavior. For Freud, we delude ourselves as to reasons for doing things, and this self-deception limits our choice. By becoming aware of our unconscious wishes and our defenses against them, we increase the degree of choice available to us. In a sense then, we decrease the degree to which we are driven by unconscious factors and assume a greater degree of agency.

Emotional Insight

There has been a tendency to privilege the role of insight or understanding in psychoanalytic change. A central notion has been that psychoanalysis works by making the unconscious conscious and that the primary vehicle for doing this is through the use of verbal interpretations that give clients insight into the unconscious factors that are shaping their experience and actions. There has always been an emphasis on the importance of emotional insight—that is, combining the conceptual with the affective so that the client's new understanding has an emotionally immediate quality to it and is not relegated to the realm of intellectual understanding that has no impact on daily functioning. It has long been held that one of the key ways of increasing the possibility that the insight will be emotional is through the use of transference interpretations (Strachey, 1934), which leads clients to reflect on their immediate experience of the therapeutic relationship rather than to construct an abstract formulation. In other words, by directly observing the way in which they are construing the present moment and acting in the here and now, clients are able to develop an experience of themselves as agents in the construction/creation of their own experience.

Early on, psychoanalytic insiders such as Otto Rank and Sandor Ferenczi raised concerns about a tendency for some psychoanalysts to veer toward a more intellectualist approach that they felt was of limited value (Ferenczi & Rank, 1925/1956). And there is no doubt that the 1960s maverick psychoanalysts such as Fritz Perls (the founder of gestalt therapy) developed an intensely anti-intellectual stance in reaction to what they saw as the tendency toward overintellectualization in psychoanalysis. In general, my impression is that the contemporary American psychoanalytic sensibility has taken the critique of the intellectualist tendencies of psychoanalysis to heart and has placed an important emphasis on the affectively grounded experiential aspects of the change process.

Articulation of Feelings and Wishes

The process of articulating feelings and wishes is another key mechanism of change in psychoanalytic treatment. As discussed earlier, emotions are a biologically based form of information about the self in interaction with the environment that are wired into the species through an evolutionary process and that play an adaptive role in the survival of the species. Healthy functioning involves the integration of affective information with higher level cognitive processing to act in a fashion that is grounded in organismically based need but not bound by it. Emotions are associated with wishes, which when experienced and articulated can lead to adaptive behavior. Thus, for example, the individual who has difficulty experiencing anger in an appropriate context may be deprived of information that will help him or her to act in an appropriately aggressive or self-assertive way. An individual who has difficulty experiencing feelings of sadness may have difficulty seeking comfort or nurturance from others.

A variety of intervention principles in psychoanalytic treatment help clients to access emotions and associated wishes that are being defended against. These include empathy, the interpretation of dissociated experience, and the interpretation or exploration of the defenses that interfere with the experience of potentially adaptive wishes and experience. At a more implicit level, the client's experiencing and expressing feelings and associated wishes in the context of a safe and validating therapeutic relationship can play an important role in challenging the unconscious relational schemas that interfere with the experience of these wishes.

Creating Meaning and Historical Reconstruction

People often come to therapy with varying degrees of difficulty in the construction of meaningful narratives about their lives. These failures of meaning can include both the absence of narratives that help them make sense of important aspects of their experience or their lives in general, as well as the existence of maladaptive narratives that they have constructed to make sense of their experience.

The process of constructing a viable narrative account of the role that one's childhood experiences played in contributing to one's problems can also decrease the experience of self-blame that typically complicates and exacerbates emotional problems. By coming to understand one's emotional problems as arising from psychological coping strategies that were adaptive and made sense in the context of a dysfunctional childhood situation but are maladaptive in the present context, the client can become more tolerant and accepting toward himself and begin the process of developing coping strategies that are adaptive in a present context.

Often the problems that clients bring to therapy extend beyond a concern with specific symptoms to a more pervasive sense of meaninglessness and existential despair. When this is the case, the process of exploring and clarifying their own values and engaging in a meaningful dialogue with the therapist can help clients to reorient themselves and develop a more refined sense of what is meaningful to them. For clients, this process of meaning construction often involves becoming more aware of and articulating the nuances of their emotional experience in the context of the relationship with the therapist, so that they can begin to get a sense of feeling more vitally alive and in touch with their inner experience.

Awareness of Unconscious Motives

Developing an awareness of unconscious motives is one of the earliest principles of change delineated in psychoanalytic treatment. Freud's fundamental assumption was that we are motivated by forces that we are not aware of and that this lack of awareness deprives us of choice. On top of this, the motives behind our actions are complex and often contradictory. In psychoanalytic terms, this is referred to as the *principle of overdetermination*. For example, an individual cultivates an attitude of humility and self-sacrifice through his exposure to spiritual teachings. The desire to be humble and prize the welfare of others is genuine. At the same time, however, that stance of humility may mask or partially defend against a need to be recognized as special, and the ethic of self-sacrifice may be partially an expression of a self-righteous desire to be morally superior to the other, combined with disowned anger and aggression. To the extent that we are unaware of our motives, our degree of choice is reduced. We do things for reasons that are opaque to us and are then surprised and disappointed by the results. This contributes to a sense of being a victim rather than an agent.

Increasing the Experience of Agency

Clients often begin treatment with a diminished sense of personal agency. They experience themselves to be at the mercy of their symptoms or to be victims of misfortune or of other people's ill-intent or neglect. They often fail to see the relationship between their symptoms and their own internal and interpersonal conflicts.

It is also common not to recognize our own roles in contributing to the conflictual patterns that we repeat in our lives. As clients gain a greater appreciation of the connections between their symptoms and their ways of being, and of their own contributions to the conflictual patterns in their lives, they come to experience a greater degree of choice in their lives and to experience themselves as agents rather than as victims. This growing awareness or understanding of one's personal agency must be experientially based rather than purely conceptual.

Appreciating the Limits of Agency

Coming to experience a sense of agency is, however, only half the battle. The other half involves coming to appreciate and accept the limits of our agency (Safran, 1999). In a culture such as ours that promotes the myth that we can "have it all" if only we drink the right wine or drive the right car, it is easy to feel that something is missing or that somehow we are being left behind. Although in America psychoanalysis tends to have a more romantic sensibility than many European variants of the tradition, there is still recognition that the freedom we experience is freedom within the constraints of our character structures, environmental realities, and uncontrollable contingencies of life. Winnicott (1958, 1965) spoke about the importance of what he referred to as *optimal disillusionment* in the maturational process. According to him, as children we begin without a clear distinction between fantasy and reality and with the expectation that our needs will magically be taken care of. As we mature and experience inevitable frustrations and disappointments of living in the real world, we undergo a process of disillusionment. If our parents and our environment are unresponsive to our needs, then this disillusionment can be traumatic and we can lose our inner sense of vitality, possibility, and authenticity. We can become overadapted to the needs of others and develop what Winnicott (1958, 1965) referred to as a *false self*—that is, a way of being that is responsive to the demands of external reality but that loses contact with an inner sense of vitality and realness (Winnicott, 1958, 1965). If, however, our parents are sufficiently responsive to our inner needs, then this inevitable process of disillusionment takes place in an optimal or "good enough" fashion, and we surrender some aspects of our childhood fantasies without having the vitality and playfulness of our childhood completely extinguished. Building on Winnicott as well as other sources, some contemporary psychoanalytic writers have spoken about this as an experience of "surrender" in which we are able to "let go" and accept things as they are rather than attempting to make them into something they are not (e.g., Aron, 2006; Benjamin, 2004; Ghent, 1990; Safran, 1993, 1999). This psychoanalytically oriented sense of the role of surrender in the change process in some respects comes closer to a paradoxical Eastern perspective on change than to the traditional Western emphasis on change through willpower and determination.

New Relational Experience and Internalization of the Therapeutic Relationship

In addition to the emphasis on emotional experience, psychoanalytic theory also emphasizes the role that the therapeutic relationship itself plays as a change mechanism. While the precise role that the therapeutic relationship plays has been controversial, there is a general movement toward the view that by acting in a way that is different from the way in which the client's parents did, the therapist can provide the client with a new relational experience that challenges his or her maladaptive relational schemas, working models, or internal object relations. This thread in psychoanalytic theory can be traced back to the 1930s to the work of Sandor Ferenczi (1980a, 1980b) and also to a seminal article by James Strachey (1934). In the 1950s Franz Alexander, a Hungarian analyst who had immigrated to the United States, developed a theory of change that he termed the *corrective emotional experience* (Alexander, 1948). Alexander argued that it was essential for the therapist to develop a formulation of the client's distorted beliefs about the nature of relationships with other people and to then intentionally position himself or herself in a way that challenged it. For example, for the client whose parents were overly intrusive, it might be important for the therapist to be particularly respectful of the client's need for privacy. Alexander's position was extremely controversial at the time, as it was seen by his contemporaries as manipulative. It also hit a nerve among analysts who had always believed that what distinguished psychoanalysis from other therapeutic approaches was its emphasis on discovering the truth rather than on the use of the power of suggestion to heal.

Loewald (1960), in a classic paper, also emphasized the therapeutic relationship itself as a mechanism of change, but unlike Alexander he made it clear that he was not advocating for a new technical procedure. Instead, he argued that in the same way that children grow through identifying with their parents and internalizing interactions with them, patients grow through internalizing interactions with their therapists. According to him, the therapist's interpretive activity provides a regulating and integrating function for the client, and it is the client's internalization of this integrative experience with the therapist that leads to change.

Modified versions of Alexander's and Loewald's positions are widely accepted by contemporary psychoanalytic theorists who have argued that the therapist's ability to function as a new object for the client (rather than an old object who resembles his parents) is a key mechanism of change (Cooper, 2000; Greenberg, 1986). According to this perspective, clients unconsciously recruit others, including the therapist, to play a role in their relationship that corresponds in important respects to the role played by their parents. Thus, for example, the client who had critical or sadistic parents will act in ways that evoke critical or sadistic behavior from the therapist. As discussed earlier, the therapist's task is to gradually disembed from the relational scenario that is being played out so that the therapeutic relationship can ultimately function as a new relational experience rather than a repetition of an old one. In contrast to the notion of the corrective experience, the contemporary perspective does not suggest that the therapist should or can develop an a priori formulation of the type of new relational experience that the client needs and then intentionally play a particular role viz-a-viz the client. Rather, the emphasis is on accepting the inevitability of playing the role of an old object (i.e., being recruited into one of the client's characteristic relational scenarios) and then working toward extricating or disembedding from this role and becoming a new object.

Affect Communication

There is a basic assumption in psychoanalytic theory that an important portion of the communication that takes place between people occurs at an unconscious level. What exactly is meant by this? Early psychoanalytic theory is somewhat vague and unclear on this point, and yet references to this notion of unconscious communication can be found in Freud's early technical papers. For example, in an early paper, Freud recommended that the therapist learn to

> turn his own unconscious like a receptive organ towards the transmitting unconscious of the client. He must adjust himself to the client as

a telephone receiver is adjusted to the transmitting microphone. Just as the receiver converts back into sound waves the electric oscillations in the telephone line which were set up by sound waves, so the doctor's unconscious is able, from the derivatives of the unconscious which are communicated to him, to reconstruct that unconscious, which has determined the client's free associations. (S. Freud, 1912/1958, p. 115)

Contemporary research on emotion has suggested that people are remarkably good at reading others' affective displays without conscious awareness (e.g., Parkinson, 1995). Many contemporary analysts who are influenced by developmental research have argued that early mother–infant communication takes place at an affective, bodily felt level prior to the development of any conceptual or symbolic abilities on the infant's part. Developmental researchers such as Ed Tronick (2007) and Beatrice Beebe (Beebe & Lachmann, 2002) have observed that there is an ongoing process of mutual influence between mother and infant's nonverbal behavior (e.g., gaze, posture, affective tone), in which both mother and infant communicate with one another through nonverbal language or at a presymbolic level (Tronick, 2007). Our first relational experiences thus take place outside of the verbal domain and are symbolized or encoded at a presymbolic level, or as what Lyons-Ruth (1998) referred to as *implicit relational knowing*. Implicit relational knowing is a felt sense that is expressed not in what we say, but rather in the way we act and feel in relationships. It is thus a kind of procedural knowledge, a knowing about being in relationships that is not encoded at a linguistic level.

Historically, the process of making the unconscious conscious or of transforming implicit relational knowing into symbolic form has been privileged as a change mechanism by psychoanalysts. The process of symbolizing implicit relational knowledge linguistically gives people an opportunity to reflect on the way in which their prelinguistic, implicit, or unconscious assumptions shape the way they understand relationships, construe other peoples actions·and intentions, act in relationships, and shape their relationships with others through their own actions. There is a growing emphasis in psychoanalytic theory, however, on recognizing the vital role that affective, nonverbal exchange between therapist and client plays as a change mechanism in and of itself.

Containment

Over time I have come to believe that one of the most important skills for therapists to develop is an internal skill, rather than a technical one. This internal skill involves attending to our own emotions when working with clients and cultivating the ability to tolerate and process painful or disturbing feelings in a nondefensive fashion. How do we help our clients hold on to some sense of faith that things will work out when we ourselves are beginning to feel hopeless? How do we work with own feelings as therapists when working with an extremely hostile or devaluing patient? How do we work with our own feelings when we begin to feel the same sense of despair that our client feels?

The British psychoanalyst Wilfred Bion (1970) referred to this process as *containment*. According to Bion, as part of the normal developmental process, children defend against feelings that are too threatening or toxic for them to experience by projecting them onto the parent. Bion argued that children (and clients) not only imagine that unacceptable feelings belong to the caregiver or therapist, but also exert subtle pressures that evoke the dissociated feeling in the therapist. So, for example, the client who experiences nameless feelings of dread and terror dissociates these feelings and in subtle ways evokes these feelings in the therapist. Bion also theorizes that children need their parents to help them process their raw emotional experience and learn to tolerate, symbolize, and make sense of this raw experience.

How do children or clients evoke powerful and sometimes dissociated feelings in parents or therapists? Although Bion did not elaborate on the precise mechanisms, contemporary emotion theory and research suggests that (a) it is not uncommon for people to experience the nonverbal aspects of emotion in the absence of conscious awareness, and (b) as indicated earlier, people are remarkably good at reading and responding to other people's emotion displays without conscious awareness (e.g., Ekman, 1993; Greenberg & Safran, 1987). The process of containment is conceptual and affective in nature. Helping the child or client to put feelings into words is certainly one component of it. The more challenging component involves processing and managing powerful feelings that are evoked in us as parents or as therapists, so that our own affective responses can help to regulate the other's emotions rather than to further disregulate them.

Self- and Interactive Affect Regulation

On the basis of a variety of research findings, Beebe and Lachmann (2002) developed a balance or midrange model of self- and interactive regulation. They argued that the psychologically healthy individual has the capacity to flexibly move back and forth between (a) using his or her own self-soothing skills to regulate distressing emotional experience and (b) using the relationship with the other to help regulate emotions. It turns out that mother–infant observational research has found that attachment security tends to be associated with a midlevel degree of affect attunement between mother and infant. Not surprisingly, infants whose mothers are consistently misattuned to them affectively tend to be insecurely attached. When this pattern ensues, there tends to be an excessive reliance by the infant on the use of self-regulation strategies. These may involve activities such as thumb sucking or gaze aversion or distraction.

Perhaps less obvious, however, is the finding that infants whose mothers are consistently affectively attuned tend to be insecurely attached as well. It may be that excessive attunement on the mother's part reflects an anxiety about the infant's independence or separation, or alternatively that excessive vigilance on the infant's part reflects insecurity about the relationship, or both. The pattern of mutual attunement that tends to be associated with attachment security is in the midrange—somewhere between the two extremes of emotional neglect and preoccupation with affective connection.

Self-regulation plays an extremely important role in the individual's functioning from birth onward. Self-regulation consists of various strategies and actions used to manage arousal, maintain alertness, dampen arousal when overstimulated, process and manage various feelings, and make constructive use of affective feedback. Self-regulation plays a critical role in the capacity to pay attention to and engage with the environment. As previously indicated, for infants self-regulation strategies include activities such as gaze aversion and thumb sucking. In adults, they can include such activities as fantasy, daydreaming, symbolic elaboration, defenses, rational self-coping strategies, and self-reassurance.

The ability to regulate one's emotional experience in a healthy fashion is an important developmental process. This ability develops in infants through the experience of being part of an interpersonal system in which they have the experience of both influencing and being influenced by the caregiver. For example, the infant cries, the mother soothes, the infant calms down, and the mother in turn feels soothed. It takes time after the infant is born for the caregiver to adapt to the specific temperament and character- istic patterns of shifting mood states of the infant. But gradually over time and through a process of mutual adaptation, a certain predictability in the interpersonal system develops. Each partner in the system transforms and in turn is transformed through a process of moment-to-moment coordina- tion of rhythms of nonverbal behavior. And to the extent that a healthy developmental process takes place, both partners come to trust the pre- dictability of the system. This type of implicit trust in the predictability of the system allows the infant to become self-regulating, even if the caregiver is not attending at the moment, and at the same time to know how to seek comfort from the caregiver when necessary and to experience the caregiver's response as soothing.

Although research investigating the role of self- and interactive regula- tion in the therapeutic process is in its early stages, the existing mother–infant observational research can provide a useful model for speculating about some of the nonverbal processes of change that take place in treatment and to refine our theoretical understanding of the mechanisms involved in containment.

For example, James, a 50-year-old lawyer, began treatment with me 1 year after having recovered from serious major depression. Although not chronically depressed, this had been his second major depression, and he was eager to begin the process of treatment to reduce the possibility of relapse in the future. One of the things that impressed me about James early on was his self-contained style. He showed very little emotion in our sessions, and although he seemed eager for help from me, there was another level at which I felt that he had difficulty finding value in anything I said or did. James was an intelligent, well-educated, and thoughtful man who had read a considerable about of psychology, and there was a way in which he seemed to have all the answers in advance. Over time, as I developed an understanding of his developmental history, I came to speculate that he was excessively reliant on the use of self-regulation skills and had tremendous difficulty making use of relationships with others to regulate emotional experience.

In contrast, Elizabeth presented with a desperate need for soothing, comfort, and reassurance from me. She seemed to have no capacity for emotional self-regulation. Furthermore, although sometimes the things I said or did seemed momentarily reassuring or soothing to her, the effects were always short lasting. She also had a tendency to express her need for reassurance and comfort from me in an intense, angry, and coercive fashion, as if she anticipated that whatever she needed from me would not be forthcoming. Over time I began to get a sense that Elizabeth's parents had been traumatically emotionally misattuned and neglectful and that she had often been left alone in states of overwhelming emotional terror. Without the presence of any type of containing environment, Elizabeth was not able to develop any self-regulation skills, and her desperate attempts to coerce soothing from others reflected both a complete lack of self-regulation skills and a pained and angry expectation of continuing neglect by others.

With both James and Elizabeth, part of the therapeutic process involved an ongoing attempt to understand how their styles of self- and interactive regulation made it difficult for me to provide them with what they needed. This involved an ongoing exploration of what is going on between them and me in the here and now of the therapeutic relationship. It also involved a process of thinking out loud together about how important developmental experiences may have played a role in the development of their current affect regulation styles. Just as important, if not more important, however, was a type of organic process through which our evolving relationships helped me to develop a greater capacity to regulate my own affective experience while we were working together. Simultaneously, James's and Elizabeth's evolving shift in implicit relational knowing allowed them to be more open to what I could provide and to make use of our relationship in ways that they were not able to at the beginning. There was thus a type of mutual evolving relational dance taking place that allowed both me and my clients (James and Elizabeth) to change at the same time.

Rupture and Repair

Tronick (2007) demonstrated that in normal mother–infant face-to-face interactions, affective coordination between the two occurs less than 30% of the time. Transitions from coordinated to miscoordinated states and back to coordinated states occur about once every 3 to 5 seconds. Tronick hypothesized that this ongoing process of interactive disruption and repair plays an important role in the normal developmental process. It helps the infant to develop a form of implicit relational knowing that represents both the self and the other as capable of repairing disruptions in relatedness. This type of secure implicit relational knowing plays an adaptive role in everyday life because it allows people to negotiate their ongoing needs for attunement and relatedness throughout the life span and provides them with both the sense of self-efficacy and faith in others to know that interpersonal conflicts and misunderstandings do not have to be catastrophic. This paradigm provides a useful model for understanding an important nonverbal mechanism through which the process of working through the inevitable misunderstandings and disruptions in relatedness that take place between client and therapist contributes to a change in the client's implicit relational knowing.

The principle of relationship rupture and repair has come to assume a central role in the thinking of many psychoanalytic theorists as an important element of the change process. For example, Heinz Kohut (1984) came to see the process of working through the therapist's inevitable empathic failures as a central therapeutic mechanism. From his perspective, when the therapist is able to empathize with the client's experience of having been failed, a process takes place in which clients begin to internalize the therapist's empathic presence and results in a type of structural change for clients that allows them to take over some of the therapist's empathic or mirroring functions. These functions are essential in order for the individual to be able to maintain a sense of self-cohesiveness.

Along similar lines, I have written about the role that repairing ruptures in the therapeutic alliance can play as a vitally important change process (e.g., Safran, 1993, 1998; Safran, Crocker, McMain, & Murray, 1990; Safran & Muran, 1996, 2000, 2006; Safran & Segal, 1990). This emphasis on the importance of repairing ruptures in the therapeutic alliance has now received attention from theorists and researchers across a range of therapeutic traditions, and there is a growing body of empirical evidence supporting the importance of this change mechanism (for reviews of this literature, see Safran, Muran, & Eubacks-Carter, 2011; Safran, Muran, Samstag, & Stevens, 2001, 2002).

Moments of Meeting and Dyadic Expansion of Consciousness

Two related change mechanisms were delineated by a group of psychoanalytically oriented mother–infant researchers who applied ideas on the basis of their empirical findings to the development of theory regarding the process of change in adult psychotherapy. This group, the Boston Change Process Study Group (BCPSG), has focused extensively on the nonverbal aspects of the change process (BCPSG, 2010). For example, the BCPSG (2010) has maintained that each client and therapist dyad develops unique, repetitive patterns of interaction that are based on the intersection of their respective relational schemas. Both client and therapist bring their own implicit relational knowing to the therapeutic relationship and develop their respective understandings of the relationship, as it develops, at least partially at an implicit level. According to the BCPSG, one of the important vehicles through which implicit relational knowledge changes in treatment is the experience of heightened moments of intersubjectivity between client and therapist. Intersubjectivity in this context is conceptualized differently from the way it is conceptualized by theorists such as Jessica Benjamin (as described earlier). It is conceptualized here as the sense of cognitive–

affective connection that two humans experience when it feels to both that they are grasping the same version of reality.

These experiences of heightened intersubjectivity, referred to as *moments of meaning,* involve a sudden transition toward grasping a similar version of "what is happening, now, here, between us" (Stern et al., 1998, p. 908). Although this transition may seem to take place at a conceptual level, it is important to note that it takes place at an affective level as well. A moment of meeting is not just a "meeting of minds" but also a "meeting of hearts." It creates a new intersubjective environment that alters the domain of implicit relational knowing. When this happens, therapist and client both momentarily step outside their usual roles, and a new dyadic state emerges. The stage for a moment of meeting is typically set when a client acts in a way that questions or challenges the current understanding of the implicit relationship. This is referred to a *now moment.*

In order for a moment of meeting to take place, the therapist cannot respond with a prescribed technique or in a way that is guided by theory in any simple or direct way. A now moment doesn't allow much time for the therapist to reflect on the best response. For example, a client I have been seeing for a year walks into my office one day and suddenly sits in my chair rather than hers. How should I respond? A client asks me a very personal question, and I'm not sure whether it's better to explore the motivation behind the question, tell him that I don't usually answer such personal questions, simply respond honestly, or respond in a way that I wouldn't necessarily have anticipated in advance.

A moment of meeting takes place when the therapist responds to this challenge in a spontaneous or authentic fashion that bears the stamp of his or her personal signature. An example comes from a clinical anecdote of Irwin Hoffman's. Hoffman (1998) recalled an experience he had as an analyst in training when one of his clients asked him, "Dr. Hoffman, is it really necessary for me to lie on this couch?" Hoffman reflected for a brief moment and then replied, "It is if I'm going to graduate from my institute." Both he and his client burst out laughing.

Ed Tronick (2007), a one-time member of the BCPSG, delineated another change principle that emerged out of his earlier described research on mother–infant affect coordination and miscoordination. He asked the question, "Why do humans so strongly seek states of emotional connectedness and intersubjectivity and why does the failure to achieve connectedness have such a damaging effect on the mental health of the infant?" (p. 403). Tronick hypothesized that each human being is a self-organizing system that creates his or her own states of consciousness that can be expanded into more complex and coherent states in collaboration with another self-organizing system. From this perspective, part of what happens in the therapeutic process is that by forming an affectively intense intersubjective connection with the therapist, the client is able to expand his or her mind in a way that it incorporates new information and becomes more complex and coherent. From this perspective, it is not just that the therapist is imparting new conceptual information to the client, but rather that the process of intersubjective connection with the therapist allows the client to expand and reorganize his or her consciousness at a higher level of complexity.

Mentalization

In recent years the theoretical and empirical work of Peter Fonagy and his colleagues on affect regulation and mentalization has become increasingly influential among psychoanalysts (e.g., Fonagy, Gergely, Jurist, & Target, 2002). Building on attachment theory and research, Fonagy and colleagues conceptualized the capacity for mentalization or reflective functioning as the ability to see ourselves and others as beings with psychological depth. It allows us to respond to our experience not only on the basis of observed behavior or immediate reaction but also on the basis of our experience and understanding of the underlying mental states of self and other, including desires, feelings, and beliefs. It thus involves a capacity both to access and reflect on our own thoughts, feelings, and motivations and to reflect on the mental states of others. As such, mentalization can be thought of as a combination of or perhaps a dialectic between self-awareness and perspective taking (Holmes, 2010).

In this respect, the construct of reflective functioning can be further clarified by elaborating on Benjamin's (2004) previously mentioned conceptualization of intersubjectivity. According to Benjamin, the capacity for intersubjectivity is a developmental achievement that involves a capacity to hold on to one's own experience of oneself as a subject with a valid perspective, while at the same time experiencing the other as a subject with his or her own independent wishes, needs, and beliefs that are important in their own right (Benjamin, 1988, 2004). To the extent that one has the capacity for intersubjectivity, one is thus able to access one's feelings, wishes, and desires and accept their fundamental validity, while at the same time to appreciate the other as a subject with equally complex and meaningful wishes, intentions, and needs rather than as an object or a character in one's own internal drama. One of the ways in which therapy can facilitate change is thus through promoting an improved capacity to mentalize. An improvement in this capacity should in theory be important because mentalization can play an important role in allowing the individual to recognize and accept his or her own feelings and needs while also managing the complexity of interpersonal relationships in an adaptive fashion by providing the tools to negotiate the needs of self and other.

How does the therapeutic process lead to an improvement in the client's capacity to mentalize? There are a host of different factors at play here. First, as is the case in a healthy developmental process, the therapist's ability to serve as a secure attachment figure for clients provides the conditions that are conducive to developing the capacity to mentalize. The security of the therapeutic relationship helps clients to explore feelings and intentions that have traditionally been dissociated. Second, the process of exploring the transference and countertransference allows clients to develop a greater capacity for mentalization by helping them to become aware of their internal experiences and the way in which their actions impact the therapist's experience. Judicious self-disclosure by the therapist in this context can help the client to develop a greater appreciation of the other's subjectivity.

Third, the process of working through ruptures in the therapeutic alliance or therapeutic impasses also helps clients to develop a greater capacity to mentalize. It is inevitable that therapists will at times fail to live up to their clients' idealized fantasies of what they can provide (e.g., perfect attunement, magically transforming the client's life). When this happens, the therapist's task is to work through these ruptures constructively and to empathize with the client's wishes and desires even if he or she is not always able to fulfill them. As described earlier, this leads to a type of optimal disillusionment that helps clients to begin experiencing the therapist as good enough (Winnicott, 1958, 1965) and as a real subject rather than an idealized object of their fantasies. At the same time, the therapist's capacity to empathize with the client's unmet needs and wishes helps the client to experience his or her desires as valid even if they cannot be fulfilled (Safran, 1993, 1999).

Finally, to the extent that therapists are able to hold in mind a representation of their clients as having their own subjective feelings, intentions, and desires, clients are better able to come to see themselves through their therapist's eyes as separate subjects with their own valid feelings and experiences. Especially in the case of more disturbed clients (e.g., clients with borderline pathology), over time a growing appreciation that the therapist is able to hold them in mind between sessions or during breaks in the therapy (e.g., vacations) plays a role in helping them develop an experience of object constancy (i.e., they are able to hold on to a representation of the therapist as a real person who cares about them even in his or her absence).

PRINCIPLES OF LONG- VERSUS SHORT-TERM PSYCHOANALYTIC TREATMENTS

In this section, I discuss the principles of both long-term and short-term psychoanalytic treatment. Although there are important similarities, there are important differences as well. I also provide clinical illustrations of both modalities.

Long-Term, Intensive Treatment

Whether or not it is helpful to see one's therapist three or four times a week, contemporary culture, with its emphasis on speed and efficiency, does not readily support this type of intense involvement in the work. In my own practice, I see clients at a range of different frequencies, with some coming three or four times per week but the majority coming once or twice a week.

At one time it was believed that frequent sessions per week and long-term treatment were necessary for the transference to develop. These days a more common perspective is that both transference and countertransference are present from the very beginning. Nevertheless, it can take time and frequent contact for the therapist to become the type of key figure in the client's life with whom the more intense feelings that are typically kept out of consciousness emerge. For example, one's romantic partner can bring out the more primitive childlike feelings of affection and aggression that one would typically not display in the workplace. Moreover, because an important aspect of the change process takes place through the relational experience with the therapist in and of itself, the more important the therapist becomes in the client's life, the more likely it is that experiences within the therapeutic relationship will have a constructive impact on the client.

I am sometimes asked by students whether it is possible to do real psychoanalytic work that involves the development of intense transferences and the careful exploration of transference/countertransference dynamics when the client only comes once a week. My experience is that it depends on the client. Some clients are able to form a strong alliance with the therapist and also have the capacity to explore intense and conflicting feelings about the therapeutic relationship when frequency of treatment is kept to once a week. With others, this is more difficult, and more frequent contact is important. Some clients simply do not have the psychological and emotional capacity to benefit from this type intense exploration of what is taking place in the therapeutic relationship, no matter how frequent their sessions are. This does not mean that they cannot benefit from psychoanalysis or psychoanalytically oriented therapy, but it does mean that the exploration of transference/countertransference dynamics cannot be a primary vehicle of change for them.

One of the important features of long-term, open-ended psychoanalytic treatment is a sense of evolving process, discovery, and openness to the emergence of new themes. This stance requires a certain tolerance of ambiguity by both client and therapist. In situations in which the client presents with an urgent need or is in crisis, this type of open-ended approach may be problematic. In such cases, it is critical for the therapist to be responsive to the client's need to focus on the specific problem in a more active and directive fashion. Once the immediate crisis or sense of urgency has passed the client may be interested in continuing treatment in a more open-ended, discovery-oriented fashion or alternatively may feel that it is time to terminate treatment. Either way, it is important for the therapist to be responsive to the client's needs.

Simone: An Illustration of Longer Term Psychoanalytic Treatment

Simone was a young African American woman with whom I worked for 4 years. During this period I saw her three times per week. At the time she began treatment, she was 26 years old. Simone initially sought treatment because of a "general feeling of emptiness" as well as a moderate problem with bulimia, which involved both binging and purging. She was working in a health food store on a part-time basis and was primarily supported financially by her father. In college, Simone had majored in fine arts, but at the time she was in treatment with me, she was not doing anything related to her college education. She was extremely attractive, intelligent, articulate, and well dressed. From the beginning I was struck by her lively and playful manner and her sense of humor. I also began to notice early on a tendency on her part to vacillate between states of narcissistic grandiosity during which she denied any needs or self-doubts and (less frequently) states of openness and vulnerability during which she was able to admit to feeling extremely alienated and lonely.

Simone was brought up in a middle-class family in the suburbs. She attended a relatively affluent, predominantly White school. When I asked what the experience of being one of the only Black children in the school had been like for her, she denied any feelings of discomfort or of not belonging. She told me that most of her friends throughout her life had been White and that she had never given it much thought. During the course of treatment, we explored whether being in treatment with a White therapist had any significance for her. At first she denied that this was the case, in the same way that she had denied having any feelings about being one of the few African Americans in a predominantly White school. Gradually over time, however, we were able to explore this issue in greater depth.

Simone had two older brothers and one younger sister. Her father had an MBA and was a business executive when she was growing up. Her mother was a nurse. Simone's father left her mother when Simone was 6 years old. Her father and mother had maintained an on-and-off-again relationship over the years, and her mother had always maintained the hope of reuniting with him.

When Simone was a child, her father's presence was very unpredictable. He would periodically (e.g., once every 1 or 2 months) come home to spend a weekend and then invariably leave early after having a fight with her mother. Simone described poignant memories of running down the road after his car, crying. She maintained that initially she would be very excited when she knew that her father would be visiting. Eventually she stopped feeling any excitement (as a form of self-protection) and then transitioned into a third state in which she experienced no feelings but pretended to be excited to avoid alienating her father.

Simone's father continued to maintain a relationship with her as she grew older and even now would periodically contact her, take her out for lunch or dinner, make plans to see her again, and then inevitably disappear from her life again. When Simone spoke about her father, I often had the feeling that there was a semi-incestuous quality to the relationship. It was difficult for me to put my finger on why I felt this way. Simone never acknowledged a literal sexual boundary violation in their relationship (and it seemed to me quite possible that there never was one). But the way she discussed their relationship often had a type of romantically charged quality. She conveyed a sense of awkwardness and shame about their interactions, and her perception was that her father felt awkward ("as if he was on a date") as well. Another factor contributing to my speculation that there may have been some time of sexual boundary violation in Simone's childhood was that she sometimes spoke about experiencing a type of "disgusting energy" emanating from her that drove people away (my experience has been that feeling disgusting in some fundamental way is not unusual for clients who have been sexually violated as children). The possibility of a sexual boundary violation having taken place in Simone's childhood was not a topic that we ever fully explored in our work together. I speculated to myself, however, that a boundary violation of this type may have affected her ability to have romantic relationships with men. I also wondered to myself whether some type of sexual trauma with her father or another man in Simone's childhood may have had an impact on her way of relating to me and her difficulty in accepting support and nurturance from me.

Simone maintained that when she was a child, her mother had been very erratic, alternating between episodes of intense anger and periods of fragility and dependency on her. She remembered learning to be very vigilant to shifts in her mother's mood to avoid triggering an outburst. She also remembered learning to take care of her mother emotionally—a way of being that had become characteristic for Simone. She described her mother as very emotionally needy and dependent and felt very judgmental of her. This critical perspective on her mother contrasted with an idealized view of her father, whom she viewed as independent and whom she identified with.

Simone was extremely shy in school and saw herself as "ugly." Her first romantic relationship was at the end of high school. She was involved with a boy for a year but had no sexual relationship with him. When he left school to attend college, Simone became briefly involved with his best friend. On one occasion, she had sexual intercourse with him and experienced this as traumatic. When she described the reasons why she had experienced the event as traumatic, it was the first point in our work together that I began to get a sense of some pockets of semi-delusional ideation in Simone's thinking that were generally kept well contained. Simone told me that prior to this incident, she had believed that she would give birth to a child through immaculate conception and that now this could never happen.

Subsequent to her relationship with this boy, she began to have lesbian relationships and was involved in a lesbian relationship at the beginning of treatment. Prior to beginning treatment, Simone's longest romantic relationship (subsequent to her first high school boyfriend) had lasted 1 month. Her typical pattern would be to end romantic relationships when she began to experience her partner as being too "emotionally needy," apparently an inevitability in her mind. When Simone began treatment, she did not see the absence of long-term romantic relationships in her life as a problem or as something she wished to change.

Over the course of treatment, Simone and I spent considerable time exploring the factors contributing to her feelings of emptiness as well as her binging behavior. She fluctuated dramatically (both within sessions and various stages of the treatment) in her ability to look at her own feelings and actions in a self-reflective fashion. But at times when she was feeling safer and more open, she was able to express a desire to improve the quality of her relationships with people, a wish to be in a long-term romantic relationship, and a curiosity in understanding interfering factors. We explored the way in which her father's unpredictability had contributed to the development of a counterdependent stance on her part. In addition, we explored the way in which she had identified with her father (and his apparent emotional aloofness) and repudiated the more vulnerable dependent aspects of herself that she associated with her mother (whom she saw as pathetic). We also explored the way in which her binging was connected to a desire to fill an experience of emptiness inside of her and the relationship between her dissociation of dependent feelings related both to her feelings of disgust when she experienced romantic partners as "needy" and her own difficulty in allowing others to relate to her in a nurturing fashion.

At different points in the treatment, Simone revealed additional elements of semidelusional ideation (e.g., a continuing belief that she would still give birth to the messiah, a belief that certain people she met had special powers, a belief that she could read other people's minds). At such times, Simone disclosed information tentatively and with a somewhat self-deprecatingly humorous style, as if to say, "I don't take this completely seriously." She vacillated in terms of how trusting of me she felt and how willing she was to reveal beliefs of this type. Her fear that I would not understand or could not fully embrace her beliefs was an ongoing focus of discussion.

Throughout the treatment Simone was preoccupied with various new age beliefs and ideas. She would spend hours browsing new age books on the shelves in bookstores in what seemed like a desperate attempt to fill what she described as a "hole" or "emptiness" inside of her. Inevitably Simone would leave the store feeling unsatiated—bored with the activity but not fulfilled. In time we came to understand this activity as similar in function to her binging behavior (i.e., a desperate attempt to fill an internal experience of emptiness).

A few months after beginning treatment with me, Simone became involved with a cult, and this involvement continued and intensified over the first 2 years of her treatment. An important focus of exploration involved her concern that her spiritual interests were incompatible with psychotherapy. In addition, the impact of Simone's dissociated dependency needs emerged more fully in the cult. Although at first she felt quite skeptical of the cult and its leader, over time she became more involved in the cult. The allure for her of being able to completely surrender to the cult and its leader became more and more apparent. The prospect of having somebody take charge of her life completely and tell her what to do and what not do in any given situation was undeniably appealing to her.

As discussed previously, there was a continuous alternation in treatment between periods when Simone seemed quite open and able to engage in an exploratory process and periods when she was highly defended and rejected any attempt on my part to explore underlying feelings or look for deeper meaning. Although these alternating states never completely disappeared, over the course of treatment they became less frequent and intense, and Simone became better able to explore both her internal experience and the meaning of our relationship to her.

At the beginning of treatment I had the sense that Simone had one foot in treatment and one foot out the door. She would often miss sessions (claiming that she had forgotten) or arrive 15 to 20 minutes late. For the most part, she would resist any attempt to explore feelings or factors underlying her inconsistent and late attendance, although occasionally she would be more receptive to exploration. I found myself feeling anxious that she would leave treatment precipitously and concerned that any attempt on my part to explore her ambivalence would hasten her departure. I also found myself feeling concerned that she would experience my attempts to explore her ambivalence as reflecting my own neediness, and I was more hesitant than I usually am to explore a client's ambivalence about treatment as a result.

Over time part of our work together involved exploring the way in which her skittishness about committing to treatment evoked anxious feelings in me that in turn made it difficult to bring myself fully into the relationship and express my own feelings of caring toward her. I began to conceptualize what was taking place as an enactment in which Simone's own anxieties about dependency led to a lack of investment in our relationship, which in turn fueled feelings on my part of both anxiety and shame about my insecurity. My own conflicts about dependency and a concern about seeing myself as needy were being triggered by Simone's avoidant style and interfering with my ability to constructively explore Simone's contribution to what was taking place between us.

Another, more subtle, element of my countertransference feeling emerged more clearly over time. When I first met Simone, I experienced her as very attractive and was impressed by her lively, playful manner and sense of humor. I had found myself looking forward to working with her, and I won't deny that my attraction to her played some role in this. Over time, however, it occurred to me that Simone's physical attractiveness developed a type of abstract, disembodied quality for me. Although Simone continued to have a playful manner, I did not experience it as flirtatious at all and was somewhat surprised by what I experienced as a complete absence of any sexual attraction on my part toward her, despite the fact that I continued to find her beautiful in an abstract sense. I wondered to myself whether this aspect of my countertransference might be related to a tendency on her part to desexualize me in her mind in order to make our relationship safe for her. This is not a theme that evolved more fully or that we had time to explore during our work together.

Over time I became aware of the quality of narcissistic grandiosity in Simone—a belief on her part that she had all the answers and that nobody else, including me, had anything of value to say to her. This attitude is not one that emerged explicitly at first, but rather gradually over time as I became aware of my own countertransference feelings of not being able to say things that she really took in, and I was able to use my feelings as a point of departure for exploring what was going on in our relationship. Gradually Simone was able to acknowledge her lack of belief that I might have anything useful to say to her. And ultimately she was able to articulate an underlying fear that if she did become more receptive, she would become dependent on me and vulnerable to abandonment. Over time Simone and I were able to collaboratively make sense of her counterdependency and narcissistic defenses in terms of her experiences of abandonment as a child, and she became more open to input from me. A central dilemma that emerged for her was the conflict between, on the one hand, fearing dependency on others and feeling that nobody (including myself) had anything of value to offer her, and on the other hand, desperately wishing that others would be able to introduce their subjectivity in a way that would help her feel less alone.

We explored these themes in a variety of different ways throughout treatment. To provide one example, I describe the way in which a dream that Simone reported in the 5th month of our work together led to an exploration of her ambivalent feelings regarding dependency in our relationship and provided hints of her complex feelings about sexuality, men and dependency, and our relationship. She reported this dream shortly after her father had invited her to temporarily move into an apartment he owned, that he would stay in periodically when he came to the city on business trips.

Simone: I'm with some people on a beach and they're playing with a puppy. And they've got the puppy partially submerged under the water . . . maybe to soothe it. But it's not happy. And so I decide to take over. . . . I see a male dog who I think is its father . . . but it's interesting because this male dog has udders. So I take the puppy and put it on its father's udders, and then the puppy seems happy.

Safran: What do you make of the dream?

Simone: Well, maybe the dog is actually my father, and maybe it has to do with me moving into his place.

Safran: That makes sense . . . and I'm also thinking . . . and this is really just playing around with the images . . . so don't take what I'm saying too seriously, maybe the male dog is me [I say this in a very tentative way, so it will be easy for her to dismiss without feeling too dismissive, but also in an attempt to gauge how capable she is of acknowledging feelings of intimacy and dependency in our relationship at this point].

Simone: I hadn't thought of that.

Safran: How does it feel?

Simone: I don't know. . . . I'd have to think about it.

She then goes on to tell me another dream fragment.

Simone: And then in the dream, I see my old advisor from college, Emma . . . she's a woman, but then I look at her shadow and it's the shadow of a man.

Safran: What do you make of it?

Simone: I don't know.

Safran: I know from what you've told me previously that last time you visited Emma you felt uncomfortable with her because she felt needy to you. [Earlier Simone had told me that Emma symbolizes neediness to her.]

Simone: Well, it's like the way she was always trying to look after me and offer me guidance, it felt like there was a kind underlying desperation . . . or neediness . . . like maybe she needs to relate to me as a daughter or something.

I wonder to myself if this might be another reference to our relationship. Perhaps Simone experiences my attempts to help her as representing a form of neediness on my part. But I decide not to explore this potential allusion to our relationship because of a concern that she will find it too threatening. Simone continued talking about the dream at the following session.

Simone: I was thinking about that dream I had about that male dog with the udders . . . and it makes me feel uncomfortable.

Safran: Are you willing to explore what feels uncomfortable about it? [This is a form of defense analysis.]

Simone: Well, there's something yucky about it. I don't really like to think of myself as getting nurtured by you. There's something scary about it.

Safran: Scary in what way?

Simone: Well, it would mean that I'm dependent on you, and that brings up a whole bunch of feelings.

We continue to explore the range of feelings it brings up: fear, yearning, revulsion, fear of abandonment, and so on.

Simone: You're not really a father figure for me . . . it's like you're not really male. It's like you just exist in my head.

Safran: Can you say more about me not being male?

Simone: Well, you don't give me advice or tell me what to do.

Safran: Would you want me to give you advice?

Simone: No.

Safran: Why not?

Simone: Because then I would become dependent on you. You're not like my father that way. Things are complicated with him.

At this point Simone transitions into talking about her complicated feelings about what she refers to as the "sexual energy" between her and her father. She speaks about how her father always makes it clear to people that she is his daughter when he takes her out to dinner, as if to make sure that no one assumes they have a romantic relationship. She speaks about the fact that on occasion she has slept at her father's place when he is out of town and that she feels uncomfortable sleeping in his bed because she knows that he "entertains people there."

I speculate to myself that it is important for Simone to desexualize me in her mind because the potential of my playing a paternal role with her may have threatening sexual connotations for her. But again, I don't say anything at this point because I feel it would be premature.

The following session, Simone spontaneously brought up the possibility that maybe the male dog with udders in her dream does represent me. We continued to explore what this possibility meant to her during this session and the intertwined threads of conflict around dependency, sexuality, and romantic relationships with both men and women continued to unfold and become further illuminated throughout the treatment.

Approximately halfway through treatment, Simone became romantically involved with Jim, a 30-year-old African American musician. Jim was the first male Simone had been romantically involved with since her adolescence. Over a period of time Simone was able to genuinely contact her desire for Jim and her hope that things would work out between them. I never expressed a preference for Simone to become romantically involved with men rather than women, nor was I aware of experiencing such a preference. Although Simone was not able to explain her new interest in a romantic relationship with a man, I speculated to myself that perhaps the process of becoming more trusting of me, a male therapist, helped her to begin to experience men in general as safer and less likely to abandon her in the same way that her father had. This possibility was not, however, something I felt Simone was ready and able to explore explicitly in treatment, so I did not introduce it.

Ultimately Jim rejected Simone. My impression was that she experienced this as excruciatingly painful and subsequently shut down and began again to deny her need for him or for anyone else, including me. During this period she flirted with the idea of leaving both treatment and the city to join an ashram associated with the cult she had joined. After a futile and extended attempt on my part to explore what was going on for her, I settled into providing more of a supportive, containing environment for her in which I would attempt to mirror or empathize with the manifest level of her experience. After approximately 2 months of this, Simone began to become more emotionally open again, more receptive to exploration, and she stopped talking about leaving treatment.

Subsequent to this, she began dating a number of men and ultimately settled into a relationship with a man named Scott. It was in the context of this relationship that she had sexual intercourse with a man for the first time since her adolescence. She subsequently moved in with Scott in a rather precipitous fashion and continued living with him for approximately 3 months. During this period, she struggled with intensely ambivalent feelings about the increased intimacy and fears of dependency and engulfment. We spent considerable time in therapy exploring the difficulty she had in negotiating between his needs and her own and also explored the parallel between the issues emerging in her relationship with Scott and the transference.

Over time, Simone found living with Scott increasingly intolerable, alternating between feeling that he was too needy and very occasionally acknowledging fears of abandonment and rejection. Eventually she left him to move in with another man who was a member of the cult. At the same time, she began to discuss the possibility of leaving treatment again, maintaining that she was feeling better and that she had accomplished the goals she had at the beginning of treatment. Over a period of time I gently and tentatively explored with her the possibility that her wish to leave treatment was motivated (at least in part) by a desire to avoid the type of intensely ambivalent feelings evoked by the intimacy of our relationship. Gradually she came to acknowledge that this was true and then began to settle into a phase of treatment during which she remained considerably more trusting and open for an extended period of time.

Although during this phase Simone continued to vacillate between periods of self-reflection and periods of shutting down and emotional withdrawal from me, the intensity of these swings decreased considerably. Also during this phase Simone substantially decreased her binging behavior and became less preoccupied with eating. She began to work on her art for the first time since ending college and was able to experience this as a source of satisfaction. Simone and I continued to explore her feelings of ambivalence about intimacy and her fear of dependency both in our relationship and in relationships in general. She also began to talk more openly about feelings of being "different" because most of her friends were not Black, and we began to explore ambivalent feelings about being in therapy with a White therapist. We explored the way in which Simone did not feel completely at home either in the White world or the Black world and the way this contributed to her general feeling of alienation and isolation.

In the final 6 months of our work together, Simone became romantically involved with a new man in her life named Jamal, and this relationship developed a more stable quality than her previous relationships. Although she was not without feelings of ambivalence, she was also better able to tolerate her feelings of dependency on Jamal and was less self-critical of her need for him. She began working on a more consistent basis in the health food store and developed a plan to save up enough money to return to college with the help of her father's financial assistance and take some specialized courses in graphic design.

Two months before ending treatment, Simone began to raise the possibility of termination. This time, however, things had a different feeling about them than they had previously. It was clear to both of us that she had made some important changes in her life, and although it was far from clear what the future would hold in terms of her current romantic relationship or her plans to return to college, there was a mutual sense that she had started on a different path than the one she had been on at the beginning of treatment. We set a termination date in advance and, over the remaining time, explored both ways in which she had changed over the course of our work together and her feelings about termination.

At first she denied any ambivalent feelings about leaving treatment and expressed an eagerness to "do things on her own" now that she no longer needed my help. I wondered to myself whether it might be a bit premature for her to leave treatment and had some concern that she would not be able to maintain the gains she had made. I also wondered whether her plans to terminate were once again related to her fears of intimacy and abandonment and distaste for dependency. At the same time, however, I considered the possibility that my reactions reflected my own reluctance to let go of her and perhaps a certain degree of narcissism on my part and an overestimation of the significance of my own role in her life.

I disclosed some of these feelings to her and this facilitated an ability on her part to begin to explore some of her ambivalent feelings about leaving treatment. She was ultimately able to acknowledge anxiety about becoming too dependent on me, fears about how her life would go after she left treatment, and—toward the end—feelings of sadness about ending our relationship. When we ended treatment I made it clear that she was welcome to contact me any time, just to let me know how things were going or to schedule another session if she wished.

I received a letter from her about 2 years later. In it she told me that things were basically going well in her life. Apparently she had left Jamal approximately 4 months after she had terminated with me. Three months later she had become romantically involved with another man, and they were still in a stable relationship. She was working for a small group as a graphic designer and was finding the work challenging but satisfying. Simone wrote that periodically she would still lapse into periods of binging, especially during difficult periods in her life (e.g., breaking up with Jamal).

But she wrote that in general, her binging was much more in control than it had been when she began treatment. Overall Simone felt that her treatment with me had been helpful, and I concurred. I had a sense that our work together had reached a level of depth that allowed her to make some significant changes in her life and significant internal changes as well. I also had the sense that there were many themes left unexplored and that Simone could have benefited from more treatment. It seems possible that she may go into treatment again at some point in her life, and that she may even contact me in the future to explore the possibility of further treatment. At the same time, however, I believe that no story ever completely unfolds in any treatment and that at any given point in time a specific client and therapist are able to reach the depth and accomplish what they are both ready and able to accomplish at that time.

Short-Term Treatment

Although psychoanalysis has become almost synonymous with long-term, open-ended treatment, brief-term psychoanalytic treatments have a long history and have become increasingly common in the last 20 years. As previously indicated, all of the original psychoanalytic treatments were short term in nature (relative to contemporary psychoanalytic standards). Sandor Ferenczi experimented with a wide variety of active interventions to speed up the process of change, including the establishment of time limits. Ferenczi also collaborated with Otto Rank (Ferenczi & Rank, 1925/1956) to write about the use of active and directive interventions to promote a more rapid and effective treatment. Rank (1929) subsequently experimented with the use of short-term, time-limited treatments as a way of mobilizing the client's will and highlighting dependency and separation issues.

There is now a profusion of short-term psychoanalytic or short-term dynamic treatments in existence. Messer and Warren (1995) categorized existing forms of short-term psychoanalytic treatment into two types: drive/structural and relational. Drive/structural approaches all subscribe to an ego psychological approach and emphasize the interpretation of wish/defense conflicts as a central ingredient of change. These tend to be quite confrontational in nature and by and large assume a one-person psychological perspective, paying little attention to the therapist's contribution to enactments that are taking place. Some of the best-known examples of the drive/structural approach are the approaches of David Malan (1963) and Peter Sifneos (1972).

Perhaps the best-known variants of the relational approach are the approaches of Lester Luborsky (1984) and Hans Strupp and colleagues (Binder, 2004; Levenson, 2010; Strupp & Binder, 1984). These approaches conceptualize problems as the result of recurrent maladaptive patterns of interpersonal behavior resulting from configurations of internal object relations, which are themselves the result of disturbances in relationships with early caretakers. Although these approaches do not preclude an emphasis on wish/defense conflicts, they pay particular attention to the relationship between the interpersonal context of these wish/defense conflicts and the way in which recurrent interpersonal patterns occur both in the client's everyday life and in the therapeutic relationship.

Although there are important theoretical and technical differences in these two general types of short-term treatments, most share certain features that distinguish them from longer term psychoanalytic treatments. These include the following characteristics: an emphasis on developing a case formulation early in treatment, the use of this formulation to establish and maintain a focus throughout the treatment, a high level of therapist activity relative to many forms of long-term psychoanalytic treatments, the establishment of a set number of sessions or a clear termination date in advance, and an emphasis on working through the meaning of termination for the client. In addition, many of the short-term psychoanalytic or dynamic approaches use termination as an opportunity to focus on issues of separation–individuation and loss that are conceptualized as playing a central role for people in their everyday lives.

Because contemporary psychoanalytic practice tends to be more long-term and open-ended in nature, it is often a challenge for therapists who are trained in a traditional psychoanalytic model to make the necessary shifts in attitude relevant to doing short-term therapy. As Messer and Warren (1995) pointed out, there are a number of emotional challenges for therapists in shifting from a long-term to a short-term orientation to psychoanalytic treatment. These include feelings of guilt over not being able to offer the client more, struggling with one's grandiose and perfectionist ambitions in light of the constraints of a short-term approach, and dealing with feelings revolving around separation and termination (e.g., feeling guilty about abandoning or rejecting a client, mourning the end of a meaningful relationship).

Short-term dynamic therapists use many of the interventions used by long-term psychoanalytic therapists, including interpretation of unconscious feelings, wishes, and defenses; interpretation of the resistance; transference interpretations; extratransference interpretations; and genetic transference interpretations. There is often a higher level of therapist activity in short-term dynamic therapy than in longer term analytic therapies and a higher concentration of interpretations. There is also often a likelihood of making more frequent transference interpretations to maximize the impact of the treatment in the short amount of time available. In practice, there is often more of a confrontational nature to short-term dynamic therapies than in many approaches to long-term therapy given the need to speed up the change process. This was particularly true in the first generation of popular short-term dynamic approaches (e.g., Sifneos, 1972; Davanloo, 1980), although more recent developments in the short-term dynamic approach appear to be learning from experience and now place more emphasis on emotional attunement, establishing an alliance, and allowing clients to work at their own pace (e.g., Fosha, 2000; McCullough Valliant, 1997).

As previously indicated, the majority of short-term dynamic approaches attempt to deal with the time constraints by establishing an explicit formulation of a core dynamic theme for the client to serve as a guiding focus for interventions throughout the treatment. The assumption is that this type of focus is essential to make efficient use of the time (Safran & Muran, 1998). Although formulation plays an important role in any psychoanalytic approach, this emphasis on establishing an explicit formulation so early in the treatment is in some respect at odds with the sensibility of a long-term open-ended psychoanalytic treatment that emphasizes the importance of cultivating an openness to the emergent process. In other words, establishing an early formulation is in tension with the stance of evenly suspended attention, which is designed to also allow the therapist's unconscious processes and associations to be receptive to the client's associations and the unconscious processes to which they are linked.

Despite this concern, most short-term dynamic therapists feel that establishing an ealy dynamic focus is necessary if one is going to accomplish anything in a brief time. Different short-term models use different approaches for developing dynamic formulations, and although there are similarities between the formulation procedures associated with different approaches (as well as the types of formulations developed), there are also differences that are influenced both by theoretical differences and differences in the components that are considered essential to a formulation.

The approach to short-term psychoanalytic treatment that has been most extensively influenced by recent developments in relational psychoanalysis is brief relational therapy (BRT; Safran, 2002; Safran & Muran, 2000; Safran, Muran, Samstag, & Stevens, 2001). BRT shares a number of similarities with other short-term dynamic treatments, but it is also distinguished by the fact that its development has been substantially influenced by principles emerging out of relational psychoanalysis and by findings emerging from our empirical research program on ruptures in the therapeutic alliance. The key characteristics of BRT are as follows: (a) it assumes a two-person psychology, (b) it involves a focus on the here and now of the therapeutic relationship, (c) it involves an ongoing collaborative exploration of both the client's and the therapist's contribution to the interaction, (d) it emphasizes in-depth exploration of the nuances of the client's experience in the context of unfolding enactments and is sparing in the use of interpretations that draw links between the transference and other relational patterns, (e) it makes use of countertransference disclosure and therapeutic metacommunication, and (f) it assumes that the impact of any intervention is always mediated by its relational meaning. Consistent with a two-person psychology, BRT emphasizes that the therapist's formulation must always be informed by an evolving understanding of the nature of his own participation in relational scenarios that are being enacted with the client. BRT thus places less of an emphasis than many other short-term dynamic approaches on the importance of developing a clear-cut dynamic formulation early in the treatment.

Amanda: An Illustration of a Short-Term Psychoanalytic Treatment

The case of Amanda provides an illustration of psychoanalytically oriented treatment administered in a highly abbreviated form (i.e., six sessions). This case has some unique characteristics because I treated Amanda for an American Psychological Association (APA) DVD illustration of psychoanalytic therapy. Because of the nature of the series, I saw her for only six sessions, which is certainly toward the low end of the continuum (short-term therapies that are typically studied in randomized clinical trials usually range in duration from somewhere in the area of 12 to 25 sessions). I also want to emphasize at the outset that from a psychoanalytic perspective, Amanda is someone who would be highly suitable for longer term, open-ended treatment and that given the chronic and severe history of her problems, her history of abandonment (which I discuss shortly), and her potential receptiveness to long-term treatment, I would not normally recommend short-term therapy as the treatment of choice for her (and in fact I did refer her for long-term treatment at the end of our time together).

It is also important to bear in mind that our work together was inevitably influenced by the fact that it took place in a production studio with cameramen and high-tech equipment present and that both Amanda and I were aware that this was not "ordinary therapy" but rather a treatment conducted specifically for purposes of filming a training DVD. This placed a considerable amount of pressure on both Amanda and me and certainly compromised the type of privacy and safety that under normal conditions are so critical to psychotherapy. On the other hand, my feeling is that the process that unfolded as we worked was sufficiently similar to the process that takes place in a regular psychoanalytic treatment to make it a useful illustration, especially since the DVD is available from APA and allows for a more detailed examination of the process.[2] Furthermore, the exploration of the impact of the videotaping on the treatment became a central focus of our work, thus allowing for an exploration of the impact of this aspect of the therapeutic frame on the transference and countertransference.

Prior to agreeing to participate in the project, Amanda had read a brief description and rationale for psychoanalytic treatment that I had written. In response to the DVD production teams' request that I provide a description of the type of client to select for the demonstration, I decided that it was important to screen for someone who had some sense of what the tasks and goals of treatment would be like and felt that this seemed like a meaningful way of working to them. The rationale emphasized such factors as the importance of exploring unconscious feelings and thoughts, examining self-defeating patterns that are enacted unconsciously, and using the therapeutic relationship as a specific focus of exploration to shed light on unconscious self-defeating patterns that are potentially enacted in other relationships. I mention this here because it became particularly relevant in my third session with Amanda.

Let me begin by providing some information about Amanda, her background, and her reasons for seeking treatment in the first place. Amanda was a young Caucasian woman from a working-class background with a history of serious depression and substance abuse. Before seeking treatment with me, she had experienced three serious and incapacitating major depressive episodes, and she claimed that she had been depressed for as long as she could remember. She also had a long history of addiction to both street and prescription drugs. In addition, she had a history of involvement in romantic relationships with abusive men. At the time of our first interview, Amanda had already begun to make some important changes in her life. She had joined Narcotics Anonymous and had been drug free for over a year. She had also been depression free for over a year and was working part time. Her stated goal in seeing me for six sessions was to continue working

---

[2] The DVD, which can be purchased at http://www.apa.org/pubs/books, is titled *Psychoanalytic Therapy Over Time* and is copyrighted by the American Psychological Association. It is important to note that the client's name and other identifying information have been changed here to protect her confidentiality. The reader who watches the DVD may notice some discrepancies.

on developing the psychological resources to begin to change her pattern of self-destructive romantic involvements.

Session 1 with Amanda was spent for the most part gathering information about her presenting problems and goals, history of problems, personal history, and current life situation and level of functioning in an attempt to develop a sense of whether I could be at all helpful to her in this context (i.e., only six sessions, once a week, on camera, etc.). I also attempted to lay the groundwork for the establishment of a therapeutic alliance by both empathizing with her and working collaboratively with her to develop a shared understanding of her problem and her goals and how we were going to work toward them. I was also beginning to attend to my own counter-transference feelings, to see if I could begin to get a hint or a felt sense of what it would be like to relate to her. For the most part, my sense was that things flowed smoothly between Amanda and me in this session. There was a quality of synchrony between us, almost a dance. I felt that I was able to empathize with her and that she was able to take in my empathy.

I also noticed that on the few occasions when I asked Amanda more open-ended questions and allowed her an opportunity to take the lead and elaborate, things started to feel a bit awkward. At these points she would talk about feeling "on the spot," and I found myself automatically rushing in to pick up the slack. It felt like I had to do this to keep things running smoothly, and I found myself noting these feelings to myself and filing the experience away for potential exploration at some later point.

In the session, Amanda revealed that she had experienced a traumatic childhood. Her biological father abandoned the family when Amanda was 4 years old. Her stepfather (whom her mother married when Amanda was 6 years old) was a firefighter. He was also an alcoholic and physically abusive toward her mother. Amanda had memories of her stepfather coming home in a drunken rage, getting into arguments with her mother, breaking furniture, and hitting her mother. When this would occur, Amanda recalled playing the role of the mediator, trying to break up the fights by actually placing herself physically between her mother and stepfather and separating them. Amanda remembered that at one point when she was 9 or 10 years old, she had called the police to break up the fight and that her mother had to be taken to the hospital. In contrast to this physical violence toward

Amanda's mother, Amanda claimed that her stepfather was never abusive (either physically or emotionally) toward her. She thought of him as her "best friend." Amanda's stepfather committed suicide when she was 15, and over the years she had gone though a whole range of feelings about this: guilt for not being able to save him, hurt, anger, betrayal, and abandonment.

In this session, I began to develop a very preliminary sense of certain recurrent interpersonal themes in Amanda's life that might be relevant to developing a working formulation. I began to wonder if abandonment was a recurrent issue in her life. I also began to think about Amanda's role as the mediator between her mother and her stepfather. What a tremendous sense of responsibility for a young child. It's not unusual for this type of developmental experience to lead to a kind of parentification and a precocious maturity in which the child adapts to the situation by learning to take care of other people's needs rather than her own. In my experience, it's not unusual for children in this position to simultaneously feel helpless and abandoned and at the same time to feel special and empowered by their role in the family dynamics. But these feelings of power and specialness are often hidden or partially unconscious. This type of experience can thus lead to the development of a way of being with others in which an individual adapts by learning to take care of other people's needs rather than his or her own (what Winnicott, 1965, referred to as a *false self* organization). The child in this type of situation can develop a sense of overwhelming personal responsibility, difficulties in truly depending on others, and unconscious or semiconscious feelings of both grandiosity and resentment.

I want to emphasize that all of these thoughts were fleeting in nature and that I have reconstructed them after the fact. They were not part of a formal or articulated formulation. In addition, I want to emphasize that although in Amanda's case I was beginning to develop certain feelings and hunches that I felt might later be relevant to a fuller understanding of her, it's not unusual for this process to take much longer or for me to find out that my initial hunches and intuitions lead nowhere or are only partially relevant.

Despite Amanda's traumatic background and history of serious psychological problems, she had (as I was about to learn) a number of significant emotional and psychological strengths. She was intelligent, had completed an undergraduate college degree, and had a network of friends she could rely on (through her work with Narcotics Anonymous). I was also beginning to get a glimpse of a feisty and lively side to her and a sardonic sense of humor, which intrigued me. By the end of our first session, I found myself admiring Amanda's strength, resilience, and feistiness. I also found myself deeply concerned about her and wanting to help her. At the same time I sensed a hint of underlying wariness or mistrustfulness in Amanda. Although our first session went relatively smoothly, I wondered to what extent this smoothness would continue over our time together.

In our second session, the international dynamic that had previously begun to emerge between Amanda and me in subtle ways started to emerge more clearly. I began to sense that as long as I was taking the lead and asking her factually oriented questions, things would continue to go relatively smoothly. And I found myself doing this reflexively, while at the same time continuing to make a mental note of it, wondering about where it was leading. I began the session by continuing to collect information about Amanda's background. I asked her for information about her relationship with her mother and her biological father (whom she had gotten to know again as an adult), in part because I felt it could provide important background information, but also perhaps in part because I intuitively sensed that this type of active relational stance on my part would help to maintain Amanda's anxiety at a manageable level and help to build the alliance.

At the same time, I was beginning to develop a vague sense that there may have been something a little bit off about the quality of Amanda's affective engagement in the session. I found myself wondering if she was talking about something that was emotionally vital and alive for her in the moment or, alternatively, was perhaps only dutifully responding to my questions. And I was becoming increasingly aware of a feeling of pressure on my part to continually introduce new topics. As these feelings intensified, I decided that rather than continuing to reflexively pick up the slack, or to intentionally shift to a less active role (which I speculated might lead to a power struggle or an impasse), I would begin attempting to explore what was going on between us. And so I began to metacommunicate with her—to engage her in the process of collaboratively exploring what was taking place between us by explicitly focusing on our relationship.

I thus said something to the effect of

> I find myself reflexively moving toward asking you more questions, in part I think as a way of keeping things going smoothly between us. But I'm also a bit concerned that if I continue doing this, it will get in the way of you talking about what feels most alive and important for you.

As I finished speaking, I felt Amanda tense up and a sense of awkwardness began to emerge more clearly between us. She responded by saying, "I have no idea what you want me to talk about." In response to her statement, I made a number of attempts to explain what I was trying to get at and how exploring this further might be helpful. Rather than responding to my invitation to explore what was going on between us, however, it felt like Amanda was consistently attempting to put the ball back in my court in an attempt to get me to take the lead again.

Even though I considered the possibility of going back to asking for more factual information as a way of easing the tension, I now began to feel at a loss for something to ask her. I was also beginning to feel that even if I could find more questions to ask Amanda, it would just be a way of going through the motions rather than talking about what was really happening, which is what seemed most meaningful to me at the moment. I began to get a sense of the two of us beginning to move into an impasse. At the same time, experience has taught me that impasses of this type, although uncomfortable, are often part of an important emerging enactment that, if worked through constructively, can be an important part of the change process.

At this point, however, rather than risk alienating Amanda by trying to explore further, I attempted to strengthen the alliance by reiterating the rationale for my intervention (thereby increasing the possibility of collaboration on the therapeutic task). I attempted to explain to Amanda that by exploring what was going on between us in the moment, we might be able to begin to shed some light on dynamics and relational patterns that were relevant to her current problems. She responded by saying, "I don't know what you're talking about. I don't understand."

In terms of my own countertransference, I was aware of starting to feel inadequate, frustrated, and—to be frank—somewhat irritated. I found myself wondering if anything I said would be adequate for her right now. And I was also beginning to wonder whether there was more to Amanda than was immediately apparent. At one level, I had begun to develop a sense of her as this sweet, fragile young woman who needed to be taken care of. And yet at the same time, I was starting to feel that she was really putting me on the spot and that I was squirming. And as is often the case in these types of situations, I was not sure how much to trust my own countertransference feelings. To what extent were my growing feelings of inadequacy and irritation providing meaningful information about Amanda, and to what extent were my feelings simply "my problem"—something that I was bringing to the table?

At this point, in an attempt to clarify the connection between my attempts to explore what was going on between us and the problems that brought Amanda into treatment in the first place, I made the following transference interpretation:

> It seems to me that one of the things you and I are struggling with right now in our relationship is the question of who is going to take the lead. I'm wondering in your relationships with men in general, who tends to take the lead?

In response, Amanda began to elaborate on a history of getting into relationships with domineering, abusive men who "take charge" in the relationship and whom she tended to "submit to." It emerged that she was used to following their lead, rather than expressing her own needs and desires. In response to further probes, Amanda was able to talk about a need on her part to know what men want so that she would be able to provide it for them. She would then find herself submitting and feeling resentful. Amanda also described a common pattern in her interactions with boyfriends in which initially she might explicitly disagree with them about something, but inevitably they would talk her into relinquishing her position and she would submit to them. And I began to wonder if there might be some element of this type of scenario being enacted in our relationship, in which my attempts to convince her of the value of exploring our relationship were fitting this type of template.

As the discussion continued, I began to speculate to myself about the nature of the enactment that might be playing out between us—I feel provoked by her but try to maintain a sympathetic and understanding stance. Despite my best efforts to control my feelings of irritation and frustration, I begin to express my hostility indirectly and to play the role of the perpetrator in a sado-masochistic enactment. And to complicate things further, I am feeling badly about having negative feelings. I certainly don't like to think of myself as sadistic. And to be frank, knowing that we were being filmed, I was particularly concerned about coming across as cruel or sadistic. In this context, my experience of internal conflict about my countertransference feelings was intensified by the unusual setting, but it is important to note that therapists often experience internal conflict about their countertransference feelings and that recognizing and working through these feelings of conflict is an important part of the therapist's internal work. For the time being, however, it felt like we had returned to safer ground. I was asking questions about Amanda's relationships, she was responding cooperatively, and the feeling of tension between us had receded into the background.

Following a rather extensive and revealing discussion of Amanda's habitual pattern of getting into relationships with men who take the lead as well as the price she pays for this, I then attempted to return the topic to the potential relationship between this pattern and what was going on in our relationship. To my surprise, Amanda denied seeing any connection between the two themes, and she did not acknowledge the possible value of exploring a potential connection. Furthermore, she continued to push me to explain the possible relevance of this type of exploration to her problems despite the fact that I had just struggled to do so. And I again returned to my experience of feeling on the spot, inadequate and speechless.

Although I responded with another attempt to provide Amanda with a rationale, it once again fell on deaf ears, and it seemed more and more to me that any such attempts on my part would be futile. As the session came to an end, I attempted to reestablish some sense of collaboration with her by telling her that prior to the next session, l would think of how to explain things in a way that would be meaningful to her and encouraged her, in turn, to think about what we had been discussing and to reflect on whether she might be able to make sense of any part of what I had said or come up with any questions to ask me that might help clarify things for her.

Over the week between Sessions 2 and 3, I gave considerable thought to our session. At one level, it seemed likely that our current impasse was an enactment that was related in meaningful ways to a core theme in Amanda's problematic pattern in romantic relationships. On the other hand, part of me couldn't let go of the fantasy that if I could just come up with the right way of offering a rationale, Amanda would begin to see what we were doing as meaningful and feel that I really was trying to help her. I considered the possibility of giving her various materials to read that would provide a more clear-cut rationale for the value of the type of exploration I was attempting to engage her in.

And then I remembered the written rationale that had been given to Amanda to read prior to her agreeing to participate in the project. At this point, I printed out a copy of the rationale from my computer and read it. I was struck by the fact that it would be pretty difficult for me to improve on what I had already written in the rationale. "And this," I thought (feeling indignant and vindicated), "is the rationale that she had read and said made sense to her, before she agreed to participate in the project!" I toyed with the idea of actually reading the rationale to Amanda in the next session. And then it occurred to me that doing so might well be my way of continuing to play out the current enactment—a way of proving to her that I was right and she was wrong (the type of "doer or done to" scenario described earlier).

Instead, I came up with a tentative plan for the next session of self-disclosing the nature of my internal processes between sessions as a way of leading into exploring and beginning to collaboratively make sense of the enactment that was taking place between us. I nevertheless put a copy of the rationale in my pocket so that I could refresh my memory just before the session, in case I ended up finding myself, once again, struggling to explain the purpose of the approach to her.

Toward the beginning of our third session, as a prelude to telling Amanda about my thinking between sessions, I asked her if she remembered the written rationale she had read before starting our work together. To my surprise, she denied having ever seen the rationale.

Now I was feeling completely stuck. I could imagine trying to explain the rationale another time, but it was difficult for me to imagine any such attempt being more meaningful to her than it had been previously. Moreover, I anticipated that given my complicated feelings of anxiety, inadequacy, hopelessness about her being receptive, and irritation, it would be difficult for me to convey the rationale in a particularly articulate or compelling way.

And then in an act of desperation, I found myself reaching into my pocket to pull out a crumpled copy of the rationale. Perhaps I felt that reading from the written version that I had put considerable thought into composing would give me a greater sense of security and help me manage complex feelings that I anticipated were likely to undermine my ability to convey the rationale in an articulate and compelling way.

So I began to read the rationale to Amanda, checking in with her periodically to see how she was reacting and whether things made sense to her. And as this process continued, I began for one of the first times since early in our second session to experience an emerging sense of confidence and mastery. Moreover, to my surprise, Amanda seemed to be engaging with me as I was reading and checking in with her. She was nodding, asking questions that I felt I could answer meaningfully, and apparently beginning to "get it."

At one level, I found myself skeptical that the rationale really made sense to her in a way that it hadn't in our previous session. I was essentially repeating the same things I had said before. Yet at the same time, I was sensing that something was beginning to shift in the dynamic of our relationship. In retrospect, I wonder if what really influenced the shift was not that I had conveyed new information to her, but rather that my internal movement toward greater confidence and my assumption of a more authoritative, dominant stance allowed her to engage with me in a way that was more comfortable and familiar to her, that is, following the lead of a dominant male who was taking charge in the relationship. In retrospect, perhaps that was unconsciously part of my motivation for choosing to read the rationale in the first place—it was an attempt to regain some sense of mastery and control.

But in any event, once I had finished reading, I felt that something was different, and I asked Amanda if the rationale made sense to her now. She responded "yes." And then after a short pause, she asked me, "But does it work?"

"Okay," I thought, "I was right to be skeptical." Nevertheless, I felt like an important shift had occurred because now Amanda's stance was beginning to move from one of "I don't understand" to an articulation of an underlying skepticism and a desire for me to reassure her that I could help her. This allowed an opening for me to begin exploring her skepticism, a critical psychoanalytic process that can be conceptualized as a form of resistance analysis. As we continued to explore Amanda's underlying skepticism and she was able to experience me listening in an empathic and validating way, the alliance continued to strengthen.

After some exploration, I became concerned that to continue in this vein might feel too overwhelming to Amanda, especially given her previous reluctance to talk about our relationship and what was happening between the two of us in the here and now. I checked in with her to ask how she would like to proceed at this point (i.e., continue talking about her skepticism or move on to another topic). True to form, Amanda responded, "What do you think?"—once again asking me to take the lead.

As in the previous session, I make an observation about the process between us (i.e., "It feels like I'm asking you to take the lead and you're asking me to take the lead"). Now however, something had shifted, and Amanda seemed more open to exploring things. In response to my observation, Amanda explained, "I turn to you because you're in charge here. You're the doctor." There was something about my experience of her saying this in the context of the current climate of our relationship that felt like a bit of a revelation to me. I was now struck by the fact that Amanda was really experiencing a vast power imbalance in our relationship. Although Amanda's perception of this power imbalance was completely understandable, until now it had been hard for me to fully grasp it at an experiential level, given that I had been feeling anything but authoritative in my relationship with her. This shift in my experience of Amanda in conjunction with her growing receptiveness allowed me an opening to explore further. And in response to my exploration, Amanda continued to open up. She spoke about not wanting to disappointment me and not wanting to "screw up" my "agenda." After all, she said, "We *are* here to produce a videotape."

And then it struck me that the same dynamic that tends to play out in many of Amanda's relationships—her pattern of trying to take care of the needs of the other person, submitting to their needs rather than asserting her own and then feeling resentful—might be playing out between the two of us as well. And although it might be tempting to simply see this as a form of transference on Amanda's part (i.e., a tendency to play out her typical patterns in the context of the therapeutic relationship as well), there was more to it than that. Amanda's attempt to take care of my needs at the expense of her own was not taking place in a vacuum. Therapists always bring their own needs to the situation, whether it is the need for validation, the need for self-esteem, the need to help, or financial need. And in this situation I had a pressing need to provide a good demonstration of my skills as a therapist. It is important to recognize that inevitably therapists have needs that clash with the client's needs and that this is part of the underlying subtexts of any therapy that sometimes need to be addressed explicitly and worked through.

My sense was that while Amanda was enacting a characteristic pattern of submitting to the needs of others, feeling resentful, and expressing her resentment in a passive–aggressive fashion, she was also demonstrating what I was coming to think of as a characteristic ability to read the subtlety of interpersonal situations and the courage to speak out and in a sense "talk about the elephant in the room." So I was impressed by her perceptiveness and inner strength (which I believed she has a tendency to disown), and I felt that it was important for me to validate her perceptions. Rather than commenting on Amanda's characteristic pattern of accommodating to others (an intervention that I was concerned she would experience as critical), I sensed it was more important to validate her perception and to highlight her disowned strengths. I thus acknowledged to Amanda that she was right that at least part of my agenda was selfish even if I was trying to help her. And I commended her on her ability to pick up on this. In retrospect, my impression is that my acknowledgement and acceptance of responsibility for my mixed agenda was another critical point in the positive shift in our alliance. The particular form of my mixed agenda (i.e., wanting to help Amanda vs. wanting to demonstrate a successful treatment for the DVD) was shaped by the context of the APA project in which we were both participating. It is important to point out, however, that as therapists we always have mixed agendas that are part of the context of the work, even if they are not talked about explicitly (Hoffman, 1998; Slavin & Kriegman, 1998). The most obvious one is that we are there to help the client, and at the same time we are there to earn money.

In any event, Amanda seemed to appreciate my recognition of her perceptiveness, courage, and strength and my willingness to acknowledge my own conflicting agendas with her. And this paved the way for Amanda to begin recognizing the way in which her tendency to look after my needs was preventing her from using this situation as an opportunity to meet some of her needs by making use of what I had to offer her. In the rest of this session, we continued to explore and work together in a much more collaborative fashion.

We developed a style of shifting seamlessly back and forth between focusing on Amanda's current life situation, her past, and our own relationship and this helped to deepen the depth of exploration of Amanda's feelings, thoughts, and previously unarticulated experience in all three areas. From the very beginning of our work together, I had been struck by her sense of fragility, and then subsequently I began to see a stronger, more aggressive side of her as well. As the sessions progressed and I came to experience an oscillation back and forth between the two of us in the roles of aggressor and victim, I began to develop a tentative formulation of Amanda as tending to dissociate her healthy aggression as part of her long-standing role of playing the caretaker and then needing to express her aggression indirectly or passive aggressively, rather than through healthy self-assertion of her needs.

I continued to give Amanda feedback about my experience of these two different sides of her (i.e., strength vs. fragility), and she was intrigued and interested in exploring both sides. Amanda acknowledged feeling pleased by my feedback about her strength and courage, but also a little afraid, overwhelmed, and reluctant to fully take this feedback in. This led to an exploration of her fears of seeing and acknowledging her strengths as well as the defensive function of her fragile posture (what would traditionally be conceptualized as the interpretation or analysis of defense). If she were to fully accept her own strength and healthy aggression, without being able to retreat into her defensive posture of fragility, it would be too much responsibility for her to bear right now. Rather than attempting to break through or do away with this aspect of her defensive style, I thus framed it in affirmative terms (i.e., it serves as kind of a safety net for her, and it's essential for her to hold onto that safety net as long as she needs it).

At one point in the context of exploring Amanda's tendency in her life to put other people's needs before her own (as she had been doing in our relationship), I asked her if she could remember how it had felt for her to play the role of the mediator between her mother and stepfather when she was a child. She recalled feeling a tremendous sense of responsibility, always having to make sure that things didn't get out of hand between the two of them.

I empathized with the dread and pain that she must have experienced as well as the heavy burden. In response, Amanda acknowledged that indeed it was only in the context of our work together that she was beginning to see how this whole experience must have (in her words) "screwed me up." At the same time, she said, she was also beginning to see that this developmental experience was part of where her current resources and strengths had come from. I responded something to the effect of, "Obviously there was a tremendous negative side to it, in that you were scared and had an overwhelming responsibility, but I imagine that the flip side is that it may have made you feel important, maybe even powerful."

This interpretation reflected an emerging semiarticulated formulation on my part of Amanda experiencing a type of secret narcissism and grandiosity. Amanda responded, "I thought of that word but didn't want to say it." This led to an exploration of her fears of acknowledging her strengths and the dangers of not having the safety net of her stance as a victim to retreat to. Session 3 ended with Amanda expressing positive feelings about our work together and an impression on my part that a vitally important shift in the therapeutic alliance was beginning to take place.

In Sessions 4 and 5, our relationship continued to deepen, and Amanda gradually became more trusting and open. Among other things, she explored how difficult it had been in the past for her to trust and depend on other people, as well the ongoing impact of her need to take care of other people. As Amanda spoke about both her fears of dependency and her fears about changing (an exploration of her resistance), the quality of her speech had a type of freshness and vitality that marked it as a genuine, emotionally immediate exploratory process. Amanda then transitioned into speaking about her growing sense of trust or faith that things would work out for her and that she would be able to continue to change after the end of our work together. In general I was impressed by how engaged and animated Amanda seemed in Sessions 4 and 5. In contrast to earlier sessions in which it felt like I had to work hard to generate questions to keep things going, Amanda seemed to be bringing herself to the session in a spontaneous and authentic way. During these sessions, she expressed a range of feelings, including sadness, hopelessness, and optimism about the future. Now there was no question on my part (as there had been, for example, during Session 2) as to whether we were talking about things that felt affectively alive and meaningful to Amanda. During these sessions, Amanda also showed more of the feisty and lively quality that I had begun to get a glimpse of in our first session, and our relationship was beginning to develop somewhat of a playful quality to it.

Session 6 (our final session) was a difficult but meaningful one. In some respects it had a tense, rough feeling to it not unlike some of our earlier sessions. There is an old psychoanalytic adage that important themes often reemerge around the time of termination, as both client and therapist deal with the realities of impending separation. I had a concern that given Amanda's history of abandonment (beginning with her mother's separation from Amanda's biological father, her stepfather's suicide, and also a more general theme that we had discussed in our work together) and the fact that she had begun to open up to me and trust me, she would experience the end of our work together as an abandonment.

I believe it is important to emphasize here that from a psychoanalytic perspective, Amanda would ideally benefit from a longer term treatment in which she would have the opportunity to develop and sustain a trusting relationship with a therapist over a period of time. She could really learn to trust someone and gradually modify her sense of implicit relational know-ing or her internal object relations over time, through her experience of developing a relationship with a trustworthy and reliable therapist. Six ses-sions is an extremely short period of treatment for someone with Amanda's history, and I had been concerned that she would begin to open up and trust, only to be traumatized by a feeling of abandonment at the end.

But all things considered, I believe it was a meaningful final session with moments of real engagement and connection between the two of us in reviewing our time together. I remember feeling pressured and tense at the beginning of the session and wanting things to end on a good note. And I imagine Amanda may have had some similar feelings. I normally consider it important to explore clients' feelings about termination, and find that they are typically ambivalent. Clients are often reluctant to fully explore their feelings when things go poorly and they are dissatisfied. And they can also be reluctant to fully explore their feelings when things go well. In these cir-cumstances clients often have feelings of gratitude mixed with feelings of loss, abandonment, anxiety, and sometimes resentment about some of the things they did not get from their therapist. Often ambivalent feelings of this type may be dissociated to varying degrees.

In Amanda's case, however, I was particularly concerned about not wanting to pressure her to talk about feelings that might be difficult for her to fully experience, acknowledge, and express, especially given how difficult it had been for her to open up in the first place. I am thinking here of the dynamic that had emerged between us in the early stages of our work together, in which she would experience open-ended questions as difficult and invasive and respond by clamming up or putting the ball back in my court. I could easily imagine the same dynamic reemerging in our last ses-sion if I pushed too hard.

At the beginning of the session, I already sensed more reserve and cau-tiousness on Amanda's part than had been the case in the previous two ses-sions. And I in turn felt more cautious and more of a need to tread delicately.

I began somewhat warily by asking Amanda how she felt about this being our last session. In response, she acknowledged experiencing some ambivalent feelings: feelings that she would miss our sessions, combined with a sense of relief that she would no longer have to perform in front of a camera. I acknowledged having similar feelings as a way of helping to emphasize the mutual aspects of our relationship and of countering Amanda's tendency to feel powerless in our relationship and resentful because of this. By self-disclosing my own ambivalent feelings, I wanted to implicitly give her permission to speak more about her ambivalent feelings without putting any pressure on her to do so.

I asked Amanda if there was anything in particular that she wanted to talk about today and she responded with an abrupt "Nope." Now I had a sense that if we were going to avoid getting into a power struggle, it would be important for me (at least at this juncture) to do more of the talking and to take more of the lead again. I told her that during our previous session, she had seemed to be "on a roll" and I had been reluctant to speak too much because she seemed very present and vitally alive, and I didn't want to inter-rupt her.

She responded that she didn't feel "on a roll" in this session. I told her that there were many things I wanted to ask her but that I felt cautious about not wanting to pressure her and put her on the spot. She seemed to relax with this disclosure, and then I told her that I felt curious about what she made of the time we had spent together, and whether there was anything in particular that stood out for her on reflection.

Amanda then told me that she was feeling a considerable difference between now and when we had first started. She felt that our time together had helped confirm her sense that she had made important changes in her life over the past year or so and that since we had started working together she felt she had made even more progress. She was feeling more confident and more aware of her own strengths. She was feeling more trust in me, more trusting in general, and more hopeful about the future. Amanda also said that she was beginning to have greater faith in herself and her ability to be more discriminating in her romantic choices.

During this final session, I also probed for any sense Amanda might have that I was abandoning her. As I indicated previously, I was particularly concerned about this theme given Amanda's history of abandonment. She responded that she felt fine about our work together ending because she had known from the beginning that we would be seeing each other for only six sessions. I had some concern that there might be more to Amanda's feelings here than she was able to acknowledge or verbalize, but I was reluctant to push too hard.

I responded that what she was saying made perfect sense rationally and that rationally I felt fine about us ending as well. I told her that, nevertheless, I felt sad ending our work together and concerned about not being able to be there for her in the future. My hope was that by disclosing this aspect of my experience, I would be giving Amanda permission to contact any complementary feelings that she might have even if she was not able to fully acknowledge or talk about them. At the end of the session, I gave Amanda some information about a local therapy clinic with a sliding scale (something I had promised to do previously). When the camera was turned off, Amanda and I walked over to the corner to briefly say goodbye. She spontaneously gave me a big hug, and I felt a sense of sadness and warmth toward her.

One year later, Amanda e-mailed me to let me know that she was doing well. She was still drug free and depression free, had gone into open-ended therapy with someone at the clinic to which I had referred her, and was finding the ongoing treatment helpful. She was also working full time and had begun a romantic relationship that sounded healthier than her previous romantic relationships.

In this chapter, I have discussed principles of intervention and underlying mechanisms of change in psychoanalytic treatment. I have also provided illustrations of change principles and the mechanisms through which they are hypothesized to operate in the context of both long-term and short-term psychoanalytic treatment. In Chapter 5, I review empirical evidence regarding the effectiveness of psychoanalytically oriented treatment and examine the application of psychoanalytic principles with diverse client populations.

5

Evaluation

This chapter evaluates psychoanalysis with respect to a number of different dimensions. These include relevant empirical research and range of applicability of more traditional psychoanalytic approaches. I place particular emphasis on the dimensions of racial and cultural diversity and social class. In this context, I examine theoretical and technical principles relevant to adapting psychoanalytic treatment to a range of different contexts.

RESEARCH SUPPORTING THE EFFECTIVENESS OF PSYCHOANALYSIS AND PSYCHOANALYTIC THERAPY

Historically, psychoanalysts have been slow to take up the challenge of evaluating the effectiveness of psychoanalytically oriented treatment for many reasons. These include a belief that systematic empirical research cannot do justice to the complexity of the psychoanalytic process, a concern that asking clients to participate as subjects in empirical research studies constitutes a violation of their privacy and can have a negative impact on the therapeutic process, and a belief that empirical research studies will inevitably influence and distort the process that is being investigated. Despite these concerns and the traditional antipathy of the psychoanalytic world toward empirical research, a growing body of research on the efficacy of psychoanalytically oriented treatment has accumulated in the last 30 years. A recent Medline search identified a total of 94 randomized clinical trials of psychodynamically oriented treatments published in English language journals between 1974 and May 2010 (Gerber et al., 2011). In a recent *American Psychologist* article, Shedler (2010) reviewed the results of eight different meta-analyses of studies evaluating the efficacy of psychodynamic therapy. The studies in these meta-analyses included only well-designed randomized clinical trials comparing psychoanalytically oriented treatments with a range of different control conditions, including cognitive and behavioral treatments. Client populations in these studies included adults presenting with a range of disorders including depression, anxiety, panic, somatoform disorders, eating disorders, substance-related disorders, and personality disorders. The majority of the psychodynamic treatments included in these studies were short term in nature (which is typically the case for randomized clinical trials). The meta-analyses reviewed found substantial effects for psychodynamic treatments, with effect sizes as large as or larger than those commonly found for cognitive and behavioral treatments. In addition, the results indicate that clients who receive psychodynamic therapy maintain therapeutic gains and appear to continue to improve after treatment ends.

It is difficult to estimate the exact number of studies included in Shedler's (2010) review because there is some degree of overlap among the studies included in different meta-analyses. To provide the reader with some sense of the amount of data summarized in the review, however, one of the larger meta-analyses included (Abbass, Hancock, Henderson, & Kisley, 2006) analyzed 23 randomized clinical trials with a total of 1,431 clients.

In addition to the studies included in these meta-analyses, three recent studies provided evidence that psychoanalytically oriented treatments can be effective in the treatment of borderline personality disorder and challenged the conventional wisdom that dialectical behavior therapy (DBT) is the treatment of choice for this population. In the first study involving a head to head competition between DBT and a psychoanalytically oriented treatment that makes extensive use of transference interpretations, Clarkin, Levy, Lenzenweger, and Kernberg (2007) randomly assigned borderline clients to either DBT or the psychoanalytically oriented treatment and found the analytically oriented treatment to be as effective or more effective than DBT. They also found significantly fewer dropouts in the analytically oriented treatment. Finally, they found that clients in the analytically oriented treatment were significantly more likely than DBT clients to change their attachment status from the insecure to the secure category as assessed by the Adult Attachment Interview.

Bateman and Fonagy (2008) evaluated the effectiveness of a psychoanalytic treatment that they developed, designated as *mentalization-based treatment,* which is designed as an intervention for clients with borderline personality disorder. Their research demonstrated that with this population, mentalization-based treatment is significantly more effective than treatment as usual (partial hospitalization) on a range of outcome measures at both termination and at an 18-month follow-up. In a longer term follow-up study with the same sample, Bateman and Fonagy found that 5 years after discharge, the clients treated psychoanalytically continued to show statistical superiority to treatment-as-usual clients on a number of important dimensions, including suicidality (23% vs. 74%), service use (2 years vs. 3.5 years of psychiatric outpatient treatment), use of medication (0.02 vs. 1.90 years taking three or more medications), global function above 60 (45% vs. 10%), vocational status (employed or in education 3.2 years vs. 1.2 years), and diagnostic status (13% vs. 87% continued to meet diagnostic criteria for borderline personality disorder).

Finally, McMain et al. (2009) evaluated the efficacy of DBT combined with medication relative to psychodynamically informed treatment combined with medication for clients diagnosed with borderline personality disorder. Treatment length in both conditions was 1 year. This was the largest randomized clinical trial that included DBT as a treatment modality to date. Counter to McMain et al.'s expectation, both treatment groups showed significant improvement across a range of outcome measures at termination, and there was no significant difference between the two groups. Although in one sense there is nothing dramatic about findings that fail to find a significant difference, these findings take on particular significance for the following reason, given the widely acknowledged *researcher allegiance effect* in psychotherapy research (i.e., the finding that the theoretical allegiance of the researcher is the most powerful predictor of treatment outcome; Luborsky et al., 1999) and the fact that McMain is a DBT proponent.

A number of practical and logistical problems make it extremely difficult to conduct randomized clinical trials of long-term, intensive treatments of any type, including psychoanalysis. One practical problem is that tracking the progress of clients over a significant length of time in treatment (4–6 years or more) requires a significant investment of time and resources. In addition, it is extremely difficult to find clients who are willing to be randomly assigned to one of two treatments that differ radically with respect to both treatment duration and intensity.

Because of these constraints, most studies evaluating the effectiveness of long-term psychoanalysis tend to be of a more naturalistic nature (e.g., clients either self-select their treatments or are assigned to the treatment condition on the basis of assessed suitability) and are thus subject to various methodological problems. The majority of the research on the effectiveness of medium to long-term psychoanalytic and psychoanalytically oriented treatment is conducted in European countries in which the public health care system covers the cost of long-term psychoanalytically oriented treatment. For example, in Germany, Leichsenring, Biskup, Kreisch, and Staats (2005) reported the results of a naturalistic study of the effectiveness of psychoanalytic therapy for 36 clients seeking treatment for chronic psychological problems (e.g., depression, anxiety, obsessive–compulsive disorder, and nonorganic sexual dysfunction), with the majority of clients presenting with comorbid diagnostic pictures. Therapy was conducted by psychoanalysts who had completed training in local psychoanalytic institutes and who were in private practice at the time of the study. Although there was no control group, the effect size of a control group from another study was used as a point of reference. The average duration of treatment was 37.4 months, and on average 253 sessions were conducted. It would thus appear that frequency of treatment was on average somewhere between 1 and 2 sessions per week. Thus, although the treatment in this study was longer term and more intensive than were treatments typically studied in randomized clinical trials, this was really a midlength treatment rather than a long-term intensive psychoanalysis. In general, effect sizes were large for changes in symptoms, interpersonal problems, quality of life, well-being, and the target problem formulated by the clients themselves at the beginning of treatment. These changes were stable at 1-year follow-up, and in some areas actually increased.

An extremely ambitious naturalistic outcome study conducted in Sweden by Sandell et al. (2000) evaluated the outcome of over 400 clients who received either psychoanalysis or psychoanalytically oriented psychotherapy. Clients selected their own treatments. Given that clients could not be randomly assigned to treatments, it is more difficult to rule out the possibility that client characteristics influenced treatment outcome. Nevertheless, various statistical procedures were used to establish that this was unlikely to be the case.

The mean duration of treatment in psychoanalysis was 51 months, and the mean frequency was 3.5 sessions per week. The mean length of treatment in psychotherapy was 40 months, and the mean frequency of sessions was 1.4 times per week. In general both treatments were found be effective, but (a) at the 3-year follow-up interval clients in psychoanalysis achieved better outcome on a number of dimensions than clients in psychotherapy, and (b) more experienced psychoanalysts achieved better outcome than therapists with less psychoanalytic training and experience. Finally, the variable of frequency and duration interacted to mediate outcome in a positive direction (i.e., interaction of higher frequency with higher duration).

An important recent study by Huber, Henrich, Gastner, and Klug (in press) used a partially randomized, quasi-experimental design to evaluate differences in the effectiveness for depressed patients of intensive psychoanalytic treatment (average duration between 160 and 240 sessions; session frequency 2–3 sessions per week), less-intensive psychodynamic treatment (average duration 50–80 sessions; session frequency 1 time per week), and cognitive–behavioral therapy (average duration between 45–60 sessions; session frequency 1 time per week). At termination, significantly more clients in the psychoanalytic group (91%) than clients in the cognitive–behavioral condition (53%) no longer met diagnostic criteria for depression. Patients in the less-intensive psychodynamic condition fell in between, with 68% no longer meeting criteria for depression.

At 1-year follow-up, 89% of the psychoanalytic clients, 68% of the psychodynamic clients, and 42% of the cognitive–behavioral clients no longer met diagnostic criteria for depression. The differences were significant between psychoanalytic and cognitive–behavioral therapies, between psychoanalytic and psychodynamic therapies, and between psychodynamic and cognitive–behavioral therapies. The findings indicating significant differences between psychodynamic and cognitive–behavioral conditions at follow-up were striking, given the fact that the two treatments were provided at approximately the same duration and intensity.

Finally, there are extensive reviews of a large number of naturalistic studies investigating the effectiveness of intensive, long-term psychoanalytic treatments (e.g., Fonagy et al., 1999; Galatzer-Levy, Bachrach, Skolnikoff, & Waldron, 2000; Richardson, Kachele, & Renlund, 2004). I will not review these studies here, but in general the results are quite promising. All of these reviews note both the methodological strengths and weaknesses of the various studies included.

In summary, a growing body of empirical evidence supports the efficacy of psychoanalytically oriented interventions for a range of disorders. Moreover, an emerging body of evidence suggests that the impact of psychoanalytically oriented interventions continues to increase after termination (a finding that is not emerging to the same extent in the case of cognitive–behavioral interventions). At this point in time, for practical and logistical reasons, the evidence for the effectiveness of intensive, long-term psychoanalysis is garnered from naturalistic studies rather than randomized clinical trials.

It would be a mistake, however, to ignore the findings of the many naturalistic studies supporting the effectiveness of long-term psychoanalysis. In fact, as many have argued (e.g., Seligman, 1995; Westen, Novotny, &

Thompson-Brenner, 2004), naturalistic studies (despite their limitations) have certain advantages over randomized clinical trials with respect to external validity and generalizabilty. Unlike subjects in randomized clinical trials, in real life clients choose the type of therapy they are receiving, as well as their therapists, and they remain in treatment until they decide that it is time to terminate. Moreover, therapists as a rule do not adhere to standardized rigid protocols and are more likely to modify what they are doing in response to the client's needs in any given session and over time. As psychology students learn in introductory research methods classes, empirical research inevitably purchases internal validity (the ability to infer causation and rule out alternative hypotheses) at the expense of external validity (generalizabilty to real-life situations). If the yield of psychotherapy research is to be of any real value, it is essential for us to adopt a pluralistic perspective that weighs the evidence yielded by a range of different methodologies in light of an understanding of the strengths and weaknesses of any given methodology (Safran, 2001).

OBSTACLES OR PROBLEMS POTENTIALLY ASSOCIATED WITH PSYCHOANALYTIC TREATMENT

No treatment is effective for all individuals, and psychoanalytically oriented treatments are no exception to this rule. This is especially true when it comes to the use of certain specific psychoanalytically oriented interventions. For example, because of either intellectual, psychological, or emotional factors, some clients have a limited capacity for self-reflection, and interventions designed to promote reflective capacity such as interpretation are simply not helpful. Some clients find any attempt to explore the transference or the therapeutic relationship too threatening. Clients who are too psychologically disorganized or disturbed may find any attempt to explore defenses or unconscious wishes too threatening. Clients who are in a state of crisis may find any insight-oriented treatments meaningless because they have an immediate need for guidance, structure, and support. Interventions that involve the use of therapist self-disclosure of their own countertransference may be experienced as threatening or intrusive by some clients. The psychoanalytic emphasis on focusing on underlying psychodynamic issues and character changes rather than on immediate symptom relief may be of little use for a client who is currently in intense emotional distress and does not have the luxury or interest in focusing on underlying issues.

Similarly, when it comes to parameters related to treatment length or session frequency, many clients may not have the interest, time, or financial resources to be in long-term treatment. And many clients may not have the interest, time, or psychological resources to be in treatment more than once a week, or even once a week. For all of these reasons, psychoanalysis, when defined in a rigid or purist fashion, is most appropriate for clients with a more neurotic level of personality organization (as opposed to borderline or psychotic), who have a relatively high level of ego strength and cohesiveness and the capacity for self-reflection.

If, however, psychoanalysis is conceptualized in a more flexible fashion as a broadly based psychoanalytic theoretical framework that incorporates an understanding of the role that a diverse range of change mechanisms can play in the treatment process and is thus open to the incorporation of a broad range of different treatment interventions (e.g., empathy, interpretation, guidance, advice giving, collaborative problem solving), then it can be useful for a broad range of clients. As described earlier, this type of broadened conceptualization of psychoanalysis needs to recognize that the ongoing negotiation of treatment tasks and goals (at both explicit and implicit levels) between therapists and clients is an intrinsic part of the therapeutic process. Although there will always be theoretical purists who cling to a more rigid definition of psychoanalysis, there is a growing trend in the direction of a more pluralistic and flexible psychoanalytic perspective in North America and in many other parts of the world.

PSYCHOANALYTIC TREATMENTS AND DIVERSE CLIENT POPULATIONS

Psychoanalysis was originally developed as a form of treatment by and for educated, middle-class Western Europeans. As psychoanalysis became the dominant theoretical influence within the public health care system in the

United States, a paradoxical process took place. Therapists influenced by psychoanalytic thinking were placed in the position of treating a broad range of clients from different cultures and social classes. At the same time, they were being guided by theoretical premises and intervention principles ill-equipped to fit the diversity of clients being treated. In recent years, psychoanalysts have written extensively about the importance of recognizing middle-class, Euro-American biases of psychoanalytic theory and practice. They have also written extensively about the importance of modifying theory, clinical stance, and interventions in a fashion that incorporates an understanding of the cultural attitudes and assumptions specific to a full range of different cultures and social classes (see, e.g., Altman, 1995; Gutwill & Hollander, 2006; Perez Foster, Moskowitz, & Javier, 1996; Roland, 1989). The discussion of culture-specific differences in attitudes regarding various themes such as individualism/collectivism, agency/dependency, social hierarchy and respect for authority, gender roles and role relationships, emotional experience and expression, and spirituality is sufficiently complex that it is impossible to begin this conversation in the space allotted to me here without hopelessly oversimplifying.

These are themes that are increasingly focused on by most traditions of psychotherapy. Contemporary psychoanalytic writing, however, is distinctive in its focus on the examination of the roles that internalized cultural attitudes, unconscious processes, and the transference/countertransference matrix play in psychotherapy. The United States is a land of immigrants that is distinguished by a rich mosaic of cultural and racial diversity. American society is officially committed to the ideal of tolerance of this diversity. Within liberal progressive circles, we pride ourselves on our commitment to multiculturalism, and the American Psychological Association has certainly done its part to promote relevant research and clinical training. The psychoanalytic perspective's unique contribution to this area is its emphasis on the role that unconscious biases and prejudices about race, culture, and class play in shaping our daily interactions.

Although it would be naïve to argue that acceptance of racial and cultural diversity is a value that is held within all segments of our society, we don't seriously question the correctness of these values within liberal progressive circles. From a psychoanalytic perspective, one of the limitations of this generally accepted consensus is that cultural and racial biases can be driven underground. We inevitably internalize societal prejudices, and these unconscious internalized attitudes influence the way in which we relate to others and to ourselves. When we treat someone coming from a different cultural background or race in therapy, internalized cultural attitudes about culture and race play out unconsciously in the transference/ countertransference matrix for both client and therapist. Neil Altman (2000) wrote a delightfully candid and self-reflective article about a failed treatment from his own practice with an African American client. In this case, Altman, a middle-class Jewish American psychoanalyst, treats an African American client, whom he calls Mr. A, for marital problems and panic attacks. Mr. A grew up in foster care, where he was abused physically and sexually by members of the extended social family. He survived by becoming a "tough kid" and a street fighter who hung around with other tough kids. At the age of 12 he was reunited with his biological parents and decided to turn over a new leaf. He worked hard at school, achieved academically, and eventually went to an Ivy League law school and became a successful lawyer. One of the themes that came up early in treatment was that Mr. A's father had been asking him to return a large financial loan that he had given him. Mr. A was angry at his father's new wife, who was urging her husband to collect the loan from Mr. A, and at his father for deferring to his new wife.

Altman initially found himself feeling tremendously admiring of Mr. A for having achieved so much despite the fact that the deck was stacked against him. Early in treatment, however, a pattern began to emerge in which Mr. A would miss appointments with Altman and bounce checks. Although Altman attempted to address the situation with Mr. A, he failed to explore the potential meaning of what was taking place between them as fully as he might with another client. In retrospect, Altman recognized that even before the first check had bounced, a marginal thought had occurred to him that Mr. A might end up not paying him. In Altman's words, the thought went something like, "I can't believe that this man, who has fought his way up from poverty and who still struggles to make ends meet, is going to give substantial sums of money to a privileged person like me." At a somewhat deeper level, Altman admits to having the racially prejudiced thought that Mr. A might stiff him because he was Black and because of Altman's own semiconscious racist stereotypes involving "Black people, irresponsibility, and criminality." In Altman's (2000) words:

> I also got caught in a tangled web of guilt, anger, and greed. A complementary anti-Jewish stereotype was activated as well. I began to feel like the stereotypically greedy Jew, like the Jewish landlord feeding off the poverty-stricken residents of the ghetto. In the face of my shame about all these feelings, it was difficult for me to confront Mr. A about the bounced checks. I was afraid that doing so would expose all these prejudices, would reveal both my own greed and my sense of him as out to stiff me. (p. 4)

Eventually Altman confronted Mr. A about the bounced checks and made an attempt to explore potential similarities between Mr. A's feelings toward his father who was asking him for the money back and the transference. Mr. A seemed to find this somewhat useful and began to explore his own pattern of letting relationships deteriorate when there is tension in them. He resolved not to let things deteriorate with Altman and to be more conscientious about paying the checks. To make a long story short, Mr. A continued to intermittently bounce checks and eventually dropped out of treatment, owing Altman a considerable sum of money. In retrospect, Altman speculated that his own feelings of shame about both his semiconscious racist feelings and his internalized anti-Semitism prevented him from exploring the situation as constructively as he might have with Mr. A. Although there is no way of knowing if a deeper exploration of the potentially unconscious racial undertones to the enactment might have resulted in a better outcome, I believe that Altman has provided a courageous and valuable example of the way in which semiconscious or unconscious race-related attitudes can potentially play out in a transference/countertransference enactment.

I have used Altman's article a number of times to stimulate conversation in courses I teach to clinical psychology students at The New School for

Social Research and have been intrigued by the range of reactions that students have to it. Whereas some students find it to be tremendously helpful, others respond by judging Altman for the racist attitudes he acknowledges and feel critical or awkward when Altman speaks about his own internalized anti-Semitism. In turn, I often feel vaguely ashamed for having assigned the article to students and for identifying with Altman in the struggles that he acknowledges—ashamed, but not ashamed enough to prevent me from continuing to assign this article. I think it is precisely this type of shame that we need to confront in ourselves as therapists on an ongoing basis if we are going to get at the core of unconscious prejudices that play out for both us and our clients in the transference/countertransference matrix.

In addition, because many of the students at the New School are international students or come from culturally diverse backgrounds, we often spend time exploring their experiences of treating clients from different cultures (including Anglo American culture) when they themselves come from diverse cultural backgrounds (e.g., Latino/Latina, Asian or Asian American, African American or Middle Eastern). Unconscious, conflicting, countertransference experiences relating to one's own cultural identity can be extremely important to explore when one is a therapist coming from the nondominant cultural background or struggling to find one's place between different cultural worlds.

Although there is a growing theoretical, clinical, and empirical literature on the role of race and culture in psychotherapy, less attention is typically given to the topic of social class. This relative neglect is consistent with the American myth that we live in a classless society. As sociologists point out, however, although the United States may not have the traditional social hierarchy of older cultures, we do in fact have a well-established class system that is structured primarily along socioeconomic lines, and within this class system there is considerably less social mobility than is acknowledged by the American dream (e.g., Keller, 2005).

The construct of social class is difficult to define because it is so intertwined with the culture, especially within a multicultural, multiracial society. Nevertheless, at a basic level, class is related to variables such as financial income, the means through which one earns one's income, the amount of physical versus mental labor involved in earning one's income, the degree of control one has over how one spends one's time, level of education, and type of residence. With the emergence of capitalism, the traditional stratification of culture into aristocracy versus peasantry began to break down, and a new distinction began to emerge between members of the working class who earned their income through physical labor and members of the middle class who earned their income through owning or managing businesses or services in which goods were produced or sold or through investing finances.

Clinical psychology students trained with a bias toward therapies that emphasize self-awareness and self-reflection can often feel powerless when working in the public sector, where many clients do not come from cultures that privilege self-reflection and where the daily aspects of their existence (e.g. poverty, social instability, physical illness, lack of control of their living environment) are so overwhelming that self-reflection and insight-oriented psychotherapy can seem irrelevant. Western psychotherapy and the project of developing self-understanding are culturally and historically situated practices. People from many traditional cultures seek out a healer or authority of one type or another (e.g., priest, shaman, family or village elder) expecting advice, guidance, or help with framing their bewildering symptoms in culturally normative terms.

Clients and therapists often have very different hopes and expectations about what will come out of treatment. The therapist is often seen by clients as a representative of the institution that has the power to provide them with resources they are deprived of or has some influence over their future (Altman, 1995; Gutwill & Hollander, 2006; Perez Foster et al., 1996). Clinics are part of a social service network that can provide benefits such as welfare, Medicaid, or Social Security. The therapist may be enlisted in an effort to obtain access to these benefits. Clients are often referred to psychology for adjunctive treatment by psychiatrists who are treating them with medication. Clients may feel compelled to see the therapist as a prerequisite for continuing to receive medication. They may just want somebody to talk to or to validate their experience of being victimized or hard done by. Or their attendance may be erratic, missing multiple sessions and then showing up unexpectedly when they are in crisis (Altman, 1995).

In the same way that internalized societal values about race play on in the transference-countertransference matrix, internalized values about social class do as well. It is not unusual for students in this situation to experience feelings of impotence and shame because their sense that they have anything of value to offer is threatened. This can lead to a type of defensive stance that contributes to devaluing working-class clients. They may tend to disown experiences and qualities in themselves such as aggression, sexuality, criminality, or exploitativeness and feel particularly critical of such qualities in working-class clients. Or they may underestimate the influence of class and social conditions on an individual's life and feel critical of clients coming from an unstable and economically disadvantaged background who are not able to "pull themselves up by their bootstraps" and choose better life options for themselves (Altman, 1995; Gutwill & Hollander, 2006). This kind of attitude in middle-class therapists or in therapists socialized into middle-class values can mirror larger societal attitudes that equate poverty with moral depravity, thereby condoning a social system that privileges the wealthy and the middle class.

As I have discussed throughout the book, a contemporary psychoanalytic perspective does not privilege "insight" as a mechanism of change, but rather emphasizes the role of a host of different change mechanisms, including new relational experience, containment, and affective communication and regulation. In this perspective it is the relational meaning of the intervention that is essential. I thus emphasize to my students that psychoanalytically oriented therapy can consist of different interventions ranging from exploring internal experience, providing guidance or advice, negotiating a common goal or task with a client, or simply attempting one's best to be there for the client in a reliable fashion while reflecting internally on the possible relational meaning of a given interaction, becoming aware of and modulating one's own affective experience, and being open to learning about the way one's own unconscious prejudices are influencing one's work.

6

Future Developments

Much ink has been spilt over the years on the topic of whether psychoanalysis even has a future. I start this section with the assumption that psychoanalysis does indeed have a future and that this future will come in a variety of different shapes and forms. One form will involve the ongoing assimilation of psychoanalytic concepts and interventions into other forms of treatment, especially cognitive therapy. When cognitive therapy first emerged as a tradition, its identity was linked not only to prescribed interventions but also to a proscription of many interventions commonly associated with psychoanalysis. Contemporary cognitive therapy now incorporates many features of psychoanalysis that were once viewed as taboo, including exploring the therapeutic relationship, using the therapeutic relationship as a vehicle of change, helping clients to become aware of feelings they are avoiding, exploring the client's past, and extending the length of treatment (with clients who are personality disordered).

I also believe that psychoanalysis will continue to survive as a distinct tradition but that to flourish and maintain its vitality, it will have to continue to evolve. One important shift will have to be the explicit recognition that the type of intensive psychoanalysis in which sessions take place four to five times per week is no longer a widespread form of treatment in North America and many other places. For example, a survey of analysts who graduated over a 15-year period from the Columbia University Center for Psychoanalytic Training and Research found that the majority were treating very few clients on a more than once or twice a week basis (Cherry, Cabaniss, Forand, Haywood, & Roose, 2004). The reality is that at least in North America, the majority of the clients undergoing a more intensive long-term psychoanalysis are analysts in training, and these are the clients who fill the caseloads of a handful of senior training analysts.

There is thus unfortunately a discrepancy between the type of psychoanalysis that candidates in many traditional institutes are trained to practice and value versus the reality of their actual practice as clinicians. Given this discrepancy, the traditional distinction between "real psychoanalysis" and "psychodynamic" or psychoanalytically informed treatment becomes increasingly problematic because this distinction ends up devaluing the type of work done by most psychoanalytic clinicians in the shadow of some idealized form of treatment that rarely takes place in practice. I thus believe that the psychoanalysis of the future will need to abandon the elitist emphasis on ideological purity (a process that is already taking place) and recognize that psychoanalysis comes in a range of different forms, treatment lengths, and intensities and that the struggle to maintain ideological and technical purity is a misguided one. Psychoanalytic training institutes of the future will also need to broaden their curricula to offer training in a variety of important areas that are not commonly covered, including brief-term therapy; integrating psychoanalysis with other treatment modalities; working with clients from diverse races, cultures, and social sectors; marital, family and group therapy; and working with specific populations including trauma victims and severe personality disorders (e.g., borderline personality disorder). Many curriculum changes of this type are already taking place, especially within the more innovative, nontraditional psychoanalytic institutes. But it will be important for changes of this type to become more widespread.

PRACTICAL PSYCHOANALYSIS

In a culture in which psychoanalysis has come to be associated with a form of indulgent self-preoccupation for the idle and financially comfortable elite, the term "practical psychoanalysis" seems like an oxymoron. There is no doubt that there is an important thrust in psychoanalysis that challenges conventional assumptions regarding the nature of "the good life" and the emphasis on quick fixes. At the same time, there is a growing realization among psychoanalysts that the reluctance to focus on clients' symptoms and to concern themselves with symptom relief can represent a failure to take clients' suffering seriously and to provide them with the type of help they are seeking. Owen Renik (2006) made the following argument:

> People who seek the help of mental health caregivers want a therapy that will provide maximum relief from emotional distress as quickly as possible. Most clinical psychoanalysts offer instead a lengthy journey of self-discovery during which too much concern with symptom relief is considered counterproductive. "Self-awareness" is the main goal; symptom relief is of secondary importance and is expected to arrive, if at all, only after a while. (p. 1)

From Renik's perspective, this type of stance is unfortunate because it all too often fails to provide clients with relief for the suffering that brings them to treatment in the first place. Although a psychoanalytic therapist may be able convince a client that the project of self-discovery is a worthwhile one, there is always a danger that the client will stay in therapy as a form of compliance even if client's symptoms are not addressed or leave treatment because he or she doesn't find it to be of any value.

Renik thus argued for the importance of collaborating with clients in the process of establishing shared treatment goals, in the same way that I earlier argued for the importance of negotiation of goals and tasks. When the therapist has a different perspective on these issues than the client, Renik argued that it is important for the therapist to be explicit about these differences to give the client an opportunity to take another perspective into consideration and decide whether he or she wishes to be influenced by it. From Renik's perspective, this type of candidness, far from using the therapist's authority to unduly influence the client (a traditional concern for psychoanalysts), actually "levels the playing field" by letting the client know explicitly where the therapist is coming from so that he or she does not end up being manipulated by a hidden agenda. As both Wachtel (1997) and Frank (1999) have argued, the traditional psychoanalytic prohibition against the therapist assuming an active or directive stance in treatment is incompatible with a contemporary relational stance that views any therapist action or lack thereof in terms of its relational meaning and challenges the myth that a neutral therapeutic stance is possible.

Renik also emphasized that regardless of what treatment goals are agreed on at the beginning of treatment, these goals have a tendency to evolve over time as both clients and therapists change their understanding of what is going on. Nevertheless, he advocated the importance of keeping track of both the client's presenting symptoms and goals as they evolve over time. He also encouraged therapists to engage in an ongoing process of explicitly exploring with the client the extent to which he or she feels that the treatment is beneficial.

Many other analysts over the years (e.g., Bader, 1994; Connors, 2006; Frank, 1999; Wachtel, 1977, 1997) have argued for the importance of taking the client's symptoms seriously and using a range of more active interventions to help the client obtain symptom relief. An emphasis on the client's symptoms does not have to neglect the underlying meaning of these symptoms or the interpersonal context in which they are embedded. Moreover, experiencing symptom relief may pave the way for the client to begin to explore other issues of a deeper nature.

Many years ago while working in a psychiatric hospital, I supervised a young trainee in the use of behavioral interventions to treat a client presenting with a needle phobia that prevented her from seeking any medical treatment because of the threat of receiving an injection. Although the behavioral treatment was apparently successful, a year later the client returned to a different clinic in the same hospital to seek treatment. She was referred back to our clinic for an assessment, and I met with her. It turned out that she had indeed been helped by her treatment with us and was no longer troubled by the same presenting problem. Now, however, she said that she was ready to work on some interpersonal concerns that, in her words, she "hadn't been thinking about so much" at the time she had initially been treated in our clinic. In recounting this case, I want to be clear that I am not rehashing the old psychoanalytic argument that treating the symptom is pointless because it is a manifestation of a deeper underlying problem, which will ultimately result in the emergence of a new symptom. Quite the contrary, I am arguing for the importance of "meeting clients where they are." If we had attempted initially to treat this client with an insight-oriented approach, she may well have dropped out of treatment. Instead, perhaps the process of engaging her at the level that was meaningful to her helped her begin to develop the sense of trust and safety to subsequently pursue deeper, more threatening psychological issues.

INTEGRATING OTHER APPROACHES

On a related note, many psychoanalysts have advocated for the value of integrating interventions from other therapeutic perspective into psychoanalytic practice. Wachtel (e.g., 1977, 1997) was an early advocate of the potential usefulness of incorporating behavioral interventions into psychoanalytic practice, arguing that behavioral interventions can actually facilitate changes at a psychodynamic level and that psychoanalytic theory could add a valuable dimension to understanding factors causing and maintaining problems that are manifested at a behavioral level. In the early to mid-1990s, I published a number of articles and books with various collaborators, articulating a theoretical framework to facilitate the integration of psychoanalytic, cognitive–behavioral, and experiential approaches that focused extensively on the fashion in which various psychoanalytic conceptualizations of the therapeutic relationship could contribute to the cognitive perspective in a number of specific ways. These include facilitating the assessment and formulations process, helping to work through therapeutic impasses, increasing treatment maintenance, and enriching our understanding of the relationship between emotion and cognition (Greenberg & Safran, 1987; Safran, 1984, 1998; Safran & Greenberg, 1991; Safran & Segal, 1990).

Frank (1999) has written extensively about the way in which the "relational turn" in psychoanalysis (i.e., the emergence of relational psychoanalysis) provides a theoretical framework that is very much compatible with the use of active behavioral interventions by psychoanalytically oriented therapists and with more contemporary theoretical developments in psychoanalysis, and he has provided illuminating clinical examples illustrating the potential fruitfulness of integrating psychoanalytic and behavioral approaches.

Finally, Connors (2006), building on the various contributions cited previously, argued for the importance of placing greater emphasis on the treatment of specific symptoms by psychoanalytically oriented therapists and illustrated the way in which the incorporation of both cognitive and behavioral interventions by psychoanalytically oriented therapists can promote the treatment of a range of specific symptoms including depression, anxiety, compulsive behaviors, and binge eating.

PSYCHOANALYSIS AND RESEARCH

As discussed previously, there is a growing body of rigorous empirical research that demonstrates the efficacy of psychoanalytically oriented treatments, and many psychoanalysts are coming to realize that investing more resources in conducting this type of research will be essential to the survival of psychoanalysis in the future. This recognition has been late in coming. Many psychoanalysts have been slow to recognize the potential importance of rigorous empirical research and, to be frank, have been dismissive of the efforts of those psychoanalytically oriented investigators who do attempt to conduct this type of research. The well-documented gap between researchers and clinicians (Bergin & Strupp, 1973; Goldfried & Wolfe, 1996; Morrow-Bradley & Elliott, 1986; Persons & Silberschatz, 1998; Rice & Greenberg, 1984; Safran, Greenberg, & Rice, 1988; Safran & Muran, 1994; Talley, Strupp, & Butler, 1994) that cuts across therapeutic orientations is particularly large in the psychoanalytic world. As is true in the field of clinical psychology in general, it is not unusual for psychoanalytic researchers to not be practicing clinicians or to have very limited clinical practices. And many psychoanalytic researchers have not received formal postgraduate psychoanalytic training.

The reasons for this are in part practical. It is extremely difficult to engage in the time-consuming activity of going through postgraduate psychoanalytic training while at the same time being a productive empirical researcher, making one's way up the formal ranks of academia in a university, and finding the time to successfully apply for the grant funding necessary to support good empirical research. Unfortunately, many psychoanalytically oriented researchers without postgraduate psychoanalytical training are treated as second-class citizens by their peers who have more formal traditional psychoanalytic credentials and who are surrounded by a psychoanalytic culture that for the most part has been split off from the university system. And within the world of academic clinical psychology, psychoanalytically oriented researchers are fighting an uphill battle, as psychoanalysis becomes increasingly marginalized within the university system.

When it comes to government-supported research funding, the bias toward biological and neurophysiological research is making it increasingly difficult to receive funding for psychotherapy research in general. And the common misconception that psychoanalytic therapy "lacks empirical support" makes it even more difficult to receive funding for psychoanalytically oriented research (I can testify to this on the basis of my experience serving on National Institute of Mental Health Grant review committees).

It is clear that the traditional psychoanalytic dismissiveness toward rigorous empirical research has been self-destructive and has had harmful effects on the development of the discipline. Although this attitude of dismissiveness often reflects a kind of narrow-minded dogmatism and insularity, it is also important to recognize that many psychoanalysts have valid concerns about the relevance to the practicing clinician of much of the psychotherapy research that is published. There are well-founded concerns about the limits of existing research paradigms' abilities to capture the complexity of the therapeutic process.

The gold standard for psychotherapy research is the randomized clinical trial, which was borrowed from medication research that assumes that it is possible to evaluate the efficacy of a particular medication independent of the interpersonal context in which it is delivered. In this framework, the medication is the "active ingredient," and all the other elements that may have an impact on its efficacy (e.g., client expectations, therapist interpersonal skill, quality of the therapeutic relationship) are extraneous, nonspecific factors that can be controlled for. The problem with applying this "drug metaphor" (Stiles & Shapiro, 1989) to psychosocial treatments is that in psychotherapy, any active ingredient of the treatment is conceptually inseparable from the so-called nonspecific factors (e.g., the emergent properties of the client–therapist relationship). It is thus conceptually impossible to separate out the therapy from the therapist (or more accurately, the therapeutic dyad). And in fact, a large and growing body of evidence indicates that factors such as the therapeutic relationship and the individual therapist variable contribute considerably more to the outcome variance than the particular brand of psychotherapy being practiced (Safran, 2003; Safran & Muran, 2000; Safran & Segal, 1990; Wampold, 2001).

Notwithstanding these concerns, many argue that it is vital to conduct randomized clinical trial research on psychoanalytically oriented treatment for purposes of influencing public attitudes and the attitudes of policymakers (both government and private insurance companies). Although I am certainly in agreement with this perspective, I also want to point out that it is important to carefully consider the rigorous and thoughtful critiques of those who argue that there are dangers of wholeheartedly embracing the enterprise of documenting the value of psychoanalytically oriented treatments through randomized clinical trials (e.g., Cushman & Gilford, 2000; Hoffman, 2009). As I indicated earlier, Cushman and Gilford (2000) argued that some of the implicit assumptions underlying the evidenced-based treatment paradigm (e.g., speed, concreteness, efficiency, systematization) can have a harmful impact on the way we understand the therapeutic process. They argued that this paradigm conceptualizes the therapist as a type of psychotechnician who delivers a standardized technique in a maximally efficient fashion. This in turn, they argued, lends itself implicitly to a view of the client as a passive recipient of this technique who varies in terms of the extent that he or she is compliant with the treatment protocol.

Along similar lines, Hoffman (2009) argued that the problem with overemphasizing the importance of demonstrating the "scientific validity" of the psychoanalytic enterprise is that valid critiques of the relevant underlying philosophical and epistemological assumptions can become marginalized. According to him, the evaluation of manual-based treatments ignores the uniqueness of each therapeutic dyad and the intrinsic indeterminacy of the therapeutic process. Moreover, from his perspective, making the claim that one can know what will be most helpful for a particular client on the basis of empirical evidence is a form of technical rationality that masks the therapist's personal responsibility for making value-based choices as to how to respond in any given moment. And finally, our assumptions about what constitutes treatment effectiveness implicitly involve assumptions about what constitutes "the good life." Such questions cannot and should not be adjudicated entirely by "science." To the extent that we give the authority of science the power to arbitrate these choices, we are falling into the worst kind of scientism, in which moral positions masquerade as scientific "findings" (Hoffman, 2009, p. 1049).

My own perspective on these issues is that notwithstanding the value of these critiques, the efforts of psychoanalytically oriented researchers are vital to the survival of psychoanalysis. Perhaps even more important, the failure to conduct randomized clinical trial research on psychoanalytically oriented treatments allows for the perpetuation of a distorted perception by the public. Debates about the intricacies of research methodology, epistemological issues, and the role that sociopolitical factors and moral deliberation play in the philosophy of science are not going to have a substantial impact on policymakers and general public attitudes. People want straightforward concrete answers about "what works," and they have little time or inclination to follow what can seem like esoteric debates among professionals.

But my concern here is more than a pragmatic or politically expedient one. For too long now, psychoanalysts have argued that rigorous empirical research is irrelevant, and this has gone hand in hand with an attitude of insularity and smug elitism that argues on the basis of appeal to authority and canonical psychoanalytic texts rather than evidence. As an active psychotherapy researcher since the beginning of my career, I have seen many situations in which empirical research is approached in an uncritical fashion and used to justify a theoretical position or a political agenda rather than to advance the process of discovery. At the same time, I have also seen that psychotherapy researchers can be open to revising their beliefs in the face of findings that challenge cherished theoretical assumptions.

SOCIAL, CULTURAL, AND POLITICAL CRITIQUE

The political agendas of authors such as Harris, Dimen, and Corbett are focused primarily on challenging the oppressive aspects of conventional theories and assumptions about gender and sexuality. There is also a thrust in contemporary psychoanalytic theory to tackle broader political issues as well. Boticelli (2004) argued that certain distinguishing features of the relational tradition in psychoanalysis (e.g., the emphasis on mutuality, deconstruction of the analyst's authority, and therapist self-disclosure) and the "liberating" and "emancipatory" possibilities of psychoanalysis (in contrast to Freud's more tempered views regarding what types of changes are possible) can be understood, in part, as a displacement of the political aspirations that inspired the protest movements of the 1960s and 1970s. To quote Boticelli:

> Dispirited by the persistence of racial and social inequality in the aftermath of the civil rights movements of the 1960s and 1970s, disillusioned by the apparent failure of socialism to provide a viable alternative to free-market capitalism, those on the political left seem to have concluded that we are basically stuck with the world we've got. (p. 640)

As a result, there has been a tendency for progressive political ambitions to be psychologized or redirected toward the internal realm. According to Boticelli (2004)

> It seems no coincidence that psychoanalysis has become interested in the deconstruction of the analyst's authority and the democratizing of the analytic relationship at a time when authority in society at large is taking increasingly imposing and seemingly unchallengeable forms, as publicly elected officials follow corporate imperatives rather than the

interests of the people who elected them. It is not by chance that an emphasis on mutuality and the analyst's participation has developed a sense that "we're both in this together," when the people who make the decisions that most affect our lives (e.g., corporate CEOs; the Federal Reserve Board chairman; members of the World Trade Organization, the International Monetary Fund, and the World Bank) operate beyond public influence and accountability. Relational psychoanalysis represents a recasting of the world as we wish it could be, projected into therapeutic space—a last bastion of utopianism. (p. 639)

From Boticelli's (2004) perspective, "We need to take ourselves more seriously and to hold onto the strength of our relational convictions after we leave our offices" (p. 649). He argued that it is imperative for us not to divorce the psychological from the political or to retreat exclusively to the psychological realm as a defensive reaction to hopelessness and our fears that actions in the political realm will prove futile.

Nancy Caro Hollander, a professor of Latin American history at California State University, Dominguez Hills, and a psychoanalyst, has written extensively about the role that politically engaged psychoanalysts played in the fight for human rights under Latin American military regimes during the 1970s and 1980s (e.g., Hollander, 1997, 2006, 2010). In her book *Love in a Time of Hate*, Hollander (1997) documented the experiences of a number of politically active psychoanalysts from Argentina, Uruguay, and Chile who had found ways of struggling for democracy and human rights under dictatorships in their countries. Some of them were imprisoned and tortured by the military governments and others escaped to countries such as Mexico, Cuba, and France. In exile they continued to work with exiled Latin Americans who had been victims of torture.

The Argentinean psychoanalyst Marie Langer (whose personal and professional odyssey I introduced at the beginning of this book) was a key figure among these politically engaged psychoanalysts (Hollander, 1997). As indicated earlier, by the 1960's psychoanalysis in Latin America had in many respects become a relatively conservative force within the culture, not unlike the situation in the United States. In the mid 1960's however, a new generation of analysts began to challenge tradition and demand a return to a more progressive and politically engaged form of psychoanalysis. The tensions within psychoanalytic circles were heightened when right wing military dictatorships began to take over various Latin American countries in the mid-sixties and early 70's. In Argentina the military coup in 1966 and the establishment of the first of a series of military dictatorships, heightened these tensions even further. While some analysts argued for an isolation of psychoanalysis from politics and promoted the ideology of psychoanalysis as a value free scientific enterprise, others became increasingly radicalized. Langer split from some of her contemporaries and allied with a younger generation of analysts who promoted political activism. Langer became a prominent figure in the human rights movement among mental health professionals in Latin America. She became an outspoken critic of human rights violations in Argentina and was forced into exile in 1974. At this point she moved to Mexico City, where she provided treatment to members of refugee communities who had fled the military dictatorships in Argentina, Chile, Uruguay and Central America (Hollander, 1997).

In recent years Hollander (2006, 2010) has drawn on her earlier documentation of the experiences of socially engaged psychoanalysts in Latin America (Hollander, 1997) to indicate parallels between the situation there and in the United States. With the growing infringement of American civil liberties, following the attacks on the World Trade Center, Hollander urged her colleagues in the United States to learn from the experience of Latin American psychoanalysts who had lived through the experience of their countries slowly drifting from democratic to totalitarian forms of government. She also warned against the dangers potentially resulting from mental health professionals dissociating the psychological from the political.

For example, following its invasion of Afghanistan, the American government made a decision that it was legal to engage in coercive interrogation practices that violate the protections guaranteed by the Geneva Convention with detainees in detention sites such as Abu Ghraib and Guantanamo. Over time, as more and more information about what was really going on at these sites emerged, there was a gradual shift in the American public's attitude from one of complacent acceptance to moral indignation. A series of news reports began to emerge alleging that psychologists and other health care professionals were playing a role in devising and consulting on the use of coercive interrogation techniques on detainees held in Iraq, Guantanamo, and various CIA "black sites."

In the wake of continuing news reports about psychologists playing a role in the use of coercive interrogation techniques, the American Psychological Association (APA) initiated an extensive review of the situation. A number of psychologists/psychoanalysts who are members of APA's Division of Psychoanalysis (e.g., Neil Altman, Stephen Soldz, Stephen Reisner, Frank Summers, Ghislane Boulanger) played a key role in spearheading a series of efforts that ultimately led to APA voting for an official policy statement responding to the situation (Altman, 2008; Harris & Botticelli, 2010; Hollander, 2010; Soldz, 2008). This policy statement explicitly and unequivocally prohibits all psychologists from working in sites where abusive interrogation techniques are used or detainees are held under abusive conditions unless they are working for the persons being detained or for independent third parties working to maintain human rights.

In describing the role that psychologist/psychoanalysts played in helping to shape APA's response at this critical juncture, I am not making the claim that psychoanalysts are a uniquely ethical group. Indeed psychoanalysts have a long history of being on both sides of important ethical divides in different cultures and historical areas. My point, rather, is that their role in helping to shape APA's response to this situation can be seen as one example of the contemporary rekindling of the socially progressive and politically engaged roots of psychoanalysis that is taking place. I believe that there is something intrinsic to psychoanalysis' fundamental recognition of the limits of human rationality, the pervasiveness of self-deception, and the long-standing interest in broader social and cultural concerns that establishes a context for this type of active and progressive political engagement.

7

Summary

M y goal in this book has been to provide an overview of key theoretical concepts and principles of intervention in contemporary psychoanalysis and psychoanalytic therapy. I have also described a range of different mechanisms of action hypothesized by contemporary psychoanalysts to underlie the process of therapeutic change. Although I have attempted to provide the reader with a glimpse of a range of different psychoanalytic traditions that have become dominant in different countries, my primary emphasis has been on American psychoanalysis and in particular on developments that have been influenced by the emergence of contemporary relational thinking.

My intention has also been to offer sufficient historical and cultural background to provide a context for understanding how psychoanalysis evolved, as well as the factors shaping recent developments in contemporary theory and psychoanalytic practice. One of my objectives has been to correct misconceptions about psychoanalysis and psychoanalytic therapy that are based on caricatures that were shaped in part by a style of psychoanalysis that is no longer dominant in the United States. I have also attempted to correct certain common misconceptions that are based on a partial or limited understanding of some of the goals, values, and practices of traditional psychoanalysis.

Psychoanalysis originated more than 100 years ago and has evolved dramatically over time. Psychoanalysis in North America has evolved in many ways to adapt to current cultural values and needs. It has become more flexible, less authoritarian, more practical, and more responsive to the needs of a wider range of clients from diverse racial, cultural, and social class backgrounds. There is a growing cohort of dedicated and rigorous psychoanalytic researchers, and there is a growing body of empirical evidence supporting the effectiveness of psychoanalytically oriented treatments. As a result of various historical and cultural circumstances, American psychoanalysis has also changed from a tradition that was dominated by physicians to one that is increasingly dominated by psychologists. This has had an important impact on the development of contemporary psychoanalytic theory and technique, and this influence is likely to increase.

By the mid-to-late 1960s, psychoanalysis was under siege: on one side by the behavioral tradition and on the other by the "third force"—the tradition of humanistic psychology. Whereas the behavioral tradition critiqued psychoanalysis for its lack of scientific legitimacy, the humanistic tradition faulted psychoanalysis for its mechanistic and reductionist tendencies and its failure to appreciate the nobler aspects of human nature and the fundamental dignity of human experience.

I believe that the traditional antipathy of many psychoanalysts to empirical research has been a serious problem—one that has served to maintain the insularity of the tradition, forestalled critical self-reflection, and treated theory as if it were fact. For these reasons, I believe that the current resurgence of interest in empirical research among psychoanalysts is all to the good. Nevertheless, it would be a mistake to disregard or devalue those dimensions of psychoanalysis that fall outside of the natural sciences—those aspects of psychoanalysis that are more accurately conceptualized as a hermeneutic discipline, a critical theory, a philosophy of life, a wisdom tradition, or a craft.

I believe that the humanistic critique of psychoanalysis for its failure to appreciate and affirm the fundamental nobility and dignity of human nature is also valuable. I know too many people (many of them friends and colleagues) who had traumatic experiences with psychoanalytic therapy when they were younger and left the treatment feeling fragmented, objectified, and pathologized rather than appreciated, understood, valued, and whole. A friend and colleague of mine, Marvin Goldfried, one of the founders of the cognitive–behavioral tradition and a leader in the psychotherapy integration movement, conducted a research project in the 1980s in which he and his students used a theoretically neutral rating scheme to code transcripts of therapy sessions identified by either psychodynamic or cognitive–behavioral therapists as "good sessions." The objective was to attempt to describe important differences between the type of interventions used by psychodynamic and cognitive–behavioral therapists in theoretically neutral terms (Goldfried, Raue, & Castonguay, 1998). When he presented the study at conferences, he would often summarize their findings (somewhat tongue in cheek) in the following way: Whereas the cognitive therapists conveyed the message to clients that "you're better off than you think," the psychodynamic therapists tended to convey the message that "you're worse off than you think."

In some respects, his way of summarizing the findings makes a certain type of sense. The traditional emphasis on psychoanalysis has been on helping clients to become aware of and acknowledge aspects of themselves that they don't like—aspects of their experience that are defended against. Traditionally the cognitive–behavioral emphasis has been on helping clients to see the way in which they selectively focus on the negative rather than the positive. The optimistic flavor of cognitive therapy and the emphasis on the positive have a historical continuity with a long tradition of optimism and positive thinking characteristic of American culture. It can be seen in the "New Thought Movement" that swept the country in the mid-19th century through the influence of figures such as Phineas Quimby and Mary Baker Eddy (the founder of Christian Science). It can be seen in Dale Carnegie's *How to Win Friends and Influence People*. And it can be seen in the massive success of the self-help industry and the New Age emphasis on healing through positive thinking.

The late Stephen A. Mitchell (1993), one of the founding fathers of contemporary relational psychoanalysis, described the difference between

Freud's perspective and a more contemporary American psychoanalytic perspective in the following fashion: "Freud was not a particularly cheerful fellow and his version of the rational scientific person is not an especially happy person. But this person is stronger, more grounded, more in line with reality even if it's a somber reality" (p. 305). According to Mitchell, the emphasis in contemporary psychoanalysis has shifted away from Freud's emphasis renouncing instinctual wishes and illusions toward the creation of personal meaning and the revitalization of the self. Mitchell (1993) wrote the following:

> Many patients (these days) are understood to be suffering not from conflictual infantile passions that can be tamed and transformed through reason and understanding, but from stunted personal development. . . . What today's psychoanalysis provides is the opportunity to freely discover and playfully explore one's own subjectivity, one's own imagination. (p. 25)

My sense is that in certain respects, contemporary American psychoanalysis has come to incorporate some of the more positive, creative, and affirmative qualities of the humanistic psychology of the 1960s. At the same time, I believe that it will be important for the future of psychoanalysis not to discard what many have described as Freud's tragic sensibility—his belief that there is an inherent conflict between instinct and civilization, his emphasis on the importance of acknowledging and accepting the hardships, cruelties, and indignities of life without the consolation of illusory beliefs. As I indicated earlier, Freud saw the goal of psychoanalysis as one of transforming neurotic misery into ordinary human unhappiness. This can be interpreted as a modest and pessimistic perspective, but it can also be viewed as a realistic and profoundly liberating perspective—not unlike the Zen perspective that enlightenment involves letting go of the fantasy of escaping the realities of everyday life.

Optimism is an important American "natural resource." It inspired the establishment of one of the world's first modern democracies and provided amazing opportunities to immigrants who lived lives of persecution, oppression, and poverty in their homelands. It has also fueled technological innovations that were once unimaginable. At the same time, however, our American optimism can lead to an insidious type of oppression that marginalizes and silences those who are suffering and judges them as failures or implicitly as morally inadequate. In a recent book written in the wake of her own personal struggle with breast cancer, the journalist Barbara Ehrenreich (2009) critiqued what she referred to as our "relentless promotion of positive thinking" in America as follows:

> Americans are a "positive" people. This is our reputation as well as our self-image. We smile a lot and are often baffled when people from other cultures do not return the favor. In the well-worn stereotype, we are upbeat, cheerful, optimistic, and shallow, while foreigners are likely to be subtle, word-weary, and possibly decadent. . . . Surprisingly, when psychologists undertake to measure the relative happiness of nations, they routinely find that Americans are not, even in prosperous times and despite our vaunted positivity, very happy at all. A recent meta-analysis of over a hundred studies of self-reported happiness worldwide found Americans ranking only twenty third, surpassed by the Dutch, the Danes, the Malaysians, the Bahamians, the Australians, and even the supposedly dour Finns. (pp. 1–3)

On a personal note, Ehrenreich (2009) spoke about her tremendous sense of isolation while struggling with breast cancer because of the cultural pressure to deal with her experience in a "positive way." For example, she tells us that at one point she posted a statement on a breast cancer support group bulletin board that conveyed some of her despair and anger. In response, Ehrenreich reported receiving a "chorus of rebukes" (p. 32).

There is a well-known anecdote that when Freud was crossing the Atlantic with Jung and Ferenczi to deliver his lectures at Clark University, Jung spoke excitedly and enthusiastically about the growing interest in psychoanalysis by Americans. Freud was much more measured in his reaction and is reputed to have replied, "Little do they realize we are bringing the plague" (Fairfield, Layton, & Stack, 2002, p. 1). As psychoanalysis became increasingly popular in the United States, many European analysts responded ambivalently. On the one hand, it is difficult to argue with success. On the other hand, they were concerned that American psychoanalysis was losing the more radical and subversive qualities that were intrinsic to the original vision of psychoanalysis. The historian Nathan Hale (1971), for example, wrote the following:

> The Americans modified psychoanalysis to solve a conflict between the radical implications of Freud's views and the pulls of American culture. . . . They muted sexuality and aggression, making both more amiable. They emphasized social conformity. They were more didactic, moralistic, and popular than Freud. They were also more optimistic and environmentalistic. (p. 332)

A number of excellent books have recently been published that are designed to reach out to an audience beyond the formal psychoanalytic community. These books attempt to present a more contemporary version of American psychoanalysis that is in tune with a contemporary cultural sensibility (Gabbard, 2010; Leiper & Maltby, 2004; Lemma, 2003; Maroda, 2009; McWilliams, 1994, 2004; Renik, 2006; Summer & Barber, 2009; Wachtel, 2007). As this book was going to press, Morris Eagle (2010) published a wonderful scholarly overview of the evolution of psychoanalysis from Freud to contemporary times. And Nancy McWilliams (2004) has done a superb job of writing about psychoanalysis in a voice that makes it accessible to a broad contemporary audience. In many ways that has been my objective as well. At the same time, however, I hope that I have managed to convey my belief that although today's psychoanalysis is very different from Freud's psychoanalysis or American psychoanalysis of the 1940s–1960s, it is important not to discard those aspects of psychoanalysis that do not necessarily assimilate easily to mainstream American culture. From the very beginning, psychoanalysis had a revolutionary and subversive quality to it that challenged conventional cultural norms and values.

In its heyday, American psychoanalysis was remarkably influential. But this success came at a cost—it became an elitist, insular, and culturally conservative force. The contemporary marginalization of psychoanalysis has in certain respects, however, brought things full circle back to the discipline's marginal status in its early days. No longer an expression of the status quo, psychoanalysis has a renewed potential of becoming a constructive countercultural force. The declining fortunes of psychoanalysis thus ironically provide us with the opportunity to recover and build on some of the revolutionary, subversive, and culturally progressive qualities that were present at the beginning.

Glossary of Key Terms

ALLIANCE (THERAPEUTIC ALLIANCE, WORKING ALLIANCE)
The client's and therapist's ability to collaborate in the therapeutic process or to negotiate a constructive collaboration.

ATTACHMENT THEORY   A developmental theory originating in the writing of John Bowlby that stipulates that human beings have a biologically wired-in propensity for maintaining proximity to attachment figures (e.g., their parents).

COMPROMISE FORMATION   A theoretical proposition emerging from the ego psychology tradition that stipulates that all experience and action is the result of a compromise between an underlying instinctually derived wish and a defense against it.

CONTAINMENT   A model of development and therapeutic change originating in the work of Wilfred Bion that stipulates that the therapist's ability to process the client's difficult or "intolerable" affective experience in a nondefensive fashion, and to help him or her make sense of it, is a central therapeutic mechanism.

COUNTERTRANSFERENCE   Historically conceptualized as the therapist's responses to the client that are influenced by the therapist's unresolved conflicts. In contemporary psychoanalytic theory, countertransference tends to be conceptualized as the totality of the therapist's experience while with the client and as an important source of information.

DEFENSE   An intrapsychic process that functions to avoid emotional pain by in one way or another pushing thoughts, wishes, feelings, or fantasies out of awareness. Common examples of defenses are intellectualization, repression, reaction formation, splitting, and projection.

DISSOCIATION   A partial or complete disruption of the normal integration of a person's conscious or psychological functioning resulting from anxiety or trauma. Involves the splitting of different self-states or self-experiences from one another.

ENACTMENT   Takes place when client and therapist unwittingly get caught in playing out a particular relational scenario that is influenced by both the client's and therapist's unique personalities, relational styles, blind spots, sensitivities, etc. Enactments are ubiquitous in psychotherapy.

EVENLY SUSPENDED ATTENTION (EVENLY HOVERING ATTENTION)   An attentive, open, and receptive listening style in which the therapist attempts to listen to whatever the client says without allowing his or her preconceptions or expectations to shape what he or she attends to.

INSIGHT   A mechanism of change that has always been considered as important by psychoanalysts. Insight involves becoming aware of a feeling, wish, fantasy, thought, or memory that has previously been unconscious. Insight can also involve becoming aware of how one's previous experiences or current unconscious expectations or beliefs are shaping self-defeating interpersonal patterns in the present.

INTERNALIZATION   The process of developing an internal representation of relationships with others that shapes our ongoing experience and actions. There are many different theories of internalization. Internalization is considered to play an important role in the developmental process and to be an important mechanism of change in psychotherapy.

INTERNAL OBJECTS (INTERNAL OBJECT RELATIONS)   Hypothetical psychic structures developed through a combination of real interactions with others, fantasy, and defensive (self-protective) processes. These psychic structures shape our experience of others, the type of partners we tend to choose (romantic and otherwise), and the way in which we experience relationships with others. There is a variety of different models of internal object relations, each with its own assumptions and both theoretical and practical implications.

INTERPRETATION   The therapist's attempt to help make sense of the client's experience, articulate a hypothesis about the client's unconscious experience, or draw the client's attention to unconscious self-defeating interpersonal patterns.

INTRAPSYCHIC CONFLICT   A conflict between unconscious wishes and defenses against them.

MENTALIZATION   The capacity to see ourselves and others as beings with psychological depth and underlying mental states including desires, feelings, and beliefs. Mentalization is also the capacity to access and reflect on our own thoughts, feelings, and motivations and to reflect on the mental states of others.

METACOMMUNICATION   An intervention that involves engaging the client in the process of stepping back collaboratively and exploring what is implicitly taking place in the therapeutic relationship.

ONE-PERSON PSYCHOLOGY   The perspective in traditional or classical psychoanalysis that assumes it is possible to understand the client's intrapsychic processes out of context of the therapist's ongoing contributions to the interaction. From this perspective, the client's transference is viewed as a distorted perception influenced by the client's past and projected onto a neutral stimulus.

PRIMARY PROCESS   A raw or primitive form of psychic functioning that begins at birth and continues to operate unconsciously throughout the lifetime. In primary process, there is no distinction between past, present, and future. Different feelings and experiences can be condensed together into one image or symbol, feelings can be expressed metaphorically, and the identities of different people can be merged. Primary process can be seen operating in dreams and fantasy.

RESISTANCE   Conceptualized as the tendency for the client to resist change or act in a way that undermines the therapeutic process. There are multiple factors underlying resistance, such as ambivalence about changing, a fear of losing one's sense of self, and a reaction to a problematic intervention by the therapist. The exploration of resistance is viewed as a central objective in psychoanalysis.

RUPTURE (RUPTURE IN THE THERAPEUTIC ALLIANCE, RUPTURE IN THE THERAPEUTIC RELATIONSHIP, THERAPEUTIC IMPASSE)   Viewed as an inevitable occurrence in therapy that varies in intensity, duration, and frequency. The process of working through alliance ruptures or therapeutic impasses constructively is viewed as an important mechanism of change.

SECONDARY PROCESS   The style of psychic functioning associated with consciousness. It is the foundation for rational, reflective thinking. It is logical, sequential, and orderly.

TRANSFERENCE   The client's tendency to view the therapist in terms that are shaped by his or her experiences with important caregivers and other significant figures in his or her developmental process. In contemporary psychoanalytic theory, the transference is always influenced to varying degrees by the therapist's real characteristics.

TWO-PERSON PSYCHOLOGY   The perspective common to many contemporary psychoanalytic models that assumes that both therapist and client are always contributing to everything that takes place in the therapeutic relationship. From this perspective, one cannot develop a meaningful understanding of the client's intrapsychic processes and actions without developing an understanding of the way in which they are being influenced by the therapist.

UNCONSCIOUS   A central psychoanalytic construct that is conceptualized in different ways by different psychoanalytic theories. Common threads running through all of these theories are the premises that (a) our experience and actions are influenced by psychological processes that are not part of our conscious awareness, and (b) these unconscious processes are kept out of awareness in order to avoid psychological pain.

References

Abbass, A., Hancock, J. T., Henderson, J., & Kisley, S. (2006). Short-term psychodynamic psychotherapies for common mental disorders. *Cochrane Database of Systematic Reviews* (Issue 4, Article No. CD004687). doi:10.1002/14651858. CD004687.pub3

Abraham, K. (1949). *Selected papers of Karl Abraham.* London, England: Hogarth Press.

Adorno, T. W., Frenkel-Brunswik, E., & Levinson, D. J. (1950). *The authoritarian personality.* New York, NY: Science Editions.

Ainsworth, M., Blehar, M. C., Waters, E., & Wall, S. (1978). *Patterns of attachment: A psychological study of the Strange Situation.* Hillsdale, NJ: Erlbaum.

Alexander, F. (1948). *Fundamentals of psychoanalysis.* New York, NY: Norton.

Altman, N. (1995). *The analyst in the inner city: Race, class, and culture through a psychoanalytic lens.* Hillsdale, NJ: Analytic Press.

Altman, N. (2000). Black and white thinking: A psychoanalyst reconsiders race. *Psychoanalytic Dialogues, 10,* 589–605. doi:10.1080/10481881009348569

Altman, N. (2008). The psychodynamics of torture. Coercive interrogations and the mental health profession [Special issue]. *Psychoanalytic Dialogues, 18,* 658–670.

American Psychiatric Association. (1980). *Diagnostic and statistical manual of mental disorders* (3rd ed.). Washington, DC: Author.

Arlow, J., & Brenner, C. (1964). *Psychoanalytic concepts and the structural theory.* Oxford, England: International Universities Press.

Aron, L. (1996). *A meeting of minds: Mutuality in psychoanalysis.* Hillsdale, NJ: Analytic Press.

Aron, L. (1999). Clinical choices and the relational matrix. *Psychoanalytic Dialogues, 9,* 1–29. doi:10.1080/10481889909539301

Aron, L. (2006). Analytic impasse and the third: Clinical implications of inter-subjectivity theory. *The International Journal of Psychoanalysis, 87,* 349–368. doi:10.1516/15EL-284Y-7Y26-DHRK

Bader, M. J. (1994). The tendency to neglect therapeutic aims in psychoanalysis. *The Psychoanalytic Quarterly, 63,* 246–270.

Bateman, A., & Fonagy, P. (2008). 8-year follow-up of patients treated for borderline personality disorder: Mentalization-based treatment versus treatment as usual. *The American Journal of Psychiatry, 165,* 631–638. doi:10.1176/appi.ajp.2007.07040636

Beebe, B., & Lachmann, F. M. (2002). *Infant research and adult treatment.* Hillsdale, NJ: Analytic Press.

Benjamin, J. (1988). *The bonds of love.* New York, NY: Pantheon Books.

Benjamin, J. (1990). An outline of intersubjectivity: The development of recognition. *Psychoanalytic Psychology, 7,* 33–46. doi:10.1037/h0085258

Benjamin, J. (2004). Beyond doer and done to: An intersubjective view of thirdness. *The Psychoanalytic Quarterly, 73,* 5–46.

Bergin, A. E., & Strupp, H. S. (1973). *Changing frontiers in the science of psychotherapy.* Chicago, IL: Aldine.

Binder, J. (2004). *Key competencies in brief dynamic psychotherapy.* New York, NY: Guilford Press.

Bion, W. R. (1970). *Attention and interpretation.* London, England: Routledge.

Bollas, C. (1992). *Being a character: Psychoanalysis and self experience.* New York, NY: Routledge.

Bordin, E. (1979). The generalizability of the psychoanalytic concept of the working alliance. *Psychotherapy: Theory, Research, & Practice, 16,* 252–260. doi:10.1037/h0085885

Boston Change Process Study Group. (2010). *Change in psychotherapy: A unifying paradigm.* New York, NY: Norton.

Botticelli, S. (2004). The politics of relational psychoanalysis. *Psychoanalytic Dialogues, 14,* 635–651.

Bowlby, J. (1969). *Attachment and Loss: Vol. 1. Attachment.* New York, NY: Basic Books.

Bowlby, J. (1973). *Attachment and Loss: Vol. 2. Separation, anxiety and anger.* New York, NY: Basic Books.

Bowlby, J. (1980). *Attachment and Loss: Vol. 3. Sadness and depression.* New York, NY: Basic Books.

Brenner, C. (1994). The mind as conflict and compromise formation. *Journal of Clinical Psychoanalysis, 3,* 473–488.

Breuer, J., & Freud, S. (1955). Studies on hysteria. In J. Strachey (Ed. & Trans.), *The standard edition of the complete psychological works of Sigmund Freud*

(Vol. 2, pp. 1–305). London, England: Hogarth press. (Original work published 1893–1895)

Bromberg, P. M. (1995). Resistance, object-usage, and human relatedness. *Contemporary Psychoanalysis, 31,* 173–191.

Bromberg, P. M. (1998). *Standing in the spaces: Essays on clinical process, trauma, and dissociation.* Hillsdale, NJ: Analytic Press.

Bromberg, P. M. (2006). *Awakening the dreamer: Clinical journeys.* Hillsdale, NJ: Analytic Press.

Buhle, M. J. (1998). *Feminism and its discontents: A century of struggle with psychoanalysis.* Cambridge, MA: Harvard University Press.

Cassidy, J., & Shaver, P. R. (Eds.). (2008). *Handbook of attachment: Theory, research, and clinical applications.* New York, NY: Guilford Press.

Cherry, S., Cabaniss, D. L., Forand, N., Haywood, D., & Roose, S. P. (2004). Psychoanalytic practice in the early postgraduate years. *Journal of the American Psychoanalytic Association, 52,* 851–871.

Clarkin, J. F., Levy, K. N., Lenzenweger, M. F., & Kernberg, O. F. (2007). Evaluating three treatments for borderline personality disorder: A multiwave study. *The American Journal of Psychiatry, 164,* 922–928. doi:10.1176/appi.ajp.164.6.922

Coltart, N. (2000). *Slouching towards Bethlehem.* New York, NY: Guilford Press.

Connors, M. (2006). *Symptom-focused dynamic psychotherapy.* Hillsdale, NJ: Analytic Press.

Cooper, S. (2000). *Objects of hope: Exploring possibility and limit in psychoanalysis.* Hillsdale, NJ: Analytic Press.

Corbett, K. (2009). *Boyhood: Rethinking masculinities.* New Haven, CT: Yale University Press.

Cushman, P. (1995). *Constructing the self, constructing America.* Reading, MA: Addison-Welsey.

Cushman, P., & Gilford, P. (2000). Will managed care change our way of being? *American Psychologist, 55,* 985–996. doi:10.1037/0003-066X.55.9.985

Danto, E. (2005). *Freud's free clinics.* New York, NY: Columbia University Press.

Davanloo, H. (Ed.). (1980). *Short-term dynamic psychotherapy.* New York, NY: Aronson.

Davies, J. M. (1996). Linking the "pre-analytic" with the post-classical: Integration, dissociation, and the multiplicity of unconscious process. *Contemporary Psychoanalysis, 32,* 553–576.

Davies, J. M. (2004). Whose bad object are we anyway? Repetition and our elusive love affair with evil. *Psychoanalytic Dialogues, 14,* 711–732. doi:10.1080/10481881409348802

Dimen, M. (2003). *Sexuality, intimacy, power.* Hillsdale, NJ: Analytic Press.

Dimen, M. (2010). Reflections on cure, or "I/Thou/It." *Psychoanalytic Dialogues, 20,* 254–268. doi:10.1080/10481885.2010.481612

Dreyfus, H. E., & Dreyfus, S. L. (1986). *Mind over machine.* New York, NY: Free Press.

Eagle, M. (1984). *Recent developments in psychoanalysis.* New York, NY: McGraw-Hill.

Eagle, M. (2010) *From classical to contemporary psychoanalysis: A critique and integration.* New York, NY: Routledge.

Ehrenberg, D. (1992). *The intimate edge.* New York, NY: Norton.

Ehrenreich, B. (2009). *Bright-sided: How the relentless promotion of positive thinking has undermined America.* New York, NY: Macmillan.

Ekman, P. (1993). Facial expression and emotion. *American Psychologist, 48,* 384–392. doi:10.1037/0003-066X.48.4.384

Ekman, P., & Davidson, R. J. (Eds.). (1994). *The nature of emotions: Fundamental questions.* New York, NY: Oxford University Press.

Erikson, E. (1950). *Childhood and society.* New York, NY: Norton.

Etchegoyen, H. (1991). *The fundamentals of psychoanalytic technique.* London, England: Karnac Books.

Fairbairn, W. R. D. (1952). *Psychoanalytic studies of the personality.* London, England: Routledge and Kegan Paul.

Fairbairn, W. R. D. (1994). *Psychoanalytic studies of the personality.* New York, NY: Routledge/Taylor & Francis.

Fairfield, S., Layton, L., & Stack, C. (Eds.). (2002). *Bringing the plague: Toward a postmodern psychoanalysis.* New York, NY: Other Press.

Fenichel, O. (1945). *Problems of psychoanalytic technique.* New York, NY: Psychoanalytic Quarterly.

Ferenczi, S. (1980a). *Final contributions to the problems and methods of pyschoanalysis* (M. Balint, Ed., & E. Mosbacher, Trans.). London, England: Karnac Books.

Ferenczi, S. (1980b). *Further contributions to the problems and methods of psychoanalysis* (J. Richman, Ed., & J. Suttie, Trans.). London, England: Karnac Books.

Ferenczi, S., & Rank, O. (1956). *The development of psychoanalysis.* New York, NY: Dover. (Original work published 1925) doi:10.1037/10664-000

Ferro, A. (2002). *In the analyst's consulting room.* New York, NY: Routledge.

Fonagy, P. (2001). *Attachment theory and psychoanalysis.* New York, NY: Other Press.

Fonagy, P., Gergely, G., Jurist, E., & Target, M. (2002). *Affect regulation, mentalization, and the development of self.* New York, NY: Other Press.

Fonagy, P., Kachle, H., Krause, R., Jones, E., Perron, R., & Lopez, L. (1999). *An open door review of outcome studies in psychoanalysis.* London, England: University College.

Fosha, D. (2000). *The transforming power of affect: A model for accelerated change.* New York, NY: Basic Books.

Frank, K. A. (1999). *Psychoanalytic participation, action, interaction, and integration.* Hillsdale, NJ: Analytic Press.

Freud, S. (1895/1955). *Studies on hysteria* (Standard Ed., Vol. 2.). London, England: Hogarth Press.

Freud, A. (1936). *The ego and the mechanisms of defense.* Honolulu, HI: Hogarth Press.

Freud, S. (1953). *The interpretation of dreams.* In J. Strachey (Ed. & Trans.), *The standard edition of the complete psychological works of Sigmund Freud* (Vols. 4–5). London, England: Hogarth Press. (Original work published 1900)

Freud, S. (1958). *The dynamics of transference.* In J. Strachey (Ed. & Trans.), *The standard edition of the complete psychological works of Sigmund Freud* (Vol. 12, pp. 97–108). London, England: Hogarth Press. (Original work published 1912)

Freud, S. (1961). *The ego and the id.* In J. Strachey (Ed. & Trans.), *The standard edition of the complete psychological works of Sigmund Freud* (Vol. 19, pp. 3–66). London, England: Hogarth Press. (Original work published 1923)

Frijda, N. H. (1986). *The emotions.* New York, NY: Cambridge University Press.

Fromm, E. (1941). *A man for himself.* New York, NY: Rinehart.

Gabbard, G. O. (2010). *Long-term psychodynamic psychotherapy.* Arlington, VA: American Psychiatric Publishing.

Galatzer-Levy, R., Bachrach, H., Skolnikoff, A., & Waldron, S. (2000). *Does psychoanalysis work?* New Haven, CT: Yale University Press.

Gay, P. (1988). *Freud: A life for our time.* New York, NY: Norton.

Gerber, A. J., Kocsis, J. H., Milrod, B. L., Roose, S. P., Barber, J. P., Thase, M. E., . . . Leon, A. C. (2011). A quality-based review of randomized controlled trials of psychodynamic psychotherapy. *The American Journal of Psychiatry, 168,* 19–28.

Ghent, E. (1990). Masochism, submission, surrender: Masochism as a perversion of surrender. *Contemporary Psychoanalysis, 26,* 108–136.

Goldfried, M. R., Raue, P. J., & Castonguay, L. G. (1998). The therapeutic focus in significant sessions of master therapists: A comparison of cognitive-behavioral and psychodynamic-interpersonal interventions. *Journal of Consulting and Clinical Psychology, 66,* 803–810. doi:10.1037/0022-006X.66.5.803

Goldfried, M. R., & Wolfe, B. E. (1996). Psychotherapy practice and research: Repairing a strained alliance. *American Psychologist, 51,* 1007–1016. doi:10.1037/0003-066X.51.10.1007

Greenberg, J. (1986). Theoretical models and the analyst's neutrality. *Contemporary Psychoanalysis, 22,* 87–106.

Greenberg, J., & Mitchell, S. A. (1983). *Object relations in psychoanalytic theory.* Cambridge, MA: Harvard University Press.

Greenberg, J., & Safran, J. (1987). *Emotions in psychotherapy: Affect, cognition, and process of change.* New York, NY: Guilford Press.

Greenson, R. (1965). The working alliance and the transference neurosis. *The Psychoanalytic Quarterly, 34,* 155–179.

Grunbaum, F. (1984). *The foundations of psychoanalysis: A philosophical critique.* Berkeley: University of California Press.

Guignon, C. (2004). *On being authentic.* London, England: Routledge.

Gutwill, S., & Hollander, N. C. (2006). Class and splitting in the clinical setting: The ideological dance in the transference and countertransference. In L. Layton, N. C. Hollander, & S. Gutwill (Eds.), *Psychoanalysis, class, and politics: Encounters in the clinical setting* (pp. 92–106). New York, NY: Routledge.

Hale, N. (1971). *Freud and the Americans: The beginnings of psychoanalysis in the United States, 1876–1917* (Vol. 1). Oxford, England: Oxford University Press.

Hale, N. (1995). *The rise and crisis of psychoanalysis in the United States: Freud and the Americans 1917–1985* (Vol. 2). Oxford, England: Oxford University Press.

Harris, A. (2008). *Gender as soft assembly.* Hillsdale, NJ: Analytic Press.

Harris, A., & Botticelli, S. (2010). *First do no harm: The paradoxical encounters of psychoanalysis, warmaking, and resistance.* New York, NY: Routledge.

Hartmann, H. (1964). *Ego psychology and the problem of adaptation.* New York, NY: International Universities Press.

Hoffman, I. Z. (1998). *Ritual and spontaneity in the psychoanalytic process: A dialectical-constructivist view.* Hillsdale, NJ: Analytic Press.

Hoffman, I. Z. (2009). Doublethinking our way to "scientific" legitimacy: The desiccation of human experience. *Journal of the American Psychoanalytic Association, 57,* 1043–1069. doi:10.1177/0003065109343925

Hollander, N. C. (1997). *Love in a time of hate.* New Brunswick, NJ: Rutgers University Press.

Hollander, N. C. (2006). Psychoanalysis and the problem of the bystander in times of terror. In L. Layton, N. C. Hollander, & S. Gutwill (Eds.), *Psychoanalysis, class, and politics: Encounters in the clinical setting* (pp. 154–165). New York, NY: Routledge.

Hollander, N. C. (2010). *Uprooted minds: Surviving the politics of terror in the Americas.* New York, NY: Routledge.

Holmes, J. (2010). *Exploring in security: Towards an attachment-informed psychoanalytic psychotherapy.* New York, NY: Routledge.

Horkheimer, M., & Adorno, T. W. (1947). *Dialectic of the enlightenment* (E. Jephcott, Trans.). Stanford, CA: Stanford University Press.

Horowitz, A. V. (2003). *The making of mental illness.* Chicago, IL: Chicago University Press.

Howard, K. I., Kopta, S. M., Krause, M. S., & Orlinsky, D. E. (1986). The dose-effect relationship in psychotherapy. *American Psychologist, 41,* 159–164. doi:10.1037/0003-066X.41.2.159

Huber, D., Henrich, G., Gastner, J., & Klug, G. (in press). Must all have prizes? The Munich Psychotherapy Study. In R. Levy, J. S. Ablon, & H. Kaechele (Eds.), *Evidence-based psychodynamic psychotherapy II.* New York, NY: Human Press.

Jacobs, T. (1991). *The use of the self: Countertransference and communication in the analytic setting.* Madison, CT: International Universities Press.

Jacoby, R. (1983). *The repression of psychoanalysis: Otto Fenichel and the political Freudians.* Hillsdale, NJ: Analytic Press.

Joseph, B. (1989). *Psychic equilibrium and psychic change.* London, England: Tavistock and Routledge.

Keller, B. (2005). *Class matters.* New York, NY: Henry Holt.

Klein, M. (2002a). *The writings of Melanie Klein: Volume 1. Love, guilt, and reparation and other works, 1921–1945.* New York, NY: Free Press. (Original work published 1955)

Klein, M. (2002b). *The writings of Melanie Klein: Volume 3. Envy and gratitude and other works, 1946–1963.* New York, NY: Free Press. (Original work published 1975)

Knight, R. P. (1953). The present status of organized psychoanalysis in the United States. *Journal of the American Psychoanalytic Association, 1,* 197–221. doi:10.1177/000306515300100201

Kohut, H. (1984). *How does analysis cure?* Chicago, IL: University of Chicago Press.

Lacan, J. (1988a). *The seminar of Jacques Lacan: Book 1. Freud's papers on technique, 1953–1954* (J. Miller, Ed., & J. Forrester, Trans.). New York, NY: Norton. (Original work published 1975)

Lacan, J. (1988b). *The seminar of Jacques Lacan: Book 2. The ego in Freud's theory and in the technique of psychoanalysis 1954–1955* (J. Miller, Ed., & S. Tomaselli, Trans.). New York: Norton. (Original work published 1978)

Leichsenring, F., Biskup, J., Kreisch, R., & Staats, H. (2005). The Güttingen study of psychoanalytic therapy: First results. *The International Journal of Psychoanalysis, 86,* 433–455. doi:10.1516/XX6F-AU0W-KWM3-G6LU

Leiper, R., & Maltby, M. (2004). *The psychodynamic approach to therapeutic change.* London, England: Sage

Lemma, A. (2003). *Introduction to the practice of psychoanalytic psychotherapy.* Chichester, England: John Wiley & Sons.

Levenson, H. (2010). *Brief dynamic therapy*. Washington, DC: American Psychological Association.

Levy, R., Ablon, J. S., & Kaechele, H. (Eds.). (in press). *Evidence-based psychodynamic psychotherapy* (2nd ed.). New York, NY: Humana Press.

Lichtenberg, J. (1989). *Psychoanalysis and motivation*. Hillsdale, NJ: Analytic Press.

Loewald, H. (1960). On the therapeutic action of psychoanalysis. *The International Journal of Psychoanalysis, 58*, 463–472.

Luborsky, L. (1984). *Principles of psychoanalytic psychotherapy: A manual for supportive-expressive treatment*. New York, NY: Basic Books.

Luborsky, L., Diguer, L., Seligman, D. A., Rosenthal, R., Krause, E. D., Johnson, S., . . . Schweizer, E. (1999). The researcher's own therapy allegiances: A "wild card" in comparisons of treatment efficacy. *Clinical Psychology: Science and Practice, 6*, 95–106.

Lyons-Ruth, K., Bruschweiler-Stern, N., Harrison, A. M., Morgan, A. C., Nahum, J. P., Sander, L., . . . Tronick, E. Z. (1998). Implicit relational knowing: Its role in development and psychoanalytic treatment. *Infant Mental Health Journal, 19*, 282–289.

Main, M., Kaplan, N., & Cassidy, J. (1985). Security in infancy, childhood, and adulthood: A move to the level of representation. *Monographs of the Society for Research in Child Development, 50*, 66–104. doi:10.2307/3333827

Makari, G. (2008). *Revolution in mind: The creation of psychoanalysis*. New York, NY: Harper Collins.

Malan, D. H. (1963). *A study of brief psychotherapy*. New York, NY: Plenum Press.

Maroda, K. (2009). *Psychodynamic techniques: Working with emotion in the therapeutic relationship*. New York, NY: Guilford Press.

McCullough Valliant, L. M. (1997). *Changing character: Short-term anxiety-regulating psychotherapy for restructuring defenses, affects, and attachment*. New York, NY: Basic Books.

McMain, S. F., Links, P. S., Gnam, W. H., Guimond, T., Cardish, R. J., Korman, L., & Streiner, D. L. (2009). A randomized trial of dialectical behavior therapy versus general psychiatric management for borderline personality disorder. *The American Journal of Psychiatry, 166*, 1365–1374. doi:10.1176/appi.ajp. 2009.09010039

McWilliams, N. (1994). *Psychoanalytic diagnosis: Understanding personality structure in the clinical process*. New York, NY: Guilford Press.

Messer, S. B., & Warren, C. S. (1995). *Models of brief psychotherapy*. New York, NY: Guilford Press.

Mitchell, S. A. (1988). *Relational concepts in psychoanalysis*. Cambridge, MA: Harvard University Press.

Mitchell, S. A. (1993). *Hope and dread in psychoanalysis*. New York, NY: Basic Books.

Mitchell, S. A. (1997). *Influence and autonomy in psychoanalysis*. Hillsdale, NJ: Analytic Press.

Moncayo, R. (2008). *Evolving Lacanian perspectives for clinical psychoanalysis*. London, England: Karnac Books.

Morrow-Bradley, C., & Elliott, R. (1986). Utilization of psychotherapy research by practicing psychotherapists. *American Psychologist, 41,* 188–197. doi:10.1037/0003-066X.41.2.188

Moskowitz, M. (1996). The social consequence of psychoanalysis. In R. M. Perez Foster & R. A. Javier (Eds.), *Reaching across boundaries of culture and class: Widening the scope of psychotherapy* (pp. 21–46). Northvale, NJ: Jason Aronson.

Ogden, T. (1994). *Subject of analysis*. Northvale, NJ: Aronson.

Parkinson, B. (1995). *Ideas and realities of emotion*. London, England: Routledge.

Parsons, M. (2000). *The dove that returns, the dove that vanishes: Paradox and creativity in psychoanalysis*. London, England: Routledge.

Perez Foster, R. M., Moskowitz, M., & Javier, R.A. (Eds.). (1996). *Reaching across boundaries of culture and class: Widening the scope of psychotherapy*. Northvale, NJ: Aronson.

Persons, J. B., & Silberschatz, G. (1998). Are results of randomized controlled trials useful to psychotherapists? *Journal of Consulting and Clinical Psychology, 66,* 126–135. doi:10.1037/0022-006X.66.1.126

Pizer, S. A. (1998). *Building bridges: The negotiation paradox in psychoanalysis*. Hillsdale, NJ: Analytic Press.

Plotkin, M. B. (2001). *Freud in the Pampas: The emergence and development of psychoanalytic culture in Argentina*. Stanford, CA: Stanford University Press.

Rank, O. (1929). *The trauma of birth*. New York, NY: Harcourt, Brace.

Rayner, E. (1991). *The independent mind in British psychoanalysis*. Northvale, NJ: Aronson.

Reich, W. (1941). *Character analysis*. New York, NY: Orgone Institute Press.

Reiff, P. (1966). *The triumph of the therapeutic: Uses of faith after Freud*. Chicago, IL: University of Chicago Press.

Reik, T. (1948). *Listening with the third ear: The inner experience of a psychoanalyst*. New York, NY: Farrar, Straus, & Giroux.

Renik, O. (1993). Analytic interaction: Conceptualizing technique in light of the analyst's irreducible subjectivity. *The Psychoanalytic Quarterly, 62,* 553–571.

Renik, O. (2006). *Practical psychoanalysis for therapists and patients*. New York, NY: Other Press.

Rice, L. N., & Greenberg, L. S. (1984). *Patterns of change: Intensive analysis of psychotherapy process*. New York, NY: Guilford.

Richardson, P., Kachele, H., & Renlund, C. (2004). *Research on psychoanalytic psychotherapy with adults*. New York, NY: Karnac Books.

Ringstrom, P. A. (2007). Scenes that write themselves: Improvisational moments in relational psychoanalysis. *Psychoanalytic Dialogue, 17,* 69–99.

Roland, A. (1989). *In search of self in India and Japan.* Princeton, NJ: Princeton University Press.

Safran, J. D. (1984). Assessing the cognitive-interpersonal cycle. *Cognitive Therapy and Research, 8,* 333–348.

Safran, J. D. (1993). Breaches in the therapeutic alliance: An arena for negotiating authentic relatedness. *Psychotherapy: Theory, Research, & Practice, 30,* 11–24. doi:10.1037/0033-3204.30.1.11

Safran, J. D. (1998). *Widening the scope of cognitive therapy: The therapeutic relationship, emotion, and the process of change.* Northvale, NJ: Aronson.

Safran, J. D. (1999). Faith, despair, will, and the paradox of acceptance. *Contemporary Psychoanalysis, 35,* 5–23.

Safran, J. D. (2001). When worlds collide: Psychoanalysis and the empirically supported treatment movement. *Psychoanalytic Dialogues, 11,* 659–681. doi:10.1080/10481881109348635

Safran, J. D. (2002). Brief relational psychoanalytic treatment. *Psychoanalytic Dialogues, 12,* 171–195. doi:10.1080/10481881209348661

Safran, J. D. (2003). The relational turn, the therapeutic alliance and psychotherapy research: Strange bedfellows or postmodern marriage? *Contemporary Psychoanalysis, 39,* 449–475.

Safran, J. D., Crocker, P., McMain, S., & Murray, P. (1990). Therapeutic alliance rupture as an event for empirical investigation. *Psychotherapy: Theory, Research, & Practice, 27,* 154–165. doi:10.1037/0033-3204.27.2.154

Safran, J. D., & Greenberg, L. S. (1991). *Emotion, psychotherapy, and change.* New York, NY: Guilford Press.

Safran, J. D., Greenberg, L. S., & Rice, L. N. (1988). Integrating psychotherapy research and practice: Modeling the change process. *Psychotherapy: Theory, Research, & Practice, 25,* 1–17. doi:10.1037/h0085305

Safran, J. D., & Muran, J. C. (1994). Toward a working alliance between research and practice. In P. F. Talley, H. H. Strupp, & J. F. Butler (Eds.), *Psychotherapy research and practice* (pp. 206–226). New York, NY: Basic Books.

Safran, J. D., & Muran, J. C. (1996). The resolution of ruptures in the therapeutic alliance. *Journal of Consulting and Clinical Psychology, 64,* 447–458. doi:10.1037/0022-006X.64.3.447

Safran, J. D., & Muran, J. C. (1998). *The therapeutic alliance in brief psychotherapy.* Washington, DC: American Psychological Association. doi:10.1037/10306-000

Safran, J. D., & Muran, J. C. (2000). *Negotiating the therapeutic alliance: A relational treatment guide.* New York, NY: Guilford Press.

Safran, J. D., & Muran, J. C. (2006). Has the concept of the alliance outlived its usefulness? *Psychotherapy: Theory, Research, & Practice, 43,* 286–291. doi:10.1037/0033-3204.43.3.286

Safran, J. D., Muran, J. C., & Eubacks-Carter, C. (2011). Repairing alliance ruptures. In J. C. Norcross & B. Wampold (Eds.), *Psychotherapy relationships that work* (2nd ed., pp. 224–238). New York, NY: Oxford University Press.

Safran, J. D., Muran, J. C., Samstag, L. W., & Stevens, C. (2001). Repairing therapeutic alliance ruptures. *Psychotherapy: Theory, Research, & Practice, 38,* 406–412. doi:10.1037/0033-3204.38.4.406

Safran, J. D., Muran, J. C., Samstag, L. W., & Stevens, C. (2002). Repairing alliance ruptures. In J. C. Norcross (Ed.), *Psychotherapy relationships that work* (pp. 235–254). New York, NY: Oxford University Press.

Safran, J. D., & Segal, Z. V. (1990). *Interpersonal process in cognitive therapy.* New York, NY: Basic Books.

Saks, E. (2008). *The center cannot hold: My journey through madness.* New York, NY: Hyperion Press.

Sandell, R., Blomberg, J., Lazar, A., Carlsson, J., Broberg, J., & Schubert, J. (2000). Varieties of long-term outcome among patients in psychoanalysis and long-term psychotherapy: A review of findings in the Stockholm Outcome of Psychoanalysis and Psychotherapy Project (STOPP). *The International Journal of Psychoanalysis, 81,* 921–942. doi:10.1516/0020757001600291

Sayers, J. (2001). *Kleinians: Psychoanalysis inside out.* Oxford, England: Blackwell.

Schafer, R. (1968). *Aspects of internalization.* Madison, CT: International Universities Press.

Schon, D. (1983). *The reflective practitioner.* New York, NY: Basic Books.

Seligman, M. E. P. (1995). The effectiveness of psychotherapy: The *Consumer Reports* study. *American Psychologist, 50,* 965–974. doi:10.1037/0003-066X.50.12.965

Shedler, J. (2010). The efficacy of psychodynamic psychotherapy. *American Psychologist, 65,* 98–109.

Sifneos, P. E. (1972). *Short-term psychotherapy and emotional crisis.* Cambridge, MA: Harvard University Press.

Slavin, M. O., & Kriegman, D. (1998). Why the analyst needs to change: Toward a theory of conflict, negotiation, and mutual influence in the therapeutic process. *Psychoanalytic Dialogues, 8,* 247–284. doi:10.1080/10481889809539246

Soldz, S. (2008). Healers or interrogators: Psychology and the United States torture regime, *Psychoanalytic Dialogues, 18,* 592–613.

Steele, M., & Steele, H. (2008). *Clinical applications of the Adult Attachment Interview.* New York, NY: Guilford Press.

Sterba, R. (1934). The fate of the ego in analytic therapy. *The International Journal of Psychoanalysis, 15,* 117–126.

Stern, D. (1985). *The interpersonal world of the infant: A view from psychoanalysis and developmental psychology.* New York, NY: Basic Books.

Stern, D. (1997). *Unformulated experience.* Hillsdale, NJ: Analytic Press.

Stern, D. (2010). *Partners in thought: Working with unformulated experience, dissociation, and enactment.* New York, NY: Routledge.

Stern, D., Sander, L., Nahum, J. P., Harrison, A. M., Lyons-Ruth, K., Morgan, A. C., . . . Tronick, E. Z. (1998). Non-interpretive mechanisms in psychoanalytic therapy: The "something more" than interpretation. *The International Journal of Psychoanalysis, 79,* 903–921.

Sternberg, R., & Jordan, J. (2005). *A handbook of wisdom: Psychological perspectives.* New York, NY: Cambridge University Press. doi:10.1017/CBO9780511610486

Stiles, W., & Shapiro, D. (1989). Abuse of the drug metaphor in psychotherapy process-outcome research. *Clinical Psychology Review, 9,* 521–543.

Strachey, J. (1934). The nature of the therapeutic action of psychoanalysis. *The International Journal of Psychoanalysis, 15,* 127–159.

Strupp, H. H., & Binder, J. L. (1984). *Psychotherapy in a new key: A guide to time-limited dynamic psychotherapy.* New York, NY: Basic Books.

Sullivan, H. S. (1953). *The interpersonal theory of psychiatry.* New York, NY: Norton.

Summer, R. F., & Barber, J. P. (2009). *Psychodynamic therapy: A guide to evidence-based practice.* New York, NY: Guilford Press.

Talley, F., Strupp, H., & Butler, S. (1994). *Psychotherapy research and practice: Bridging the gap.* New York, NY: Basic Books.

Taylor, C. (1992). *The ethics of authenticity.* Cambridge, MA: Harvard University Press.

Thompson, C. (1957). *Psychoanalysis: Evolution and development.* New York, NY: Atlantic Monthly Press.

Thompson, M. G. (2004). *The ethic of honesty: The fundamental rule of psychoanalysis.* New York, NY: Rodopi.

Tronick, E. (2007). *The neurobehavioral and social-emotional development of infants and children.* New York, NY: Norton.

Turkle, S. (1992). *Psychoanalytic politics* (2nd ed.). London, England: Guilford Press.

Veblen, T. B. (1919). *The place of science in modern civilization and other essays.* New York, NY: Huebsch.

Wachtel, P. L. (1977). *Psychoanalysis and behavior therapy: Toward an integration.* New York, NY: Basic Books.

Wachtel, P. L. (1997). *Psychoanalysis, behavior therapy, and the relational world.* Washington, DC: American Psychological Association. doi:10.1037/10383-000

Wachtel, P. (2007). Relational theory and the practice of psychotherapy. New York, NY: Guilford Press.

Wallerstein, R. W. (1998). *Lay analysis: Life inside the controversy.* Hillsdale, NJ: The Analytic Press.

Wampold, B. (2001). *The great psychotherapy debate: Models, methods, findings.* Northvale, NJ: Erlbaum.

Westen, D. (1998). Unconscious thought, feeling, and motivation: The end of a century long debate. In R. Bornstein & J. Masling (Eds.), *Empirical perspectives on the psychoanalytic unconscious. Empirical studies of psychoanalytic theories* (pp. 1–43). Washington, DC: American Psychological Association. doi:10.1037/10256-001

Westen, D., & Gabbard, G. (1999). Psychoanalytic approaches to personality. In L. Pervin & O. John (Eds.), *Handbook of personality: Theory and research* (pp. 57–101). New York, NY: Guilford Press.

Westen, D., Novotny, C., & Thompson-Brenner, H. (2004). The empirical status of empirically supported psychotherapies: Assumptions, findings, and reporting in controlled clinical trials. *Psychological Bulletin, 130,* 631–663. doi:10.1037/0033-2909.130.4.631

Winnicott, D. W. (1958). *Through paediatrics to psycho-analysis: Collected papers.* New York, NY: Basic Books.

Winnicott, D. W. (1965). *The maturational process and the facilitating environment.* New York, NY: International Universities Press.

Index

About the Author

Jeremy D. Safran, PhD, is a professor of psychology and former director of clinical training at the New School for Social Research in New York City. He is also senior research scientist at Beth Israel Medical Center. In addition, he is a faculty member at the New York University postdoctoral program in psychotherapy and psychoanalysis and a faculty member at the Stephen A. Mitchell Center for Relational Studies. He is also past president of the International Association for Relational Psychoanalysis and Psychotherapy.

Dr. Safran is an associate editor for the journal *Psychoanalytic Dialogues* and is on the editorial boards of *Psychotherapy Research* and *Psychoanalytic Psychology*. He has published more than 100 articles and chapters and several books, including *Negotiating the Therapeutic Alliance: A Relational Treatment Guide; Emotion in Psychotherapy; The Therapeutic Alliance in Brief Psychotherapy; Interpersonal Process in Cognitive Therapy;* and *Psychoanalysis and Buddhism: An Unfolding Dialogue.*

Dr. Safran and his colleagues have conducted research (partially supported by the National Institute of Mental Health) on the topic of therapeutic impasses for the past 2 decades. He is also known for his work on emotion in psychotherapy and for his integration of principles from Buddhist psychology into psychoanalysis and psychotherapy.

About the Series Editors

Jon Carlson, PsyD, EdD, ABPP, is distinguished professor of psychology and counseling at Governors State University in University Park, Illinois, and a psychologist at the Wellness Clinic in Lake Geneva, Wisconsin. Dr. Carlson has served as the editor of several periodicals, including the *Journal of Individual Psychology* and *The Family Journal.* He holds diplomas in both family psychology and Adlerian psychology. He has authored 150 journal articles and 40 books, including *Time for a Better Marriage, Adlerian Therapy, The Mummy at the Dining Room Table, Bad Therapy, The Client Who Changed Me,* and *Moved by the Spirit.* He has created more than 200 professional trade videos and DVDs with leading professional therapists and educators. In 2004. the American Counseling Association named him a "Living Legend." Recently he syndicated an advice cartoon, *On The Edge,* with cartoonist Joe Martin.

Matt Englar-Carlson, PhD, is a professor of counseling at California State University–Fullerton. He is a fellow of Division 51 of the American Psychological Association (APA). As a scholar, teacher, and clinician, Dr. Englar-Carlson has been an innovator and professionally passionate about training and teaching clinicians to work more effectively with their male clients. He has more than 30 publications and 50 national and international presentations, most of which are focused on men and masculinity and diversity issues in psychological training and practice.

Dr. Englar-Carlson coedited the books *In the Room With Men: A Casebook of Therapeutic Change* and *Counseling Troubled Boys: A Guidebook for Professionals* and was featured in the 2010 APA-produced DVD *Engaging Men in Psychotherapy*. In 2007, he was named Researcher of the Year by the Society for the Psychological Study of Men and Masculinity. He is also a member of the APA Working Group to Develop Guidelines for Psychological Practice With Boys and Men. As a clinician, he has worked with children, adults, and families in school, community, and university mental health settings.